A Century of
NORTH SEA
PASSENGER STEAMERS

The Wilson liner *Tasso* was a typical example of a late 19th century North Sea passenger steamer, depicted here out of context during a Mediterranean cruise. (See page 53). *Author's collection*

A Century of
NORTH SEA
PASSENGER STEAMERS

AMBROSE GREENWAY

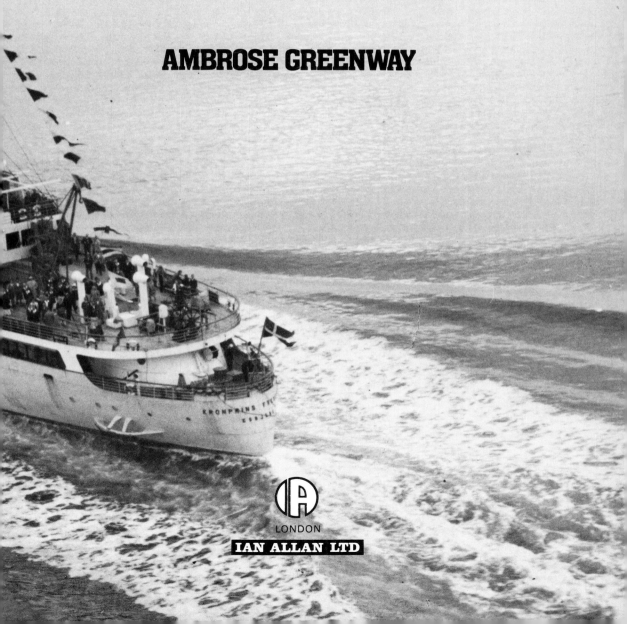

IA

LONDON

IAN ALLAN LTD

Abbreviations

AHL	Associated Humber Lines Ltd
ALA	Angleterre–Lorraine–Alsace
BAOR	British Army of Occupation, Rhine
BTC	British Transport Commission
bp	between perpendiculars
bhp	brake horsepower
d-e	double-ended
DR	double reduction
DFDS	Det Forenede Dampskibs-selskab
GCR	Great Central Railway
GER	Great Eastern Railway
GSN	General Steam Navigation Co
HSM	Holland Steamship Co
HP	high pressure
ihp	indicated horse power
IP	intermediate pressure
LMS	London, Midland & Scottish Railway
LNER	London & North Eastern Railway
LNWR	London & North Western Railway
LP	low pressure
L/V	light vessel
LYR	Lancashire & Yorkshire Railway
MoT	Ministry of Transport
MOWT	Ministry of War Transport
MSL	Manchester, Sheffield & Lincolnshire Railway
mld	moulded
NER	North Eastern Railway
nhp	nominal horse power
oa	overall
psi	pounds per square inch
s-e	single-ended
SR	single reduction

First published 1986

ISBN 0 7110 1338 1

Published by Ian Allan Ltd, Shepperton, Surrey, and printed by Ian Allan Printing Ltd at their works at Coombelands in Runnymede, England

Bibliography

Books
British Nationalised Shipping – Clegg and Styring
Cross Channel and Coastal Paddle Steamers – Frank Burtt
Ellermans, a Wealth of Shipping – James Taylor
For England & Europe – Hitchman and Driver
Great Central – George Dow
Great Eastern Railway Cecil J. Allen
100 Years of Parkeston Quay and its ships – Philip J. Cone
Honderdjaaar Engeland Vaart: Stoomvaart Maats Zeeland – Kelin & Bruijn
Hundrede Ar pa Havene (DFDS 1866–1966) – Poul Graae
Lloyd's Register of Shipping
Norway and the Bergen Line – Wilhelm Keilhau
Railway and Other Steamers – Duckworth and Langmuir
Svenska Lloyd
Une Demi-siecle d'Histoire de la Societe ALA – Louis Mechain
The West Hartlepool Steam Navigation Company Ltd – Spaldin & Appleyard

Periodicals
BNR Journal
Fairplay
Marine Engineer
Marine News
Motor Ship
Schiffahrt International
Sea Breezes
The Shipbuilder
Shipbuilding & Shipping Record
Shipping World
Ships Illustrated
Ships Monthly
Syren & Shipping

Front endpaper:
The Wilson's and North Eastern Railway Shipping Co's continental steamer *Darlington* hurries up the Humber inbound from Antwerp. (See page 65).
Author's collection

Back endpaper:
Rebuilt during World War 2 for active service in the Royal Navy as a troop landing ship, Zeeland Line's fast motor ship *Koningin Emma* took on a new appearance following a postwar refit in 1947. (See page 99).   *John G. Callis*

Title page:
The DFDS 'Harwich boat' *Kronprins Frederik*, laid down before World War 2, but not completed until 1946, shows off her lines to advantage as she cleaves the still waters of the Danish sound at 20 knots during acceptance trials. (See page 115).   *Author's collection*

Contents

Preface

The history of North Sea shipping is a long and complex one and it would take a lifetime of research and several volumes to do the subject justice. That is not the aim of this work which concentrates instead on the narrower aspect of North Sea passenger services and in particular on the development and histories of the widely different ships that maintained them.

During the early part of the 19th century many new shipping companies came into being and over the succeeding years some of these started up regular services linking the major sea ports bordering the North Sea. As there was no other means of travelling abroad, these services soon began to attract the attention of passengers, and fed by a rapidly expanding network of rail connection the initial trickle became a steady flow. Subsequently secondary, often seasonal, services were developed to cater for an interest in tourism engendered by the newly acquired wealth of the Victorian era.

Purchased from Harrison Line, the 4,200-ton *Orlando* became Ellerman Wilson's largest passenger steamer. Initially in the Baltic trade, she later became a regular visitor to Norway and Sweden before being withdrawn in 1929. *National Maritime Museum*

Throughout the first half of the period under review westbound passenger carryings were greatly augmented by an enormous number of emigrants from Scandinavia, the Baltic states and northwest Europe on the first stage of their one-way journey to a new life in the United States. It does not take much imagination to visualise the misery of many of these, unused as they were to the sea, as they rolled their way across the North Sea, packed sometimes up to a thousand at a time in the austere tween-decks of often quite small steamers. A short rail journey, usually by cattle truck, carried them on from the northeast ports to Liverpool or Glasgow from whence they had to undergo an even longer spell of misery on the Atlantic crossing – all quite a contrast to the well-to-do passenger enjoying the plush surroundings of the first class saloon before retiring to his comfortable stateroom for the night.

As there are many more ships involved than in my previous work *A Century of Cross-Channel Passenger Ferries,* to which this is a companion both in period and style, I have had to face the inevitable problem of which ships to include and which to leave out. I soon realised that it would be necessary to exclude all ships trading on through services to the Baltic, likewise those which ran from the

Continent to Iceland. Coastal passenger steamers are part of another story, so these have been excluded as well, though there was a certain amount of interchange in companies engaged in both these and Continental services. For convenience I have included ships on the Norway/Sweden to Hamburg routes in this category.

Having got thus far I was still faced with the problem of defining what constituted a passenger ship, my task being made harder by the fact that passenger carrying capacities varied over the years and were not recorded as often as other particulars. The outcome has therefore been something of a compromise and whilst I make no claim as to comprehensiveness, any decision to exclude a ship has generally been due to lack of confirmation that she carried more than 12 passengers.

Despite careful pruning I was still left with a plethora of information and in order to include as many illustrations as possible I have regrettably been obliged to condense the histories of the foreign-owned vessels which I hope will not detract from the value of the book.

The development of the ships themselves falls into two separate categories. The shorter routes nearer to the English Channel tended to favour the faster type of 'Channel packet', often paddle and later turbine-propelled, though the longer overnight services from Harwich did eventually evolve their own particular full-hulled type of ship. On the longer northern routes which often involved a voyage of 200 miles or more speed was of secondary importance to strength of construction. Hulls were at first a mix of flush and well-deck types but later evolved into a long foc'sle merging into an enlarged superstructure. Propulsion was generally by the well tried reciprocating engine but DFDS pioneered the use of the internal combustion engine

in 1925, and was quickly followed by Olsen and then Bergen Line. Strangely paddles and turbines were rare and early experiments with the latter on the part of the GCR were a failure.

Many of the ship-owning companies also ran services to destinations outside the North Sea and ships were often switched from one route to another, this being particularly true of GSN, Argo, DFDS and Bergen Line.

In compiling this work I have received help from many quarters and my curiosity has in all cases been received with patience and kindness by those whose lot it has been to suffer it. In particular I would like to record my thanks to Laurence and Jennifer Dunn without whose help and encouragement I might have faltered along the way. I should also like to add my thanks to the patient staffs of Lloyd's Register of Shipping and the library of the Institute of Marine Engineers. Many of the illustrations are from Laurence Dunn's collection but I must also record my gratitude to Colonel Gabriel, Captain Sigwart and Maurice Webster. To those others too numerous to mention I record my collective thanks.

Whereas my previous book followed an already well-trodden path, as far as I am aware no book has yet been written which treats the North Sea as a separate subject, and I hope that my efforts will go some way towards filling the gap and at the same time encourage further research into a fascinating subject.

As I write this only a handful of the 250 or so ships described in this book remain in existence and of these only two are still in commission. It cannot be long before they too disappear and sadly their like will not be seen again.

Ambrose Greenway
London, June 1985

The elegant and stylish-looking *Vega,* seen here on trials, was the largest and fastest prewar North Sea passenger ship. Despite a lower tender from Elsinore the Norwegian Government insisted on her being built in Italy as collateral for Norwegian fish exports. Her accommodation was stated to be equal to that of an Atlantic liner, but in keeping with changing social patterns second class berths outnumbered first class.

Exorbitant war risk premium demands led to her being laid up early in World War 2 after just over one year in service and she was later seized by the Germans. Her destruction by Allied planes in Eckernfjord with fleeing refugees was a sad and premature end for one of the finest passenger ships ever to sail the North Sea.
Laurence Dunn collection

General Steam Navigation Co

London/Harwich–Hamburg, etc
1824–1972 General Steam Navigation Co
Funnel colours: Black

Peregrine (1891), *Peregrine* (1892)

In a general work of this nature with space at a premium it would be impossible to try to explain the origins of the European services of the General Steam Navigation Co. Suffice it to say that from the time of its formation in 1824 to about 1880 it had become one of the best known coastal and short sea shipping companies in Europe, operating a large network of cargo and passenger services in addition to its popular excursion steamers in the Thames estuary.

Its main passenger services ran to Leith, Bordeaux and Hamburg, and whilst it is only the latter that concerns this work, it must be borne in mind that GSN tended to switch its ships from route to route at fairly frequent intervals. In 1880 there were two passenger sailings a week each way from the Pool of London to Kaiser Quay or St Pauli, Hamburg, the voyage occupying about 35–40 hours. The ships employed were generally elderly three-masters of about 1,000 tons, and *Libra* of 1869 could be cited as a typical example with accommodation for 80 first-class passengers aft and 72 second class under the foc's'le.

In 1888 a new service was started from Harwich (Parkeston Quay) to Hamburg, the first sailing being taken by the *Hawk* (1876) on 29 March. In the same year GSN took delivery of the fast new passenger steamer *Seamew* for its Leith service and after the Bordeaux run had received the new *Hirondelle* in 1890 it was the turn of the Hamburg service to acquire a new express steamer. Named *Peregrine* she was constructed by W.B. Thompson & Co which launched her at its Dundee shipyard on 7 July 1891. Fitting out took seven weeks and she was ready for trials on 29 August, in which she attained a mean speed of 15.4kt. Amongst the guests on board was a representative of the Australian firm Howard Smith Ltd who was looking for a suitable ship to combat those of the rival AUSN Co, and this was to have a considerable effect on her future career.

Peregrine was a single-funnelled, twin-screw steamer with a straight stem, elliptical stern and split superstructure amidships, the whole creating a nicely balanced profile that was quite unlike any previous GSN ship. Her main particulars were:

Length: 290ft 6in oa/280ft 0in bp
Breadth: 37ft 8in
Depth/draught: 16ft 10½in/16ft 2½in

The first *Peregrine* (1891) wore GSN colours for only a very short time before being sold, without change of name, to Howard Smith, Melbourne for Australian coastal service. She is shown here leaving Sydney in her lengthened state after 1906. *Capt. Sigwart collection*

Gross tonnage: 1,664
Machinery: 2 sets, 3-cylinder triple expansion
Boilers: 2 steel, 165lb/sq in
Power: 3,000ihp
Speed: 15kt

She was an iron ship and her hull was sub-divided by five watertight bulkheads from keel to upper deck whilst a cellular double bottom was provided for ballast. Above the upper or promenade deck was a boat deck and above this a flying bridge.

She could carry in all about 200 passengers in two classes, first and third, with some 60 berths being provided for the former under the main saloon. Electric lighting and steam heating were provided for passenger comfort and safety measures included the provision of six lifeboats.

After delivery she called at Granton on 10 September en route to London where she was much admired. She had only completed one round voyage to Hamburg however when she was sold to Howard Smith, and after some alteration by her builders left Dundee for Australia on 8 October, arriving in Melbourne on 26 November where her luxurious accommodation attracted much attention.

Meanwhile GSN had quickly placed a repeat order with Thompsons and the new ship, also named *Peregrine*, entered the water for the first time on 12 May the following year, successfully completing trials some six weeks later on 24 June. Minor differences including a full width dining saloon seating 70 and a total capacity for about 250 passengers gave her the slightly larger gross measurement of 1,681 tons. She took up station on the Parkeston Quay-Hamburg service where her speed of about 16kt reduced the previous 30hr passage time by some six hours. Over the next 10 years she was partnered in the twice-weekly service (Wednesday and Saturday) to Dalmann Quay by a number of vessels including *Gannet* (1878), *Lapwing* (1879) and *Seamew* (1888); the latter in 1899 when the single saloon fare was £1.10.0d.

The original *Peregrine* had meanwhile been performing satisfactorily on her new owner's Melbourne to Sydney, Brisbane and Queensland ports service in spite of a reputation for being a bit of a roller. In August 1893 her voyages were extended westwards to include ports in Western Australia in order to cope with a gold rush and she continued thus for five years. After a spell or two laid up she was sent to Williamstown Dock, Melbourne in May 1906 to be lengthened by 40ft in way of No 2 hold forward of her funnel. At the same time her hull was strengthened and her funnel heightened, these alterations taken together increasing her gross tonnage to 1,980. The alterations improved her seaworthiness and speed but not her looks.

She returned to her normal East Coast service in October but two years later was put on local duties out of Brisbane. After starting a new mail service to Cairns in March 1915, increasingly frequent engine trouble and a couple of accidents led to her being laid up in September. The following March she was sold to Moller & Co of Shanghai after playing a considerable part in the development of tourist traffic from the southern Australian states to Queensland.

Back in Europe World War 1 had started in 1914 and GSN's *Peregrine* had been quickly taken up by the Admiralty as a flotilla supply ship, this service lasting until 22 November 1915 when she was returned to her owners. She then started running between Harwich and neutral Rotterdam and on 8 February 1917 used her speed to escape from a submarine which tried to shell her. Later the same year she was returning from the Dutch port on the night of 29 December when she grounded on Longsand near the Sunk light vessel. She managed to slide off astern but turned broadside on to the waves and again grounded. Her starboard boats were washed away and at about midnight as the tide rose she was washed on to the wreck of the *Isis*. Some four hours later the Walton-on-Naze lifeboat arrived and took off 59 passengers, mainly French women and children, shortly after which *Peregrine* broke her back. The lifeboat returned at 7.30am and in just over an hour had lifted the remaining 33 crew members to safety.

Purpose-built for GSN's Hamburg passenger service, the elegant *Peregrine* of 1892 represented a major advance in design and was one of the fastest long distance North Sea packets of her day. *World Ship Society*

In the meantime her former sister, still bearing the name *Peregrine,* had returned to European waters from the Far East, and on 15 June in the same year stranded on rocks near Portland Bill lighthouse. She remained fast for over three weeks before being refloated and beached in Portland Roads, later being moved to a South Wales port. Her subsequent history is rather obscure but it appears that she was a reserve blockship for the Medway between May 1918 and the end of February 1919, when she was purchased by the Admiralty as a storage hulk. This final phase of her interesting and varied career lasted until 20 March 1922 when she was sold to Germany for scrap.

Alouette

In 1901 the GSN purchased the cargo/passenger steamer *Calvados* from the South Eastern & Chatham Railway which itself had only just acquired her, with two similar ships, from the London, Brighton & South Coast Railway. *Calvados* had been built in 1894 along with a sister *Trouville* for the Brighton company's Caen service, whilst a third sister, *Prince Arthur,* with increased passenger accommodation, had followed two years later. The service failed to come up to expectations and explains the ships' early sale to the SECR.

As built *Calvados* had the following main particulars:

Length: 195ft 0in
Breadth: 28ft 1in
Depth/draught: 14ft 4in/11ft 4in
Gross tonnage: 570
Machinery: 2 sets, 3-cylinder triple expansion
Boilers: 1 se, 160 lb/sq in
Power: 104nhp
Speed: 15kt

She was a steel ship with raised foc'sle and bridge deck and a rather unusual stern. Two steel pole masts surrounded a rather thin looking funnel which was painted white with a black top. Passenger accommodation was provided amidships for 44 first class travellers, whilst that of the later *Prince Arthur* catered for 66 with space for a number of third class passengers under the foc'sle. Like her sisters, *Calvados* was a twin screw ship, power being derived from two triple expansion engines; these gave her a trial speed of just under 16kt at 1,478ihp. Her bunkers could hold about 50 tons of coal.

Following her transfer to the GSN she was renamed *Alouette,* and wearing her new owner's all black funnel colours was placed in a thrice weekly service between London and Ostend, replacing the old paddle steamers *Swallow* and *Swift.* Apart from passengers, of which she could carry 233 in first class and 92 in second class, her cargo included a large amount of rabbits earning her the nickname 'Ostend rabbit boat' and she became a well known sight in the Thames in the years leading up to World War 1. She had the reputation of being quite a roller and on one occasion is believed to have lost her funnel during a particularly bad roll in a Channel gale.

She was taken up as a fleet messenger (Y4.5) in the second month of the war and after refitting at Deptford with a single 12pdr gun was redesignated an armed boarding steamer (N.54). Her duties were mainly in and around Scapa Flow and she occasionally acted as a relief for the mail steamer *St Ninian* between Scrabster and Stromness. In August 1917 she helped to salvage the mined turret steamer *Ethelwynne* of Whitby which had been beached in Yell Sound, North Shetland, leaving this task early in September to replace the armed boarding steamer *Fiona,* formerly of the London & Edinburgh coastal passenger service, which had been wrecked on Pentland Skerries while herself

Her decks crowded with passengers, GSN's 'rabbit boat' *Alouette* leaves the Pool of London on one of her thrice-weekly trips to Ostend. Originally built for the LB&SCR's short-lived Newhaven–Caen service she retained her turtle-back foc'sle and small steadying sail.
Author's collection

standing in for GER's *Vienna* on the Orkneys and Shetlands mail run.

Alouette was returned to the GSN on 21 November 1919, serving for a further four or so years before being broken up at Rainham in 1924 after a useful career of 30 years.

Hirondelle

This fast steamer was launched by Gourlay Bros & Co, Dundee for the GSN Co on 7 May 1890. She was completed the following month and on 14 June made a trial trip from Parkeston Quay to Gravesend with a large party of official guests on board, attaining over 15kt on a measured mile en route. *Hirondelle* was the largest ship yet built for her owner's short sea/Continental passenger cargo trade, eclipsing *Seamew* of 1888 by some 100 tons, and her main particulars were:

Length: 268ft
Breadth: 37ft 6in
Depth/draught: 19ft mld/17ft 6in
Gross tonnage: 1,607
Machinery: 3-cylinder triple expansion
Boilers: 2, 160lb/sq in
Power: 370nhp
Speed: 14kt

Built in 1890 for GSN's express London–Bordeaux service *Hirondelle* joined *Peregrine* on the Harwich–Hamburg run between 1905 and 1914. Despite the closeness of their construction dates her appearance, with horizontal funnel top and outfit of steam deck-cranes, looked altogether more old-fashioned, although she was later fitted with a wider funnel with sloping top. *Author's collection*

She was a two-deck steel ship with iron plating, and her hull was subdivided into five watertight compartments with a full length double bottom. Her hull gave the appearance of being flush decked but high bulwarks containing outward-swinging doors concealed a 30ft long well-deck between a foc'sle and long combined bridge and poop. A large deckhouse amidships contained a music room, smoke room and some special staterooms, whilst above this were the bridge, lifeboats and a raking horizontal-topped funnel.

She was designed to carry 70 first, 50 second, and 25 third class passengers with the majority of the first class staterooms and main saloon being placed aft of the machinery on the maindeck. Second class accommodation was forward of the engines and third class under the foc'sle, with electric lighting fitted throughout. She had a deadweight cargo capacity of some 2,500 tons, and handling equipment included four steam cranes.

Her initial service was on the Company's express route from London to Bordeaux but like all GSN ships she was interchangeable and from 1905 ran between Parkeston Quay and Hamburg. On 20 December 1913 she grounded in the Lower Elbe whilst inward bound, the weather being foggy at the time, and in refloating later at high water she struck the steamer *Tento* damaging her stem. Just before World War 1 she had again been moved and was running on the London–Leith service.

Immediately following the outbreak of war she was taken up as a Squadron supply ship, pennant number Y9.17, and continued thus until 7 June 1915 when she became a BDV water carrier. She later returned to commercial service and was presumably back on the Bordeaux run when she was torpedoed and sunk 13 miles south by east from Belle Ile, in the Bay of Biscay, on 25 April 1917, happily without loss of life.

Great Eastern Railway Co

Harwich–Rotterdam/Antwerp/Hook of Holland
1862–1922   Great Eastern Railway Co
1923–1947   London and North Eastern Railway Co
1948–1966   British Transport Commission
            (Eastern Region)
1963–1978   British Railway Board
1979–1984   Sealink UK
Funnel colours: Buff with black top
1965–   Red with black top and white BR 'linked
            rails' logo

Princess of Wales

After a number of unsuccessful attempts by various companies to start steamship services from Harwich to the Continent in the 1850s, the Great Eastern Railway finally countered strong opposition and in 1863 obtained the necessary parliamentary powers to own and run steamships. Whilst new ships were under construction chartered cargo and cattle steamers were placed in service between Harwich and Rotterdam.

The GER's first passenger ships were the Dudgeon-built two-funnelled paddlers *Avalon* and *Zealous* which opened the Rotterdam and Antwerp passenger services on 13 June and 1 August 1864 respectively; the following year the same builders delivered a second *Avalon* and *Ravensbury*, 14kt sisters of about 670 tons. In 1871 a further paddler named *Richard Young* became notable as being the first ship to arrive in Rotterdam via the newly opened New Waterway, previous access having been via the sandbank-strewn Maas estuary.

The John Elder-built *Claud Hamilton* of nearly 1,000 tons joined the GER fleet in 1875 and with her compound oscillating machinery set new standards of speed and comfort. Her 22 years in GER service did much to enhance the popularity of the Harwich continental services.

Princess of Wales was another Clydeside product, launched and delivered by the London & Glasgow Engineering & Shipbuilding Co at Govan in 1878. Her main particulars were as follows:

Length: 265ft 6in
Breadth: 30ft 5in
Depth: 14ft 2½in
Gross tonnage: 1,098
Machinery: 2-cylinder simple oscillating
Power: 2,500ihp
Speed: 15kt

Little appears to be known about her excepting that she was an iron paddle steamer with three masts, and her simple oscillating engines had a cylinder length of 68in and a stroke of 84in. She was licensed to carry about 580 passengers with berths for 111 in first- and 77 in second classes.

She sailed at first between Harwich and Rotterdam but later used the new quays at Parkeston and the Hook of Holland. After a useful but apparently uneventful career of 18 years she was sold for scrap on 16 May 1896.

Lady Tyler

Having had three ships built on both the Thames and the Clyde the GER turned to East Coast shipbuilders in 1880 for a new iron passenger steamer for its Rotterdam service. She was launched at T. & W. Smith's North Shields shipyard in the spring of 1880 after being christened *Lady Tyler*. Trials took place on 4 May and she is reported to have behaved very well in a strong swell. Her dimensions and other particulars were as follows:

Length: 261ft 0in
Breadth: 30ft 2½in
Depth: 13ft 9in
Gross tonnage: 995
Machinery: 6-cylinder compound
Power: 1,400ihp
Speed: 13kt

With a single raking funnel placed aft of the paddle boxes and two tall masts the new ship was no great beauty but she could carry some 700 passengers in first and second class and her main saloon was about 40ft in length. Her compound

The iron-hulled *Lady Tyler* built in 1880 was one of the last paddle driven steamers built for the GER's continental services. She ended her days as a coal hulk at Gravesend. *Author's collection*

machinery – which had two high pressure and four low pressure cylinders – was constructed by R. & W. Hawthorn & Co of Newcastle.

She was soon displaced by newer and more efficient screw driven steamers and after a comparatively short career of 13 years was sold in 1893 to Messrs Earle's of Hull, the well known shipbuilding company, possibly in part payment for a new ship. Two years later she had steamed round to the Irish Sea on charter to the Mutual Line of Manx Steamers Ltd, a new company trying to run a service to the Isle of Man in opposition to the old established Isle of Man Steam Packet Co. This proved abortive and she was laid up after only one season. In 1897 she was renamed *Artemis* and three years later was converted to a coal hulk. Her owner appears to have been a George Sandford, and she remained a hulk at Gravesend until 1955 when she was finally broken up.

The handsome twin-funnelled *Adelaide* was the GER's first steel ship and the Company's last continental service paddler. Note the white painted top to her foremast which was a distinguishing feature of the GER's ships for many years. *Author's collection*

Adelaide

Early in 1880 the GER ordered its last paddle driven cross channel passenger steamer from the Barrow Shipbuilding Co Ltd. Launched by Mrs Simpson, the wife of one of the Company's directors, on 8 May, the new ship was named *Adelaide*. On completion she proceeded on a 100-mile trial trip from Barrow with 250 tons of coal in her bunkers during which she averaged a comfortable 14.56kt. Her dimensions, which were broadly similar to those of her contemporary *Lady Tyler*, were:

Length: 260ft 0in/254ft 2in bp
Breadth: 32ft 4in
Depth: 14ft 3in
Gross tonnage: 969
Machinery: 2-cylinder compound oscillating
Power: 1,600ihp
Speed: 14½kt

Adelaide was a handsome two-deck steamer with well-raked funnels and was the first steel ship in the GER fleet. She was undoubtedly better looking than *Lady Tyler* as well as being faster, and her accommodation was described as being equal to that of the Barrow-built Atlantic liners, with 113 first class berths and 58 in second. Total capacity was 682.

Her career lasted only a few years longer than *Lady Tyler's* and she was sold in 1896 to T.W. Ward who passed her on to J. Bannatyne & Sons for breaking up in June of the following year.

Ipswich, Norwich

As a result of frequent disagreements with the Harwich harbour authorities concerning the extension of its dock facilities the GER decided to take matters into its own hands and early in 1879 started the construction of a new quay on marshland on the southern bank of the Stour, about two miles upstream of the old Continental Pier at Harwich. The new terminal, which took its name Parkeston Quay from the then GER chairman Mr Parkes, became fully operational in 1883, and in anticipation of this the Company had ordered two new screw steamers from Earle's Shipbuilding & Engineering Co of Hull, whose yard had previously done a good deal of repair work for the GER.

Norwich, the first of the new ships, was launched on 6 March 1883, followed by her sister *Ipswich* on 21 May. Strangely, iron was used for their construction, which was arranged on the three-island principle with short well-decks for working cargo of which they could carry substantially greater amounts than the earlier paddle steamers. Both ships had the following general particulars:

Length: 260ft 0in
Breadth: 31ft 4in
Depth: 15ft 0in (hold)
Gross tonnage: 1,065
Machinery: 2 sets, 2-cylinder compound
Boilers: 2de, 80lb/sq in
Power: 2,000ihp
Speed: 14kt

Representing a major advance over the paddle steamers both in design and efficiency, the two ships had first class accommodation for 84 passengers amidships under a long bridge deck and forward of the machinery space, whilst a further 42 were housed in second class under the poop. Electric lighting was fitted in the first class saloon and staterooms, the ladies' cabin and the engine room. The forward part of the ship was given over to cargo space and the crew were berthed in the foc'sle.

Their main machinery came from the builders and consisted of a pair of inverted surface condensing diagonal compound engines which gave a service speed of 14kt, though *Norwich* made 17½kt on her official trial between Orfordness and Aldeburgh on 21 July, albeit with 1½kt of current in favour. Her sister averaged 14kt on a 100-mile trial between Spurn and Flamborough on 9 October and arrived in Harwich the next day after a 10hr run from Hull.

The two sisters were generaly employed in the Antwerp service and both were reboilered in the course of their 22-year careers with the GER, *Ipswich* in 1895 and her sister two years later. Their disposal came in 1905, the former passing briefly through the hands of J. Constant, London before being sold to the Shah Steam Navigation Co in 1906 for service in Indian waters. In about 1908 *Ipswich* was transferred again to the Bombay & Hujaz Steam Navigation of India Co Ltd but this lasted only a short while and she was scrapped locally in May 1909.

Norwich meanwhile had been sold to Channel Dry Docks & Shipbuilding & Engineering Co Ltd and in 1906 was shown as belonging to Queenstown Dry Docks SB & E Co. Between 1908 and about 1911 she was again registered at Harwich under the ownership of The Shipping Syndicate after which she became the Portuguese *Fortuna* of Empresa of Navegacao, based at Fogo in the Cape Verde Islands. Two years later she crossed the Atlantic to Montevideo where she ran for a short while as F. Allessi's *Evelyn* before going to New York registry in about 1915, becoming the Continental Trading Co's *Neptune*. She retained this name under two further New York companies, Cuneo Importing and Federal Operating, and was finally sunk in March 1921 when under the ownership of the Mexican Fruit & Steamship Corporation. She had outlived her sister by 12 years and the final third of her 38-year career had been an interesting and varied one.

The iron *Norwich* of 1883, pictured off the old Continental Pier at Harwich, and her sister *Ipswich* introduced twin-screw propulsion to the GER fleet. Their twin-funnelled profile set the pattern for a long line of subsequent ships built by Earle's Co at Hull.
Laurence Dunn collection

Cambridge, Colchester

Such was the success of the 1883-built twin screw steamers that only three years elapsed before an improved and slightly larger version appeared from Earle's shipyard.

Cambridge was a steel ship but retained the strong scantlings of her predecessors; her launching took place on 11 October 1886. Two years later Earle's built a sister ship *Colchester* which after fitting out ran a 70-mile trial north of Spurn on 10 January 1889 during which she averaged 15kt.

The two ships shared the following main particulars:

Length: 280ft 5in/280ft 9in
Breadth: 31ft 0in
Depth: 15ft 3in
Gross tonnage: 1,194/1,160
Machinery: 2 sets, 2-cylinder compound
Boilers: 2de, 90lb/sq in
Power: 2,200ihp
Speed: 14½kt

Although very similar to *Norwich*, *Cambridge* and *Colchester* were about 20ft longer and had more superstructure amidships, whilst their hulls were specially stiffened to reduce vibration. They could carry a maximum of about 730 passengers of which 134 and 160 respectively were berthed in first class under the bridge along with a dining saloon, smoke room and ladies' cabin. Portable berths were provided for an additional 62 passengers in the tourist season. Second class accommodation was placed aft under the poop with sleeping arrangements for 56. All accommodation was electrically lit and heated by steam.

Their machinery was the same as in the earlier ships, and they owed their slightly better speed to their greater length. Deck machinery for handling cargo and baggage consisted of four steam winches and provision was made for carrying horses and cattle under the foc'sle.

They appear to have started their careers on the Antwerp service but later served both Rotterdam and the Hook, all of which entailed night crossings. In 1900 *Colchester* was re-engined with a pair of four-cylinder triple expansion engines which gave her 14kt with greater economy than before.

On 12 December 1911, in her last year of operation with the GER, *Cambridge* collided with the destroyer HMS *Salmon* killing two of the latter's crew, but she picked up the remainder. The following November, displaced by the last of three new turbine steamers, she was sold to the Anglo Ottoman Steamship Co under D. Lambiri management, but this was taken over by S. Cavounidis a year later.

Colchester continued to run after World War 1 had broken out and on no less than four occasions between December 1914 and May 1915 used her speed to escape from enemy submarines. Her luck ran out on 22 September 1916 when she was captured by torpedo boats off the Dutch coast and taken into Zeebrugge, her crew being interned. Condemned as a war prize she passed into the hands of the German navy and was converted into a

Above left:
The 1889-built *Colchester* was a younger sister of *Cambridge* (1886) and both were steel developments of the *Ipswich* pair. Some 20ft longer, they had an extra pair of lifeboats.
Author's collection

Left:
Cambridge pictured in the 1920s as the Turkish *Gul-Nehal* showing little alteration save for the removal of her forward boats. Her funnels were painted a deep yellow with black tops and the white bands carried red designs.
Laurence Dunn collection

minelayer at Bruges. She later served in the Baltic, taking part in the Oesel operation, but stranded and sank off Laboe, in Kiel Bay, on 2 March 1918. Raised and returned to the UK after the war, she was only fit for the scrapyard.

Shortly after the war *Cambridge* was renamed *Gul-Nehal* and her owners became the Administration de Navigation a Vapeur Ottomane. Ten years later her name had been amended to *Gulnihal* and her ownership retitled Turkiye Seryrisefain Induresi, subsequently shortened to Denizyollari Idaresi, both being antecedents of today's Turkish Maritime Lines. She was scrapped locally in about 1937 after a career which had spanned more than 50 years, split between two widely differing locations.

Chelmsford

Some 10 years after the pioneering *Norwich* and *Ipswich*, Earle's contracted to build a fifth passenger steamer for the GER. Her name *Chelmsford* followed Company policy in using the names of East Anglian towns for its ships, and she was launched on 21 February 1893. She was some 400 tons heavier and 20ft longer than the previous pair of sisters as can be seen from the following details.

Length: 300ft 5in
Breadth: 34ft 6in
Depth: 16ft 2½in
Gross tonnage: 1,635
Machinery: 2 sets, 3-cylinder triple expansion
Boilers: 5se, 160lb/sq in
Power: 397nhp
Speed: 17½kt

Having previously attained 18.2kt on trials her entry into service on 1 June was designed to coincide with the opening by the Dutch of a new terminal at the Hook of Holland near the entrance to the New Waterway. From then on the GER ships halted there to allow their passengers to take advantage of the new rail connections to the European hinterland. The Rotterdam passenger service was finally terminated in 1904 and thenceforward the Hook became the GER terminal.

Chelmsford's design was a logical development of the earlier ships but extra length enabled her to carry more passengers with berths being provided for 200 in first, 64 in second and a number in third class. A new feature in first class was the provision of several special private double cabins at no extra charge.

Her powerful triple expansion engines – which were the first such outfit in the Company's fleet – were inclined inwards to allow more space for passenger accommodation and special staying was employed to reduce vibration to a minimum.

She became surplus to requirements in 1910 and was sold at the end of June to the Great Western Railway which employed her on its Plymouth–Nantes cargo service under the appropriate name of *Bretonne*. When this was discontinued on 30 September 1911 she was sold once more, her new owners being the Embiricos family who renamed her *Esperia* and placed her in their National Steam Navigation Co of Greece under Andros registry. She was used on local inter-island services and was renamed *Syros* in about 1920, but reverted to *Esperia* for a short period in the mid-1920s while serving her owners' London subsidiary, the Byron Steamship Co. The Embiricos' fortunes declined in 1933 and she was sold for scrap the following year after a career of more than 40 years.

The 18kt *Chelmsford* produced by Earle's in 1893 was the prototype of a series of larger ships for the newly-opened Harwich–Hook service. She introduced reciprocating engines to the GER fleet and could be distinguished by having no boats abreast her funnels.
Author's collection

Amsterdam, (1894), Berlin, Vienna/Roulers (1894)

The GER was well satisfied with the performance of the faster *Chelmsford* and, wishing to consolidate its new accelerated service to the Hook and no doubt with an eye on the mail contract still held by Zeeland Line, quickly ordered two more similar ships from Earle's, with a third order following later. The new ships were given suitably 'Continental' names reflecting the new through services made possible by the new railway connection to the Hook. *Amsterdam* and *Berlin* were built alongside each other and were completed only weeks apart in the early spring of 1894; both exceeded their designed speed of 18kt on trials. *Vienna* was launched on 18 July and entered service in October.

Although more or less repeats of the prototype *Chelmsford* they were marginally longer with about 1½ft extra beam, but had the same engines.

Length: 302ft 6in
Breadth: 36ft 0in
Depth: 16ft 2in
Gross tonnage: 1,745
Machinery: 2 sets, 3-cylinder triple expansion
Boilers: 5se, 160lb/sq in
Power: 5,000ihp
Speed: 18kt (13 on one engine)

Their steel hulls were divided into eight watertight compartments and other safety measures included eight boats and about 1,200 lifebelts. Their long part-awning deck was joined to the foc'sle and was separated from the poop by a short well.

Accommodation was arranged on three decks with an entrance hall, some staterooms and the captain's cabin in a large house on the awning deck. Added shading gave better protection for passengers who wished to go out on deck. The dining saloon, ladies' cabin and further staterooms, including a double connecting one for VIPs, were situated on the main deck with additional cabins one deck below that. In all first class berths totalled 218. Second class accommodation for 120 was arranged in the poop and after tween-decks.

Their bunker capacity was about 150 tons and the engines consumed about four tons of coal an hour. Three winches with derricks were provided for rapid cargo handling, and stalling for horses was fitted in the forward tween-decks.

The accelerated service became firmly established with all three ships in commission and there were departures in each direction on every night except Saturdays. Going to Holland, a train left Liverpool Street station at 8.00pm and after a six-hour crossing the steamer arrived at the Hook just before 6.00am the next morning.

On 21 February 1907 *Berlin* was swept across the northern mole at the entrance to the New Waterway during a fierce northwesterly gale. Her bows broke off and sank but her stern portion remained fast on the breakwater. Despite heroic rescue attempts only 10 passengers and five crew were saved and the loss of 128 lives made this the worst peacetime disaster in the history of North Sea passenger travel.

After the delivery of new turbine steamers for the Hook service the surviving ships sometimes ran on the Antwerp route and on the night of 19 January 1911 *Vienna*, steaming at quarter speed, collided in clear weather with the Blue Funnel steamer *Patroclus* on a bend in the Scheld, striking her amidships. The latter was badly damaged and had to return to Antwerp but *Vienna* managed to continue to Harwich with a badly bent stem.

During World War 1 *Amsterdam* became an armed boarding steamer, equipped with a 4in gun and one 12pdr. *Vienna* was used as an accommodation ship for about 3½ months in 1914

This view of the ill-fated *Berlin* is representative of her class in their original guise. Her loss off the Hook of Holland with 128 lives on 21 February 1907 was one of the worst disasters in North Sea history. *Author's collection*

A later view of *Amsterdam* showing the raised navigating bridge. Note also the different boat arrangement to *Chelmsford*. *Author's collection*

followed by a brief spell early the following year as one of the first 'Q' ships, using the name *Antwerp* as well as her own. For the rest of the war she too became an armed boarding steamer with an armament of two 12pdr guns.

In 1920 *Vienna* was renamed *Roulers* and placed on a new seasonal service to Zeebrugge with departures on alternate nights. *Amsterdam* was sold for scrap in December 1928 and *Roulers* went the same way in March 1930 after 36 years of useful service.

Dresden/Louvain

Dresden was the ninth and last of the twin screw steamers built by Earle's for the GER and her design marked the final stage of evolution from that of *Norwich* built some 14 years previously. She was launched on 17 November 1896 and later completed a 100-mile steaming trial at about 19kt before being handed over early in 1897. Her dimensions were similar to those of the previous trio but with somewhat greater beam and she also had slightly finer hull lines.

Length: 302ft 1in
Breadth: 38ft 1in
Depth: 17ft 3in
Gross tonnage: 1,805
Machinery: 2 sets, 3-cylinder triple expansion
Boilers: 5se, 160lb/sq in
Power: 5,000ihp
Speed: 18kt

She was designed on the usual three-island principle and her bridge deck, which was also the first class promenade deck, was 218ft in length. Her first class accommodation – which became noted for its luxury – contained a total of 226 berths. The majority of these were on the main deck forward of the machinery with the remainder, including a deluxe cabin, on the upper deck along with the dining saloon and ladies' room. Considerable attention was paid to ventilation in both the passenger and machinery spaces and steam coils were provided for heating.

During her first year of service she took time off to represent her owners at the June Naval Review at Spithead. In April 1889 the GER finally wrested the GPO mail contract from Zeeland Line which was proof enough of the efficiency of *Dresden* and her Humber-built consorts. In October 1913 Dr Rudolf Diesel, the celebrated inventor of the internal combustion engine, disappeared whilst taking passage to Parkeston in her and is presumed to have fallen overboard.

About two months after the start of World War 1 the ship was requisitioned by the Admiralty and renamed HMS *Louvain*. The following year she was converted into an armed boarding steamer with two 12pdr guns and served as such for the greater part of the war until sunk in the Eastern Mediterranean on 20 January 1918 by the submarine UC.22.

Dresden of 1897 was a lone ship and represented the culmination of a long line of Earle's-built ships. Her solid bulwarks forwards were an innovation, as was her raised bridge. *Author's collection*

Brussels

The next time the GER required a new passenger steamer it was forced to seek new builders as Earle's had only recently been saved from bankruptcy by Thomas Wilson, and as a result had a full local order book. Gourlay Bros – no beginners when it came to building coastal passenger steamers – won the contract and *Brussels* was launched by Miss Drury on 26 March 1902, the ship's name being a particularly apt one as she was the first to be specifically designed for the Antwerp service. Like *Dresden* before her she was a single ship but was built to a new smaller design.

Length: 285ft 4in
Breadth: 34ft 0in
Depth/draught: 16ft 6in/14ft 6in
Gross tonnage: 1,380
Machinery: 2 sets, 3-cylinder triple expansion
Boilers: 4, 160lb/sq in
Power: 3,800ihp
Speed: 16½kt

Brussels did not display any marked differences from the Earle's-built ships in spite of her different yard of origin; she was a compact little ship with an appearance that was easy on the eye. Special features of her accommodation which again echoed that in the earlier ships were the provision of a large number of two-berth cabins and a special suite of rooms for lady travellers. The first class section included berthing arrangements for about 160.

In service she proved to be a popular ship and her prewar career seems to have been devoid of any great incident save for a grounding off Harwich in April 1907, which fortunately was not serious.

When war came she was not requisitioned and maintained an irregular service between Tilbury and the Hook of Holland. The first of her many brushes with the enemy came on 28 March 1915 when under the command of Captain Fryatt she tried to ram the submarine U.33 which had ordered her to stop about eight miles west of the Maas light vessel. In June of the same year she used her speed to evade submarines on no less than three occasions and on the 20th of the following month was missed by a torpedo when about 20 miles east of the South

Inner Gabbard buoy. The Germans were by now more than anxious to capture her and this was finally accomplished by torpedo boats off the Hook on 23 June 1916 when she was escorted into Zeebrugge. Her crew was imprisoned and the unfortunate Captain Fryatt was tried in Bruges on 26 July, found guilty of a warlike act in trying to ram a submarine, and shot. This brutal treatment of a non-combatant caused widespread national indignation across the Channel.

The Germans renamed the ship *Brugge* and used her as a depot ship for flying boats and submarines, but before being pushed out of the port by the Allies they sank her as a blockship on 5 October 1918. Just over a year later she was raised and taken to Antwerp by the Belgians who later presented her to the British government. After being brought to the Tyne she was put up for auction but public resentment forced the stipulation of a British buyer. Only one bidder came forward and she was sold for £2,100 on 7 August 1920 to a firm of Liverpool brokers acting on behalf of the Dublin & Lancashire Steamship Co.

She was given a thorough rebuild by Henry Robb at Leith and emerged with new accommodation and fittings for the carriage of some 600 head of cattle or 1,000 sheep. After steaming round to Preston she started her new career as a cattle carrier with a sailing to Dublin on 7 September 1921. Two years later she was taken over by the British & Irish Steam Packet Co and the prefix *Lady* was added to her name, but she continued in the Preston–Dublin trade until 1929, making her last crossing from the Irish port on 19 April. The following month she was sold for breaking up at Port Glasgow.

Brussels, **built by Gourlay Bros in 1902 specifically for the Antwerp service, was a smaller version of** *Dresden* **but could be distinguished by having thicker stanchions under her forward boats. She made the headlines during World War 1 when captured by the Germans and her master was later shot for attempting to ram a U-boat.** *Author's collection*

Copenhagen, Munich/St Denis, St Petersburg/Archangel

Length: 343ft 0in/331ft 0in bp
Breadth: 43ft 2½in
Depth/draught: 26ft 6in (shelter deck)/14ft 6in
Gross tonnage: 2,410 (*St Petersburg* 2,448)
Machinery: 1hp and 2lp Parsons turbines
Boilers: 5se, 190lb/sq in
Power: 10,000shp
Speed: 20kt

Turbine propulsion had been in use with some of the other railway companies for a number of years when the GER placed an order with John Brown & Co of Clydebank for its first turbine steamer. The new ship was christened *Copenhagen* by Miss Ida Hamilton on 22 October 1907 and by the time she was completed the following spring an order had been placed for a second ship. *Munich* entered the waters of the Clyde on 25 August but almost two years were to go by before the third sister, *St Petersburg,* was launched on 25 April 1910, entering service that July.

The new ships were fine looking examples of their type and although innovatory for their owners with regard to propulsion, they retained a certain family resemblance to their reciprocating-engined predecessors.

They were the first turbine steamers on the North Sea and the first flush-deckers in the GER fleet, but the final ship of the trio was given a raised foc'sle – possibly as a result of the others having proved rather wet forward in bad weather. Their hulls were constructed of mild steel with the GER's traditionally heavy scantlings, and were subdivided by seven watertight bulkheads.

Passenger accommodation was spread over three decks amidships with sleeping berths for 320 in first class, over 200 of which were in double cabins. Public rooms included a smoke room on the awning deck and below this a ladies' room, whilst the full-width 62-seat dining saloon was situated on the lower deck. Second class accommodation was

Above right:
A trials view of the GER's first turbine steamer, the triple-screw *Copenhagen* built by John Brown & Co in 1907. Note the solid bulwarks extending into the forward part of the superstructure to give more protection to the promenade deck.
Author's collection

Right:
***St Petersburg* of 1910 differed from her Clyde-built sisters in having a raised foc'sle with recessed anchor stowage, whilst her bridge was set further aft. She was renamed *Archangel* in 1916.**
Author's collection

arranged aft on the main and lower decks with berthing for 130.

Three propellers were driven directly by a large high pressure turbine on the centre line and two lower-powered wing turbines, each of which was fitted with small separate turbines within their casings for astern power. The five boilers were coal fired and were of the closed stokehold type employing forced draught.

Once in regular operation the three sisters did much to enhance the popularity of the Harwich-Hook route to the Continent in the years leading up to World War 1.

Shortly after the outbreak of war *Munich* was requisitioned and converted into a military hospital carrier with 231 beds. *Copenhagen* remained on North Sea service for a while carrying Belgian refugees, later being used as a trooper until 1 January 1916 when she was taken up as an ambulance carrier. Her career as such was brief as she was torpedoed without warning on 5 March 1917 about eight miles east of the North Hinder light vessel with the loss of six lives. *Munich* and *St Petersburg* were renamed *St Denis* and *Archangel* in 1916 and 1919 and both survived the war, the former being released on 18 October 1919.

After the Armistice *Archangel* was used for a time to repatriate POWs, but the daily service to Holland was not resumed until April 1920. The GER was absorbed into the LNER in 1923 and when the latter's new 'Amsterdam' class ships were delivered in 1930 the older pair were relegated to the more leisurely seasonal service between Parkeston and Zeebrugge in place of *Roulers;* remaining there until war came again in September 1939.

Initially *Archangel* was moved to Southampton for trooping and in April 1940 *St Denis* was ordered to Rotterdam with *Malines* to pick up British civilians, but was caught by the German invasion on 10 May and scuttled after being damaged in a heavy air attack. *Archangel* took part in the evacuation of troops from France and at St Valery her boat stayed on until the last troops had been ferried to safety under continuous enemy gunfire. A year later, on 16 May, she was carrying troops from Kirkwall in the Orkneys to Aberdeen when she was bombed by an enemy aircraft, losing many killed, including 17 of her crew, and her captain and 16 others were injured. Attempts to tow her were abandoned and she was beached about eight miles north of Aberdeen where she later became a total loss.

St Denis was later raised by the Germans and after repairs was used as the auxiliary minesweeper *Barbara* before becoming the miscellaneous auxiliary *Schiff 52*. In 1945 she was taken over by the British authorities at Kiel and, still wearing her dazzle paint, was leased back for use as an accommodation ship for refugees and later for students of Kiel University. On expiry of the lease in February 1950 she was towed back to Sunderland for scrapping.

Stockholm

A new passenger steamer was laid down by John Brown & Co, for the GER early in 1917, but whilst still on the stocks she was bought by the Admiralty on 27 February for completion as an aircraft carrier. She was launched under the intended name of *Stockholm* on 9 June but was renamed HMS *Pegasus* on 28 August. Her original design was a logical development of the *Copenhagen* type but incorporating geared turbines; however, her new appearance as an aircraft carrier could certainly be described as unusual.

Length: 332ft 0in
Breadth: 43ft 0in
Gross tonnage: 2,450
Machinery: 2 sets se geared turbines
Power: 9,500shp
Speed: 20kt

Having been designed from scratch so to speak she was a great advance on the channel steamers which had been converted to rudimentary aircraft carriers at the beginning of the war and she became a unit of the Grand Fleet, later joining the White Sea expedition and ending the war in the Mediterranean.

Her peacetime service was mainly of an experimental nature and by the time she was bought by T.W. Ward for scrapping at Morecambe in August 1931 she had been completely eclipsed by the more modern full flight-deck type of carrier.

Kilkenny/Frinton

In the summer of 1919 the GER was forced to purchase two second-hand ships to replace war losses and requisitions. The first was the City of Dublin Steam Packet Co's *Kilkenny,* a passenger/cargo steamer completed by Clyde Shipbuilding & Engineering Co, Glasgow in 1903 for Dublin–Liverpool service.

She was a single-funnelled ship with bridge deck amidships and three hatches, two forward and one aft. Berths for 154 first class passengers were provided amidships, with space for a large number of steerage on the main deck forward.

Length: 269ft 8in
Breadth: 36ft 2½in
Depth/draught: 16ft 3in/15ft 10in
Gross tonnage: 1,361

The Irish Sea passenger/cargo steamer *Kilkenny* was bought by the GER in 1919 as a replacement for war losses. Renamed *Frinton* she operated mainly as a cargo steamer. *Author's collection*

Machinery: 3-cylinder triple expansion
Boilers: 2 de, 190lb/sq in
Power: 3,500ihp
Speed: 14kt (trials 14.9kt)

At the time of her purchase she had been damaged by grounding on 15 May at Knockadoon Bay, west of Youghal whilst engaged on a Cork–Liverpool service for the War Department. The GER repaired her and placed her on its Antwerp route, previously operated by the chartered GCR *Marylebone* and GSN *Woodcock*. Renamed *Frinton* in December 1919 she was transferred to the Rotterdam service the following spring when replaced by *Amsterdam*.

During her time with the GER and later the LNER it would appear that her passenger accommodation was not used to any great extent and in May 1926 she was sold to Greek owners Inglessi Bros, her place being taken by the new cargo steamer *Sheringham*. Registered under the latter's Samos Steam Navigation Co she was briefly renamed *Samos* before reverting once more to *Frinton* and was generally employed on Piraeus–Brindisi service, departing Mondays and returning Wednesdays. At other times she cruised between Venice and the Ionian Islands but events in World War 2 overtook her and she was lost in Greek waters in 1941.

St George

A further second-hand ship was acquired by the GER in June 1919. She was the former Fishguard & Rosslare Railways & Harbours Co's *St George* which, with two sisters, had been built in 1906 (a fourth followed later) to inaugurate a new link between Fishguard and Rosslare under the joint control of the GWR and GS&WR of Ireland. She was the first turbine ship built by Cammell Laird & Co and was launched at Birkenhead on 13 January 1906.

Length: 364ft 0in/352ft 0in bp
Breadth: 41ft 1in
Depth/draught: 16ft 2in/15ft 0in
Gross tonnage: 2,456
Machinery: 1hp and 2hp Parsons turbines
Boilers: 8se, 185lb/sq in
Power: 10,000shp (12,420shp on trial)
Speed: 20kt (22½kt on trial)

The handsome *St George* puchased from CPR in 1919 started her career on the Fishguard–Rosslare route in 1906. Her turbines gave her a maximum speed of 22½kt making her potentially the fastest GER ship.
Author's collection

St George and her sisters were distinctive ships with unusually high foc'sles to combat the vagaries of the Irish Sea in winter and two very tall, elliptical funnels. Passenger complement was around 1,000 and sleeping accommodation was provided for about 220 in first class amidships and 100 in second class on the main and lower decks aft. Six special staterooms were situated at the after end of the main deckhouse whilst the dining saloon was placed on the main deck forward.

Large holds (including an insulated one) were provided for cargo, and electric winches facilitated its handling. Propelling machinery was arranged on the usual principle of a high pressure centre turbine with two low pressure ones on either side, each directly connected to its own shaft. Extremely smooth running, they gave *St George* a speed of over 22½ kt during trials in the Clyde in a strong southwesterly whilst developing about 12,420shp. Bunker capacity was 170tons of coal and they burned about 5½ tons an hour.

In May 1913 *St George* was sold to the Canadian Pacific Railway which had her towed across the Atlantic to operate its 47 mile St John–Digby service across the Bay of Fundy. Two years later she returned to England to become a World War 1 hospital carrier, being provided with 278 beds.

Following her purchase by the GER in 1919 her accommodation was altered to cater for some 500 passengers. A few extra first and second class cabins were added but generally her cabins were rather small and cramped in comparison with her running mates *St Denis* and *Archangel* and she was not popular with the more discerning type of traveller on the night service between Harwich and the Hook

She was made redundant by the arrival of the new *Vienna* in 1929 and was sold to Hughes Bolckow Shipbreaking Co Ltd in October for demolition at Blyth.

Bruges – pictured on trials in the Clyde – and sister *Antwerp* were built by John Brown & Co for the Antwerp service in 1920. Their design incorporated cruiser sterns for the first time but otherwise they were developments of *St Petersburg* with foc'sles extending to beneath the bridge. *Author's collection*

Antwerp, Bruges, Malines

As soon as the disturbed conditions existing after World War 1 would allow the GER put in hand a replacement building programme. Priority was given to the Antwerp service and two new sisters were ordered from John Brown, who had taken over from Earle's as principal supplier of new tonnage for the Company. *Antwerp* was put into the water on 26 October 1919 followed by *Bruges* on 20 March the following year, and both entered service in 1920. A third sister, *Malines* (her name continuing the Belgian theme of nomenclature), was launched at the High Walker yard of Armstrong Whitworth & Co Ltd, Newcastle on 6 January 1921, but for some reason she did not run trials until 9 March the following year, when she attained a speed of 21½kt. She entered service on 21 March 1922 being the last ship constructed for the GER before its disappearance in the 1923 regrouping, and the last to be built specifically for the Antwerp service.

The main particulars of the three fine new sisters were:

Length: 337ft 0in oa/321ft 7in bp
Breadth: 43ft 2in
Depth/draught: 17ft 10in/13ft 4in
Gross tonnage: 2,957/2,949/2,969
Machinery: 2 sets, SR Brown-Curtis geared turbines
Boilers: 5, 200lb/sq in
Power: 12,500shp
Speed: 21kt

As one would expect after an interval of some 18 years the new ships represented an enormous advance over the *Brussels,* the previous ship built for the Antwerp service. Although retaining the traditional two funnels their design incorporated a very long (131ft) foc'sle which continued into the boat deck, and – also for the first time in one of the Company's ships – a cruiser stern. The hull was subdivided into nine watertight compartments which extended up to shelter deck level.

Overnight berthing accommodation was arranged for a total of 263 in first class and about 100 in second class aft, but their certificates permitted maximums of about 430 and 1,250 to be carried in the two classes. Their crew numbered 60.

They had a cargo capacity of about 500 tons which could be carried in five holds, three forward of the machinery spaces and two aft, and cargo was handled by five derricks and five silent running steam winches. Discounting *Stockholm*, their single reduction geared turbines were the first to be employed in the fleet, and their boilers were arranged to burn both coal and oil fuel, respective bunker capacities being 190 and 196 tons.

Between them the three ships maintained the 'British Mail Route to Belgium' with great regularity until 1939, the 135-mile overnight crossing taking some 9–10 hours of which only about five were spent in the open sea. Several collisions took place in the Scheldt, the most serious being a violent contact between *Antwerp* and the Wilson & NER steamer *Darlington* on 9 July 1932 and the occasion when *Malines* was beached after being run down in fog by the motor tanker *Hanseat* (8,499grt).

Wartime brought the closure of all services and by the early 1940s the grey-painted *Antwerp* and *Bruges* were operating out of Southampton on trooping duties. *Malines* was sent to Rotterdam to pick up British civilians and, having survived the heavy bombing attacks preceding the German advance, picked up the crew of her scuttled partner *St Denis* and, unlit, slipped down the New Waterway at night under the noses of the German gunners already installed on the southern bank.

All three sisters took part in the evacuation of troops from France and off Dunkirk *Malines* rescued over 1,000 troops and naval ratings from the torpedoed destroyer HMS *Grafton*. *Bruges* fell victim to a bombing attack off Le Havre on 11 June, her crew escaping home in *Vienna*, and soon afterwards both *Antwerp* and *Malines* helped to evacuate civilians from the Channel Islands.

After conversion to RN convoy escorts the remaining sisters were dispatched from Avonmouth to the Mediterranean via the Cape in October 1941 but on 22 July 1942 *Malines* was torpedoed by aircraft and beached near Port Said. *Antwerp* later became the headquarters ship for the Eastern Naval Task Force during the invasion of Sicily in July 1943 and a year later was acting as a Fighter Direction Ship armed with two 12pdr AA guns. She was released in 1945 and returned to the LNER for refitting before becoming a BAOR leave ship on the Harwich–Hook run.

Malines meanwhile had been raised in September 1943 following transfer to the MoWT. Used as a training ship at Kabret early in 1944, she eventually arrived back in the Tyne in November 1945 after an eventful tow lasting nearly six months during which she twice broke adrift. She never returned to service and was broken up by Clayton & Davie Ltd at Dunston in April 1948. The final surviving sister *Antwerp* was withdrawn two years later and sold in 1951 to T.W. Ward, which demolished her at Milford Haven.

Vienna (1929), *Prague, Amsterdam* (1930)

Towards the end of the 1920s the LNER placed an order with John Brown & Co for three large new steamers for its Harwich–Hook overnight service, because the company's *Archangel*, *St Denis* and *St George* were well advanced in years.

The first of the new sisters, which revived the name *Vienna*, was launched on 10 April, completing her steaming trials on 28 June and entering service on 15 July. Her sisters *Prague* and

Left:
The elegant 4,218 ton Clyde – built *Vienna* shared with her sisters *Prague* and *Amsterdam* the distinction of being the largest North Sea passenger ships until the arrival of Bergen Line's *Venus* in 1931. *Author's collection*

Below left:
Down by the stern, the damaged *Prague* escapes from Dunkirk in tow of the Dover tug *Lady Brassey*, escorted by the Dieppe steamer *Newhaven*. *Author's collection*

Amsterdam followed in 1930 and they shared the same specification.

Length: 366ft 0in/350ft 9in
Breadth: 50ft 1in
Depth/draught: 27ft (shelter deck)/15ft 3in (load)
Gross tonnage: 4,218
Machinery: 2 sets, SR Brown-Curtis turbines
Boilers: 5se, 215lb/sq in
Speed: 21kt

The new ships were the result of a joint design by F.W. Noal, marine superintendent engineer, and Captain R. Davis, the marine superintendent of the LNER, and were the largest yet built for cross-channel service out of UK ports. They were shelter-deckers with a long combined foc'sle and bridge deck which extended about three-quarters of the way aft, and their hulls were divided by eight watertight bulkheads reaching up to shelter-deck level.

Passenger accommodation was arranged over four decks and included berths for 444 in first and 104 in second classes. The former were mainly in single cabins but four special de-luxe cabins with private baths were located at the forward end of the promenade deck. The second class sleeping accommodation was aft in two and four-berth cabins but all were fitted with washbasins with hot and cold running water. As well as the usual public rooms a novel feature was the addition of several shops.

Two large cargo holds were provided forward and there was also space in the after tween-decks for fish cargoes or cars, whilst baggage and mail were carried in a tween-deck forward on the shelter deck. Total cubic capacity was 40,000ft and handling arrangements included two three-ton derricks forward and a single 1½-ton derrick on the mainmast.

Their two sets of turbines each incorporated a high pressure and a low pressure unit with separate astern turbines for 60% power enclosed in the low pressure casing. Bunker capacity was about 230 tons of coal.

Between them the three ships maintained the important Harwich–Hook line without undue incident throughout the 1930s, but a new departure occurred in the summer of 1932 when *Vienna* inaugurated weekend cruises to nearby continental ports, for which extra lounge accommodation had been fitted and her promenade deck extended to the mainmast. These popular 'no passport' trips were continued each summer between June and September until 1939 and she visited Amsterdam, Rotterdam, Flushing, Ghent, Zeebrugge and on occasions Rouen. In July 1935 *Vienna* took time off to officially represent her owners at the Jubilee Naval Review at Spithead.

Within months of the outbreak of war all three had moved to Southampton for trooping duties and later *Prague* and *Amsterdam* took part in the Dunkirk evacuation. The former when returning from her third trip on 1 June 1940 with some 3,000

French troops was holed aft by a near miss during an air attack. One of her engines was put out of action and she had to be beached near Deal. After salvaging she was fitted with a new stern in London and later joined *Amsterdam* on the Aberdeen–Orkneys trooping service where she was again damaged by bombs.

Vienna, which had been acquired by the Ministry of War Transport in 1941, became a depot ship for coastal forces in the Mediterranean, being based first at Algiers and later Bari at the end of 1943. At about the same time *Amsterdam* was converted into an assault landing ship (LSI-H) taking part in the Normandy invasion in June 1944, after which she was quickly converted again to a hospital ship; however, she had only made two trips when she was mined off the French coast on 7 August with heavy loss of life. Her sister *Prague* was also at D-day acting as a hospital carrier for American forces, having been converted on the Tyne earlier in the year, and she continued hospital work until the end of the war.

Shortly after peace was declared *Prague* re-opened the Harwich–Hook service on 14 November 1945 with three departures a week in each direction, but her accommodation was of necessity austere. Early the following year she was joined by Zeeland's *Oranje Nassau* to make the service a nightly one and in May 1947 by the new *Arnhem*. Her final sailing that year was on Christmas day and early in the new year she returned to her builder for a much needed refit. Unfortunately she caught fire on 14 March, her accommodation was gutted, and she sank alongside the dock. She was not deemed worth repairing and after raising was towed to Barrow where she arrived on 14 September for demolition by T.W. Ward.

Vienna meanwhile had been returned to the Harwich–Hook run by the MoT in 1945 albeit in a trooping role, but she remained under LNER management. In 1947 she was refitted as a permanent leave ship for the British occupation forces with a total of 1,048 berths. At first she had a black hull and grey upperworks but was repainted later with a grey hull carrying a blue 'trooping' band, and her funnels lost their black tops. On 11 February 1952 a boiler explosion whilst she was berthed at Parkeston killed two engineers

With the introduction of air trooping imminent she was withdrawn in July 1960 and two months later was towed to Ghent by *Merchantman* for breaking up by Van Heyghen Freres, arriving on 4 September.

The name ship of her class, she had been a notable feature of the North Sea shipping scene during her 10 years of prewar civilian service and after a varied and successful war career had continued to serve the military on her original route for a further 15 years.

Duke of York

In the spring of 1948 the newly constituted British Transport Commission transferred the steamer *Duke of York* from the Irish Sea to the Harwich station to fill the gap caused by the loss of the *Prague*. She had been built by Harland & Wolff, Belfast in 1935 as an extra passenger/cargo ship for the Heysham–Belfast service to run alongside the three 1929-built 'Dukes' in place of *Duke of Abercorn*, the former *Curraghmore*. Launched on 7 March (trials on 3 June) she was of interest in being the first channel steamer to emulate North Atlantic practice in treating her third class accommodation as tourist class.

Length: 339ft 2½in
Breadth: 52ft 2½in
Depth/draught: 17ft 10in/14ft 8in
Gross tonnage: 3,743

Machinery: 2 sets, SR geared turbines
Boilers: 2
Power: 8,800shp
Speed: 21kt

As built she was a handsome two-funnelled ship with a raised foc'sle and long bridge deck, above which was an extensive observation lounge. Her first class accommodation amidships provided berths for 139 passengers, with 'tourist' sleeping arrangements for 240 below on the main and lower decks and aft. She was intended to carry large amounts of cargo and livestock and was fitted with four turret-like electric cranes. In the engine-room mechanical stokers were something of a novelty.

During World War 2 she was at first used for trooping on the south coast and later assisted in the evacuation of Dunkirk. Early in 1942 she was taken over by the Navy and converted to the assault landing ship HMS *Duke of Wellington*. As such she could carry 250 troops and 10 small landing craft and took part in the Dieppe Raid and the Normandy landings. After her release she was used for a while as a trooper out of Harwich before returning to the Irish Sea in October 1947.

Following her transfer to the Eastern Region she made her first commercial sailing on the Harwich–Hook service at the end of May 1948. In July 1950 she was briefly transferred to the Southern Region's Southampton–Cherbourg service afterwards returning to her builders in Belfast for a six-month refit. During this time she was converted to oil-firing and was fitted with a large single funnel; also her accommodation was extensively rebuilt to provide berths for 359 first and 160 second class passengers – these alterations raising her gross tonnage to 4,190. She returned to Harwich in May 1951, soon afterwards running for a spell between Holyhead and Dun Laoghaire.

On 6 May 1953, shortly after 4.15am whilst inward bound to Harwich and still some 40 miles distant, she was struck just forward of the bridge by the US military transport *Haiti Victory* and almost cut in two. Eight lives were lost and many injured but her passengers were taken off by the American

After losing her bows in collision with the US *Haiti Victory* on 6 May 1953 *Duke of York* was given an entirely new bow section with a raking stem. Her former well-deck was eliminated and her foremast moved nearer the bridge. As built for Irish Sea service she had two funnels and an oufit of deck cranes which were removed during a 1950/51 refit. *John G. Callis*

vessel and another ship. Her bows later broke off and sank but the stern half was towed first to Harwich, and later to the Tyne for repairs at Palmer's Yarrow yard. These involved the fitting of a new 90ft flush-decked bow section with a raking stem which further raised her tonnage to 4,325; the work being completed in February 1954.

With her running partners *Arnhem* and *Amsterdam* taking most of the regular sailings her duties were mainly confined to seasonal and relief work and in the summer of 1963, in anticipation of the arrival of the new *Avalon,* she was sold to the Chandris owned, Liberian registered, Marivic Navigation Inc, with delivery taking place shortly after her final arrival at Harwich on 20 July. Renamed *York* at Smith's Dock, she underwent some structural alteration which included the lengthening of her promenade deck. Sailing for Piraeus in November, she was finished off in Chandris' own yard at Ambelaki, and after re-registering as Chandris Cruises Ltd's *Fantasia* she commenced a fortnightly cruising schedule out of Venice on 15 March 1964.

In her new role she could accommodate some 380 one-class passengers in air-conditioned two, three and four-berth cabins with the usual public rooms and bars, also a night club and two swimming pools. Her itinerary included calls at Corfu–Piraeus–Heraklion – Rhodes – Cyprus – Haifa – Mykonos – Piraeus and Dubrovnik but the Cyprus call was later dropped, and later still she was employed on shorter cruises from Piraeus to Aegean. She was finally broken up at Piraeus by Prodromos Sariktzis in May 1976 after a varied career lasting 41 years.

Arnhem, Amsterdam (1950)

Immediately after World War 2 the LNER ordered a new steamer to fill the gap left in its Harwich–Hook service by the loss of *Amsterdam*. As with the previous trio the builders of the new ship were John Brown & Co and she was launched on 7 November 1946, being named *Arnhem* to commemorate the famous battle of 1944. Fitting out was completed very quickly in spite of the austerity conditions then prevailing and she was delivered in May 1947. Larger than her prewar predecessors, she had the following main particulars:

Length: 377ft 1in oa/360ft 8in bp
Breadth: 54ft 5in
Depth/draught: 27ft 0in/15ft 3in
Gross tonnage: 4,891 (*Amsterdam* 5,092)
Machinery: 2 sets Parsons SR geared turbines
Boilers: 2 oil watertube, 340lb/sq in
Power: 8,000shp
Speed: 21kt

With her raked stem, rounded bridge front and large elliptical funnel she looked quite different from the ships of the 'Vienna' class but her design was very much a logical development of the earlier ships with an extended upper deck almost reaching the stern and a more enclosed superstructure. Her accommodation was originally arranged for only one class with four special cabins and 319 singles, about one-third of which had an extra Pullman berth if required, but this was altered to cater for two classes in 1949. Her maximum passenger complement was given as 750.

Main propulsion was by four Parsons turbines – two HP and two LP – driving twin screws through single reduction gearing, and steam was supplied by two oil-fired watertube boilers working at a pressure of 340psi. Four holds were provided for cargo, cars and baggage, but she had only two three-ton derricks as handling was mainly carried out by shore-based cranes.

When *Prague* was lost by fire whilst refitting in November 1948 the British Transport Commission, which had taken over the running of the newly nationalised railways at the beginning of that year, ordered a replacement in the shape of a sister to *Arnhem*. The new ship revived the name *Amsterdam* for a third time, it being particularly complementary to *Arnhem*, and she was launched at Clydebank on 19 January 1950 with delivery taking place the following May. Her dimensions were virtually identical to *Arnhem's* but in the light of experience she had one or two minor structural differences, the most noticeable of which was the raising of her boats in gravity davits. Her accommodation however was arranged for two classes from the outset with sleeping arrangements for 321 in first class and 236 in second class. The former were berthed in two de-luxe and 56 single cabins plus 22 doubles with cot beds and 100 doubles with Pullman berths, 11 of which were fitted with an extra settee berth. Second class passengers were housed in 48 double and 35 four-berth cabins whilst public rooms for both classes were situated on the promenade deck.

In the spring of 1954 *Arnhem* underwent a two-month refit during which her overnight accommodation was altered to cater for 375 passengers in first class and about 200 in second class. At the same time structural changes which

The powerful-looking *Arnhem* of 1947 was the first single-funnelled passenger ship built for the Harwich continental services since the paddle steamer *Lady Tyler* of 1880. Note her deep hull with combined foc'sle and bridge deck reaching almost to the stern.
Author's collection

included a new window arrangement on the promenade deck raised her gross tonnage to 5,008.

Between them the two sisters maintained regular overnight sailings between Harwich and the New Waterway for a further 13 years, running in company with *Duke of York* until 1963 and afterwards with the new *Avalon*. Towards the end of 1966 British Rail and Zeeland ordered two large new car ferries from English shipyards with a view to commencing a double day and night service in the summer of 1968. In anticipation of this the 21-year-old *Arnhem* was withdrawn and laid up following a final crossing from the Hook on the night of 26/27 April 1968. No trading buyers were forthcoming and she was sold to T.W. Ward Ltd for scrap, arriving at Inverkeithing on 16 August, though

demolition did not in fact start until June the following year.

The new ships *St George* and *Koningin Juliana* arrived at Harwich in July but the opening of the new service was delayed until November due to

Below:
Although a sister to *Arnhem*, the 1950-built *Amsterdam* carried her boats in gravity davits. Other differences included a small house under the foremast, a white-painted bridge, and an extended boat deck aft.
Real Photos

Bottom:
Fiorita (ex-*Amsterdam*) leaving Corfu in September 1975 showing the extent of the alterations undertaken by her new owner Chandris in 1969/70 to convert her to a full-time cruise ship. *Author*

problems with *St George*. *Amsterdam* was kept as reserve ship during this period and stood in for *Avalon* on the night sailings between 27–30 October. She was sold the following April to the Bermuda-registered Claxton Ltd, a Chandris subsidiary, and was taken to Piraeus where work commenced on her conversion to a full-time cruise ship. This involved the extension of her superstructure fore and aft and the fitting of new masts, a streamlined funnel top and a swimming pool at the after end of the newly designated sun deck. A new bar and lounge area with a night club was created amidships on the promenade deck with the dining saloon on 'Minerva' deck below. Cabins, most having private faciities, were situated at the forward end of 'Minerva' deck and on two lower decks named 'Venus' and 'Diana'. Her new one class passenger capacity was about 480 and her fully air-conditioned accommodation also included a beauty salon and a duty free shop.

Following her conversion she was renamed *Fiorita* and on 13 May 1970 commenced a regular series of 11 and 12-day cruises from Venice, calling at Corfu, the Aegean Islands, and either Istanbul or Alexandria, returning via Piraeus. This set the pattern for subsequent summers although her itinerary varied from time to time, and later calls at Haifa and Dubrovnik were included. During the winters she was occasionally employed elsewhere and in 1970/71 made a series of 15-day cruises from Malaga to Tangier, the Canary Islands, and Dakar. In March 1976 she made an unusual cruise through the Suez Canal to visit Red Sea ports including Jeddah, Hodeidah and Port Sudan, but more often than not she was laid up in the Piraeus area. During her Chandris career her registered ownership changed from International Cruises SA to Universal Cruises SA and finally in 1974 to the one-ship company Armadores Fiorita SA.

In the spring of 1978 she was chartered to the Norwegian Akers shipbuilding group for use as an accommodation ship at Stord where she arrived on 3 April. A year later she was back in Piraeus but a scheduled series of cruises out of Venice was cancelled and she was laid up on 9 May. Various reports of her sale to Saronic Cruises as *Ariane II* proved groundless and she remained laid up until the autumn of 1982 when she was brought out for inspection by potential buyers from Newcastle, who were seeking a hotel ship. No sale materialised and she remained laid up in Piraeus until March 1983, when she was delivered at sea to new owners Ef-Em Handels Gmbh, Munich, having passed briefly through the hands of Sommerland Handels Gmbh. On 5 April she arrived at Kas, southwest Turkey for use as a floating hotel, without change of name, but reports suggest the venture was not successful and the scrapyard must surely await this last surviving example of a traditional English North Sea packet.

Avalon

In September 1961 the British Rail Board ordered a large new ship to replace the ageing *Duke of York* on its Harwich run but as three ships were not required on the route the whole year round she was also designed with off-season cruising in mind. Her builders were Messrs Alexander Stephen & Sons and she was launched at Linthouse without ceremony on 7 May 1963, the originally planned date of 10 April having been postponed due to an electricians' strike.

Her name *Avalon* revived that of an early GER favourite and she was at that time the largest passenger ship ever built for railway company service, representing the ultimate development of the purely passenger carrying ship prior to the introduction of new car ferries. After performing trials in the Clyde she steamed south to Harwich to undergo berthing trials and made her first commercial sailing on 25 July. Her construction cost BRB about £2million.

Length: 404ft 6in oa/327ft 0in bp
Breadth: 59ft 8in
Depth/draught: 21ft 0in mld/15ft 10in
Gross tonnage: 6,584
Machinery: 2 sets, Pametrada DR geared turbines
Boilers: 2 oil watertube, 350 lb/sq in
Power: 15,000shp
Speed: 21½kt

Externally she was an imposing ship with clean lines and her all-welded hull was flush for almost the whole of its length save for a very short drop in deck level right aft. Her enclosed three-deck high superstructure was streamlined at its forward end, and mounted above this were two streamlined masts and a single tapered funnel topped with a rounded smoke deflector.

Her internal accommodation was arranged over four decks for a total of 750 passengers including 331 berths in first class and 287 in second class, whilst the remainder were in aircraft-type seats. Public rooms were situated on the shelter deck and included a first class lounge and restaurant forward of the machinery casing and a second class cafeteria and smoking room aft; two further lounges were provided on the promenade deck above. For cruising her accommodation could be rearranged to cater for 320 one-class passengers in a variety of cabins ranging from two-berth de-luxe on the promenade deck to four-berth inside on the main deck.

Provision was made for the carriage of about 1,000 tons of cargo in two holds forward and one aft, the latter having a particularly large hatch to allow the loading of large cars. Her propelling

Avalon in Sealink colours crosses an unusually placid Irish Sea following her conversion to a stern-loading car ferry in 1975. *Author's collection*

machinery consisted of two Stephen-built Pametrada single casing turbines which were connected to twin shafts by means of double reduction gearing, and steam was supplied by two Foster Wheeler watertube boilers supplying steam at 350 psi and 650°F. For manoeuvrability she was fitted with a bow thruster, bow rudder and twin rudders aft, whilst for passenger comfort she was equipped with a pair of the latest Denny Brown/ AEG stabilisers.

She was generally employed on the Harwich overnight service in the summer and winter months but undertook cruises out of the Essex port in the Spring and Autumn, thus reviving a tradition started by *Vienna* in the 1930s. Her first such cruise was a modest weekend visit to Amsterdam on 24 April 1964, but in the autumn she made an eight-day cruise which included a visit to Copenhagen. By May 1966 she was venturing south to Oporto and Lisbon, calling at Tangier in the autumn, and the following year saw her in Scandinavian and Baltic waters.

On the night of 22 August 1966 she had made an unusal diversion from her normal Harwich–Hook service, being chartered by Ellerman's Wilson Line for an overnight sailing from Hull to Gothenburg on the night of 28 in place of the latter's new *Spero* which had been delayed at her builders. The following autumn she was chartered by Gulf Oil between 26 and 31 October to take a party of guests and journalists to Bantry Bay to witness the opening of the Whiddy Island refinery by the 330,000dwt VLCC *Universe Ireland*. Later that year she made a round voyage between Fishguard and Cork over the Christmas holiday period, on yet another charter.

After the car ferries *St George* and *Koningin Juliana* had started a new double day and night service in the autumn of 1967 her duties on the Hook service were confined to extra overnight summer sailings and relief work, allowing her to concentrate even more time on cruising, and she visited Gibraltar on several occasions.

The arrival of the new car ferry *St Edmund* at Harwich late in 1974 rendered her redundant and

on 29 December she sailed for the Tyne where Swan Hunters converted her into a stern-loading car ferry for Irish Sea service. This involved the gutting of her main and lower deck accommodation which was replaced with two car decks capable of carrying about 200 cars and a limited number of commercial vehicles. At the same time her superstructure was extended aft to make an enlarged cafeteria. She emerged from this £1million rebuild with a reduced gross tonnage of 5,142 and a passenger capacity of 1,200, and was sent to replace *Caledonian Princess* on the Fishguard–Rosslare service in the summer of 1975.

Her career on the Irish Sea – where she was the largest ship in operation – varied from time to time. For the first three months of 1976 she ran between Holyhead and Dun Laoghaire but over the next three years continued her regular 'one ship' service out of Fishguard. As traffic increased however its mainly commercial nature proved too much for her stern loading capability and she was replaced by the chartered Swedish drive-through ferry *Stena Normandica* in March 1979, moving to Holyhead. Later that summer however the breakdown of the newer ship necessitated her return to the Pembrokeshire run between 22 June and 23 September.

After a further year as a reserve and summer extra on the Holyhead service she was withdrawn and sent to Barrow for lay-up. In November 1980 she was sold to the Cypriot-registered Seafaith Navigation Co and was renamed *Valon*. Wearing a black funnel she left Barrow five days before Christmas on a one-way voyage to Gadani Beach near Karachi. After calling at Aden she arrived on 22 January and demolition commenced almost immediately at the hands of H.H. Steel Ltd. Thus passed the last and largest of the traditional 'Harwich packets'.

Ministry of Transport

Harwich–Hook of Holland (occasionally
Bremerhaven)
1945–1962   Ministry of War Transport/
Ministry of Transport

Empire Parkeston

In the summer of 1946 the Ministry of War
Transport purchased the Canadian Government
steamer *Prince Henry* which was lying at Falmouth
after a short post-war period on loan to the Royal
Navy, during which she had been used as an
accommodation ship at Wilhelmshaven. Bought for
around £125,000 she was taken to Harland & Wolff
at Southampton for conversion to a troop transport.
Her landing craft were removed and replaced by 10
new lifeboats in gravity davits whilst her interior
was refitted for 813 troops in three-tiered bunks
together with rather austere cabin accommodation
for 182, reserved for officers and their families as
well as members of the women's services. Upon
completion in March 1947 she was renamed *Empire
Parkeston* and placed under the management of the
GSN Co.

Prince Henry had originally been built by
Cammell Laird & Co Ltd in 1930 as the first of three
twin-screw sisters for Canadian National Steamship
Co for service on the British Columbian coast. She
was launched on 17 January by Miss MacDonald,
daughter of the Canadian Prime Minister, and later
attained over 23kt on trials. She was rather a dumpy
little ship with a large superstructure extending over
three-quarters of her length, and three short,
closely spaced funnels which carried her owners'
blue, white and red colours.

Length: 366ft 5in
Breadth: 57ft 1in
Depth: 27ft 4in
Gross tonnage: 6,893
Machinery: 2 sets, Parsons SR geared turbines
Boilers: 6, 350lb/sq in
Power: 19,000shp
Speed: 20kt

After a varied career as passenger and cruise liner on the
west and east coats of Canada and the USA followed by
World War 2 service as a Canadian AMC and later an
LSI(M), the former three-funnelled *Prince Henry* was
acquired by the MoWT in 1946 for its Harwich leave
service. Seen in the Thames in May 1948 in black and
grey livery, she later had Thornycroft-type smoke
deflectors added to her funnel tops and adopted normal
trooping colours.   *John G. Callis*

Her luxuriously appointed superstructure provided berths for 334 first and 70 third class passengers and she was used in either the Alaska or Vancouver–Seattle–Victoria services. Competition from Canadian Pacific proved too strong however and in 1932 she was transferred to the East Coast for cruising duties out of Boston and later New York, for which she was given a white hull. Late in 1937 after a short period on charter to Clarke Steamship Co of Quebec she was purchased by that firm for $500,000 and in a $108,000 refit her accommodation was altered to cater for 335 cruise passengers. Renamed *North Star* she was given yellow funnels with four narrow blue bands and initially cruised out of Miami to the West Indies, but was later put on a Montreal–New York service.

After the outbreak of World War 2 she was purchased by the Royal Canadian Navy and was converted into the armed merchant cruiser HMCS *Prince Henry* by Canadian Vickers at Montreal. Her superstructure was removed and replaced with a more functional bridge whilst her two forward funnels were trunked together into a larger single stack. Her main armament consisted of four vintage 6in guns and her subsequent duties took her to places as far apart as Newfoundland, the Caribbean, the west coast of South America and the Aleutian Islands.

In 1943 she was converted to a medium-size infantry landing ship at Burrard Dry Dock Co, Vancouver, being fitted with eight landing craft and rather basic accommodation for their crews and about 550 troops. She crossed the Atlantic and after working up in Cowes took part in the Normandy landings where she acted as HQ ship at 'Juno' Beach. Later she went to the Mediterranean to act as Rear Admiral Chandler's flagship for the invasion of Southern France and then took part in the liberation of Greece before returning to the East India Dock, London where she was paid off.

She took up her new role as a BAOR leave ship early in 1947, initially with a black hull and funnels and a grey superstructure. From 1948 she was regularly employed between Harwich and the Hook of Holland in company with two other MoWT ships, *Vienna* and *Empire Wansbeck*. She usually crossed at night, alternating with *Vienna*, and ran with two of her boilers shut down for an economical 16kt to cover the 116-mile run in 7/8 hours. During this early part of her new career she was one of the ships that went to the assistance of the Laeisz sailing ship *Pamir* which had got into difficulties on her first postwar voyage under German ownership.

Later her livery was changed to a grey hull with a blue trooping band, white superstructure and grey funnels, the latter being fitted with Thornycroft type smoke-deflecting tops. In the late 1950s her funnels were painted troopship yellow with black

tops and this improved her appearance enormously. She rarely deviated from her normal route, visiting the Mediterranean in 1956 during the Suez Crisis, and Cardiff the following year to transport the Welsh Guards to Holland.

1961 was a year of major defence cutbacks and thenceforward it was decided to carry out troop movements by air. This marked the end of *Empire Parkeston's* usefulness and after 14 years' service, during which she and her two companions had carried over eight million troops and their families, she arrived in Harwich from the Hook for the last time on 26 September, dressed overall and flying a paying off pennant. She joined *Empire Wansbeck* in lay-up and the following year was sold to Italian breaker Lotti SpA and towed by *Gele Zee* to La Spezia where she arrived on 20 February. Her 30-year career was certainly a varied one up to its mid-point, but the latter half spent crossing the North Sea was almost routine in comparison.

Empire Wansbeck

When setting up its postwar trooping and leave service for the BAOR the Ministry of War Transport (later the Ministry of Transport) acquired the German motor ship *Linz* which had arrived in Hull from Hamburg on 1 December 1945 after being handed over as part of the allied war reparation scheme the previous July. Originally laid down by Danziger Werft in 1939 as one of two fruit ships for North German Lloyd she was launched in 1940, but World War 2 interrupted construction and she was towed to Denmark for completion in 1943 by the A.P. Moller-owned Odense Steel Shipyard. Subsequently she was taken over by the German navy and used as an auxiliary minelayer.

After her acquisition by the MoWT she was renamed *Empire Wansbeck* and placed under the management of Ellerman's Wilson Line, undergoing a refit which gave her the following dimensions and particulars:

Length: 336ft 5in oa/323ft 2½in bp
Breadth: 45ft 7in
Depth/draught: 26ft 7in/18ft 0in
Gross tonnage: 3,508
Machinery: 6-cylinder MAN diesel
Speed: 15kt

She was a two-deck ship with a raked stem and cruiser stern, having a long raised foc'sle extending to her foremast. Abaft the latter was a short gap in the No 2 hold position and then a long superstructure which had a high, square bridge block dwarfing the squat funnel, but otherwise extended as a single deck almost to the stern.

Her accommodation (which was of a fairly basic nature) comprised cabin berths for over 150 officers and their dependents whilst about 700 troops could be berthed in tiered bunks in the foc'sle and tween-deck dormitories. Later her overall capacity was increased to almost 1,050.

She made her first crossing on the Harwich–Hook service in February 1946 but as the 1950s wore on acted mainly as a relief for her two larger and faster consorts *Empire Parkeston* and *Vienna*. She arrived at Parkeston on 26 September 1961 after completing 2,030 round voyages and was laid up in the Stour.

The MoT service had by this time been superceded by an air trooping scheme in 1961 and the following year she was sold to the Piraeus-based Kavounides Shipping Co Ltd. She was renamed *Esperos* (Hope) and in 1964 was extensively rebuilt, her foc'sle being extended into the superstructure whilst at the same time part of her original boat deck was enclosed and extended forward to a point just short of her foremast. A new bridge was fitted above her former one and a pair of kingposts placed at the break of her forward bulwarks.

These alterations increased her gross tonnage to 3,964 and she could then carry 116 first, 175 second, 100 tourist, and 200 dormitory class passengers as well as about 60 cars. Later her passengers figures were altered to 500 in one class.

Her service was a regular one linking Venice with Rhodes, calling at Corfu, Piraeus and Mykonos en route, and though she lacked the glamour of some of the Greek ships she soon built up a reputation for toughness and reliability, often maintaining winter sailings when others were laid up.

Subsequent alterations affecting her profile included the replacing of her foremast with a small signal mast on her bridge and the shortening of her mainmast, whilst later still her funnel was heightened and fitted with a rounded top.

Gradually her owners dropped their regular services to concentrate entirely on cruising and as *Esperos* was not really suited for this and was getting on in years she was laid up near Perama. There she remained quietly rotting until early 1980 when, with her hull 40 years old, she was sold for scrap, leaving Piraeus on 14 March in tow for Gandia, Spain where work commenced in May.

Above right:
Laid down in 1939 as a German fruiter and later serving as an auxiliary minelayer, the surrendered *Linz* became *Vienna's* partner in the BAOR leave service in 1945, running as *Empire Wansbeck* under Ellerman's Wilson management. All grey at first, she later wore the latter's funnel colours and a black hull before adopting full trooping livery as shown here. *T. Rayner*

Right:
Following her sale to Kavounides in 1962 *Empire Wansbeck* became *Esperos* and later underwent several phases of alteration. This 1971 Piraeus view shows her final guise with heightened funnel. *Laurence Dunn*

Manchester, Sheffield & Lincolnshire Railway Co

Grimsby–Hamburg/Rotterdam/Antwerp
1856–1865   Anglo-French Steamship Co
1865–1897   Manchester, Sheffield & Lincolnshire
                Railway Co
1897–1922   Great Central Railway Co
1923–1947   London & North Eastern Railway Co
1948–1966   British Transport Commission
                (Eastern Region)
Funnel colours: White with black top
  1948– Buff with black top

Gainsborough

The Manchester Sheffield & Lincolnshire Railway obtained powers through its Steamboats Act of 29 July 1864 to operate passenger and cargo services to Hamburg, Rotterdam, Antwerp and Flushing as well as to Copenhagen, Stockholm, St Petersburg and other Baltic ports. The company quickly purchased the four ships of the Anglo-French Co and ordered four ships for its own account to link Grimsby with Hamburg and Rotterdam. These two services were to become the MS&L's 'main lines' to the Continent and operations commenced in July 1865 and April 1866 respectively with two sailings a week in each direction.

By the beginning of the 1880s MS&L North Sea shipping services were well established having successfully weathered a number of early unprofitable years due to intense competition from the Great Eastern Railway and also to a certain extent from direct services between Liverpool and the Continent. The first 16 years had also been marred by an excessive number of accidents. The 1880s were to bring about an almost complete renewal of the MS&L fleet, eight older ships being disposed of and eight new ones being built to replace them. It is worth noting also that the number of serious mishaps began to decline as the newer ships came into service.

The first new ship to appear was the *Gainsborough* ordered in June 1880 from Earle's Co Ltd of Hull, who had previously built only one ship for the Company. the *Wakefield* of 1866.

Gainsborough was built to the same basic design as the Clyde-built pair of 1872, *Halifax* and *Huddersfield*, which had been the first in the fleet to exceed 1,000 tons, but the new ship only cost some £21,000 as opposed to about £23,000 apiece for the earlier pair. Like them she was a three-masted iron steamer with engines placed well aft.

Length: 231ft 0in
Breadth: 30ft 2½in
Depth of hold: 16ft 5in
Gross tonnage: 1,081
Machinery: 2-cylinder compound
Boilers: 1de, 70lb/sq in
Power: 900ihp
Speed: 12kt

Gainsborough was launched on 20 December 1880 and after reaching 12kt on trials was placed in the Company's Hamburg trade early the following year, her speed being intended to eclipse all others on this route. Her long poop was fitted with a saloon and staterooms for 40 first class passengers and a large number of emigrants could be accommodated in the tween-decks. Cattle pens were fitted on deck and also underdeck amidships. Her career was destined to be a short one and on 27 December 1883 after only two years' service she was run down and sunk some 25 miles off Spurn Head when inward bound by the Sunderland steamer *Wear*. Her seven passengers and 23 crew were all picked up by the latter.

Retford

In 1882 the MS&L ordered two more steamships from Earle's and the first of these, *Retford*, was launched on 20 January the following year. She was earmarked for the Rotterdam service and was an iron ship with the following dimensions:

Length: 230ft 7in
Breadth: 32ft 0in
Depth: 12ft 11in
Gross tonnage: 951
Machinery: 2 sets, 2-cylinder compound

Despite a 27-year career spent mainly on the Grismby–Rotterdam service the iron-hulled *Retford* (1883) remained the only example of a twin-screw steamer in the MS&LR's Continental fleet. The long quarterdeck design was not repeated in subsequent ships. *From 'Great Central' by George Dow*

Boilers: 2, 85lb/sq in
Power: about 900ihp
Speed: 12kt

Her layout was fairly conventional with a separate foc'sle and combined bridge and poop whilst her two pole masts were schooner rigged. Her propelling machinery was unusual in that it was the first twin screw arrangement to be adopted by the railway company. The MS&L routes were much longer than those of the rival GER (375 miles to Hamburg) and speed was less of a criterion than good cargo capacity. *Retford* was certainly no flyer, but the experiment with twin screw cannot be deemed a success for it was not tried again until 1906, and even then it did not work, as will become apparent later.

In accommodation *Retford* conformed to the old-fashioned arrangement of having the 36 first class passengers berthed aft under the poop whilst 12 second class were housed forward and about 250 emigrants below in the forward tween-decks when required. Later these figures were amended to 30 in first and 148 in third classes.

On 26 January 1895 she was involved in a serious collision with the Swedish steamer *Telesto* off the Norfolk coast between Cromer and Great Yarmouth which resulted in the latter ship's sinking. Some six years later on 10 December 1901 a further minor collision took place with the German

tug *Hercules* near Maasluis, and almost exactly a year later on 3 December 1902 she was again involved in a brush with the Russian steamer *Osmo* and a tug, her master being suspended for three months at the resulting court case.

Early in 1910 she became surplus following the introduction of new tonnage and was sold in March to Samuel Galbraith, being scrapped later that year after a useful 27-year career with the railway company.

Lincoln

The third ship to be built for the MS&L by Earle's of Hull and the second to be completed for the Company in 1883 was the *Lincoln*. Built alongside *Retford* she was some 20ft greater in length and marked a return to single-screw propulsion.

Length: 251ft 6in
Breadth: 32ft 2½in

Larger than *Retford* which she followed from Earle's Humberside shipyard in 1883, the 1,075 gross ton *Lincoln* differed in having a short well-deck at No 3 hatch disguised by high bulwarks. Note also the different boat arrangement and small donkey funnel abaft her stack. The container-like boxes seen in her forward well housed circus animals. *Col R. C. Gabriel collection*

Depth: 15ft 11in
Gross tonnage: 1,075
Machinery: 2-cylinder compound
Boilers: 2se, 85lb/sq in
Power: 185nhp
Speed: 12kt

Lincoln was an iron-hulled steamer with a short raised foc'sle, a long well deck incorporating Nos 1 and 2 hatches, and a combined bridge and poop extending for half her length. There was a minimum of superstructure and her small funnel was placed near to the mainmast to give a rather unbalanced profile. Unlike *Retford* her first class accommodation for some 48 passengers was situated amidships with further provision for a number of second class passengers forward whilst her main tween-decks could be fitted for the carriage of up to 288 emigrants.

Although built initially for the Hamburg service she later served on both the Rotterdam and Antwerp routes, and was given a new deck in 1892. On 11 March 1894 she collided with and sank the Danzig steamer *Lining* in the River Maas but a more pleasing occurrence took place in June 1902 when she was privately chartered to attend the Royal Naval Review at Spithead. Danger again entered her career some nine years later on the night of 20/21 January 1911 when Grimsby-bound from Antwerp she stranded in fog on Hasborough Sands. Happily the weather was calm and after her passengers had been taken off by lifeboat she was refloated, virtually undamaged, with the aid of tugs.

After serving her owners for 31 years she was sold in 1914 to the Achaia Steamship Co Ltd of Patras, but life under her new name of *Elikon* was short for she became a war loss, being torpedoed in the Bay of Biscay on 1 February 1917 on a voyage from Bilbao to Cardiff.

The advanced three-island type *Ashton* (1884), seen at Antwerp, and *Chester* were the first sisters in the fleet since 1872 and the first to be driven by triple-expansion engines. Note the donkey exhaust aft (*Chester*'s was mounted forward of mainmast) 'echoing' the horizontal topped funnel. *Col R.C. Gabriel collection*

Chester, Ashton

The first pair of sister ships to be built for the MS&L for some 12 years were ordered from the West Hartlepool shipyard of E. Withy & Co for delivery in 1884. They were quite different from their Earle's -built counterparts and were considered advanced for their day. *Chester* was launched at Middleton Yard by Miss Florence Withy on 29 April followed by *Ashton*, whose christening was performed on 12 June by Mrs James Huddart of Melbourne. The two ships shared the following main characteristics:

Length: 248ft 0in oa/238ft 7in bp
Breadth: 32ft 3in
Depth: 15ft 4½in mld
Gross tonnage: 1,010/1,007
Machinery: 3-cylinder triple expansion
Boilers: 2de, 140lb/sq in
Power: 170nhp
Speed: 12kt

Intended for the Grimsby–Hamburg route but designed to be equally suitable for the Rotterdam and Antwerp services the new sisters were built of iron to an advanced three-island design with a long bridge deck amidships and turtle backed foc'sle and poop. A measure of ice strengthening was incorporated with double plating forward. Accommodation for some 30 first class passengers was arranged in a saloon and staterooms under the bridge deck with 10 second class in the foc'sle and the usual provision for about 275 emigrants in the fore tween-deck. The captain's cabin was amidships with the rest of the officers and crew housed aft in the poop.

Their engines were constructed by T. Richardson & Son of West Hartlepool and were the first examples of triple expansion type to be employed in the MS&L fleet. Deck gear included a steam windlass and three horizontal steam winches for handling the derricks.

In service *Chester* appears to have been the unluckier of the two being twice involved in major

collisions. The first occurred on 3 December 1885 when she was run into by the same company's *Wakefield* (1865/706gt) which had left Grimsby pierhead only five minutes before. The latter sank in 10 fathoms about half a mile inside Spurn, drowning a stewardess, but all the passengers and the rest of the crew were rescued by *Chester*. Both captains were later found to blame and were dismissed.

The second incident which was to prove fatal took place in 1910, late in *Chester's* career. She was inward bound in the Elbe on 28 September when she came into collision with the Norwegian steamer *Hugin* which had just cleared the locks at Brunsbuttelkoog. Damage to *Chester* was extensive with a large hole on the starboard side, bilge keels torn off, bridge and boat deck smashed and funnel broken. She sank the following day but not before about 700 of her cargo of several thousand cases of herrings had been offloaded into lighters. The wreck was later raised and sold for scrap.

Ashton appears to have led a relatively blameless career in comparison. In May 1893 she helped to rescue some of the passengers and crew of the Tyne passenger steamer *Londoner* which had sunk following a collision with the MS&L's *Sheffield* (1877/644gt) off Cromer. She was reboiled in 1901 and in December 1908 attracted the only adverse publicity of her career when five Russian emigrants died on board as a result of inhaling toxic fumes from barrels of ferro-silicon which were stored in the forehold beneath their accommodation.

Ashton did not finally leave the fleet until 1916 when she was deemed to be no longer seaworthy and was sold for £5,250 to the Cadeby Steamship Co Ltd (Managers: A.F. & J.C. Blackater).

It has been said that the up-to-date features incorporated in these two ships was due to the eagerness of their builders to break into the passenger ship market. However, the railway company does not seem to have been impressed and apart from retaining triple expansion engines reverted to old-fashioned practice for its subsequent ships, none of which were to come from the Middleton Yard.

Northenden, Warrington

In the five years up to 1885 the MS&L had taken delivery of a like number of new ships, but none of these had conformed to any recognisable pattern, suggesting that the company was still experimenting in order to determine the best possible design to fit its services. A further pair of iron ships was ordered from C.S. Swan & Hunter, Wallsend in 1885 and in them it is possible to discern for the first time the emergence of type that was to set the pattern for MS&L ships for some years to come.

The first of the new sisters, *Northenden*, slid down the ways into the Tyne on 1 May 1886, her name honouring the small Cheshire town where the Railway Company's progressive chairman Sir Edward Watkin had made his home. *Warrington* was named by Mrs Hunter on 9 June and five days after this the earlier ship steamed out on her acceptance trials, achieving better than 12½kt average in the course of four runs on the Withernsea mile. The main particulars of both ships were as follows:

Length: 240ft 0in/230ft 0in bp
Breadth: 30ft 1¼in

Warrington, Swan Hunter-built with *Northenden* in 1886, marked the start of a recognisable MS&LR type. Basically smaller versions of the *Lincoln* design, they were the first in the Company to carry deck cranes as well as derricks for cargo handling. *Author's collection*

Depth: 14ft 7in
Gross tonnage: 843
Machinery: 3-cylinder triple expansion
Boilers: 2se, 150lb/sq in
Power: 1,100ihp/170nhp
Speed: 12kt

The newly evolved design consisted of an iron hull with single deck and cellular double bottom subdivided into four watertight compartments, and having a short raised foc'sle and long continuous bridge combined with a full poop. Notwithstanding *Chester* and *Ashton,* the first class saloon and accommodation for about 47 passengers were placed once more under the poop, with a smokeroom and saloon entrance combined in a small deckhouse above. Petty officers and crew were housed in the foc'sle and the usual provision was made for about 230 emigrants in the tween-decks.

Cargo-carrying capacity was about 800 tons and cargo handling for the first time was provided by silent running steam cranes, one for the two forehatches and two on either side of No 3 hatch aft. Their triple expansion engines were products of the Wallsend Slipway & Engineering Co and Messrs. Westgarth English & Co of Middlesbrough respectively.

On entering service both ships were placed on the Hamburg run, and it would appear to have been Company policy to install new ships on this its most important service and then later, as they in turn were replaced by newer ships, to transfer them to the Rotterdam and Antwerp routes. Sandtor Quay was the German terminal and it was in Sandtor creek that *Northenden* hit and sank a lighter on 15 March 1900. Just over a year later she grounded in the Elbe while trying to avoid a collision but was refloated two days later. *Warrington* – whose engines were overhauled by Earle's in 1901 – was less fortunate when she grounded on South

Hasborough Sands on 7 December 1903 becoming a total loss, happily without casualty to her 14 passengers and 22 crew.

Some six years later in October 1909 *Northenden* was sold for £2,750 to the Progress Co (West Hartlepool) Ltd. She later passed to the ownership of Constantinople-based B.V. Vahratoglau (manager L. Economou) who renamed her *Ouhouvet.* She was later renamed *Selamet* by subsequent managers S. Alychides and Th. B. Vahratoglau and finally became the Persian registered *Ispahan* of Bander Abbas under the same management. She became a war loss when torpedoed by HM Submarine E.11 off Haidar Pasha on 15 August 1915.

Oldham

Following the delivery of the Swan Hunter-built sisters, 2½ years elapsed before a further new passenger cargo steamer appeared on the MS&L continental services. Earle's were her builders and iron was once more used in her construction, a somewhat surprising decision in view of the fact that the same shipyard had delivered two steel ships, a paddle ferry and a tug, to the railway company in the previous year.

Oldham was launched on 1 November 1888 and performed loaded trials on the Withernsea mile on 15 January the following year, recording an average of 12¾kt during four runs. A similar speed was achieved during a two-hour steaming trial at full power. The Company's first single ship for a number of years, she had the following dimensions:

Length: 240ft 5in
Breadth: 30ft 0in
Depth: 16ft 0in
Gross tonnage: 846
Machinery: 3-cylinder triple expansion

A view believed to be of *Warrington* as built. The Earle's-built *Oldham* was similar and was the last MS&LR ship to mount her mainmast forward of the after hold.
Author's collection

Boilers: 2 steel, 150lb/sq in
Power: 165nhp
Speed: 12kt

Her design followed the pattern established by *Northenden* and *Warrington* with separate foc'sle, bridge and poop, the latter housing just under 50 first class passengers with a large dining saloon and also a small smoking room. Portable berths for about 200 emigrants were arranged in the foreward tween-decks.

In December 1890, when still less than two years old, she sank to the bottom of Grimsby's Royal Dock after a sea cock had been accidentally left open during coaling operations. At about ths time the MS&L was running nine ships on its continental services from the Lincolnshire port: five to Hamburg with sailings four times a week in both directions and two each to Rotterdam and Antwerp with twice weekly departures each way.

In February 1913 after 24 years on railway service *Oldham* was sold to the Achaia Steamship Co of Patras for a sum of £3,100. As *Eleftheria* she traded under this new ownership for a relatively short time, being burned out in August 1916.

After World War 1 the wreck was apparently rebuilt and she continued trading as *Elefteria* for Piraeus owners A. Philon & Co, her gross tonnage being by now 1,208. In about 1925 she was transferred to the Inglessi-owned Steam Navigation Co of Samos, and some three years later was renamed *Samos*, a name briefly held by another of that Company's ships, the recently purchased former GER steamer *Frinton*. She continued thus throughout the 1930s, still a passenger carrier, but became a war loss in 1941 after a long career of 52 years. This however was easily eclipsed by her former MS&L partner *Sheffield* of 1877 which remained under Turkish flag as *Seyyar* until about 1955.

Nottingham, Staveley

In 1890 the board of the MS&L turned its attention towards the provision of a daily service to Hamburg and with this in mind four new steamers were ordered, two from C & S Swan & Hunter and two from Earle's Shipbuilding & Engineering Co Ltd.

The first of the Tyne-built pair, *Nottingham* was launched from the builders' West Yard on 13 March 1891 followed by *Staveley* on the first day of May. They took their names from towns that would shortly be connected to London by the railway company's new main line. *Nottingham* was handed over in July and *Staveley* left Grimsby for loaded trials on the Withernsea measured mile on 6 August, attaining a mean speed of 12½kt.

Length: 250ft 0in oa/240ft 2½in bp
Breadth: 32ft 0in
Depth/draught: 17ft 8in/16ft 6in
Gross tonnage: 1,033/1,034
Machinery: 3-cylinder triple expansion
Boilers: 2se, 170lb/sq in
Power: 1,450ihp
Speed: 12½kt

Although their hulls were still built of iron the new ships were improvements on the *Northenden* design, with an additional deck. Some 30 first class passengers (later figures give 47) could be accommodated under the poop with facilities which included a handsome main saloon and separate ladies' saloon, whilst a gentlemen's smoke-room and saloon entrance were enclosed in a deckhouse above. The long bridge house contained cabins for the officers and engineers whilst the petty officers and crew were housed in the foc'sle. The forward tween-decks were fitted up for emigrant carriage, and the maximum number permitted was about 330 persons.

Propelling machinery was supplied in *Nottingham's* case by the Wallsend Slipway & Engineering Co Ltd, whilst her sister's came from Messrs Westgarth, English & Co. Deck machinery included two powerful steam cranes, two silent running winches and one ordinary winch.

Staveley (1891) shown entering Rotterdam on 28 June 1920, was the second of two Tyne-built sisters. Note the crows nest on the foremast and the long second hold, an integral feature of many MS&LR ships, for carrying coal to Hamburg. *Welholme Galleries*

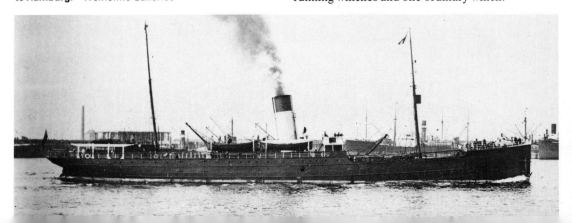

In 1912 *Nottingham* was reboilered by Smith's Dock Co Ltd, and two years later World War 1 brought the Hamburg service to a close. *Staveley* was taken up as an Admiralty store carrier (pennant No Y8.25) from 12 October 1914, and *Nottingham* – which was renamed *Notts* from 1915 to the end of the war – was loaned to the Great Eastern Railway with *Wrexham*. They were joined by *Staveley* after her release from the Admiralty on 8 July 1916 and between the three of them carried many passengers and considerable amounts of cargo mostly in the return direction from Rotterdam to Tilbury.

Both sisters survived the war and continued trading throughout the 1920s though latterly with their passenger capacity reduced to 12. In 1932 *Staveley* was sold to the British & Irish Steam Packet Co. She was renamed *Lady Glen* in 1933, but in August of that year went to T.W. Ward at Preston for breaking up. Her sister *Nottingham* followed her to the scrapyard in 1935 having become surplus following the rationalisation of Humber–Continental services under the banner of Associated Humber lines.

Lutterworth, Leicester

The second pair of sisters to be ordered by the MS&L in 1890 were products of the famous Earle's shipbuilding yard on the Humber. Their names like those of their Tyne-built consorts echoed towns on the Railway Company's as yet unfinished main line to London. *Lutterworth* entered the water for the first time on 8 April 1891 and *Leicester* followed her down the ways some two months later.

Dimensionally they were very similar to the Tyne-built pair as can be seen from the following table of particulars, but iron was still employed in their construction, despite the fact that steel had been used by competing companies for a number of years.

Length: 240ft 7in
Breadth: 32ft 0in
Depth: 14ft 8in
Gross tonnage: 1,002
Machinery: 3-cylinder triple expansion

Boilers: 2se, 170lb/sq in
Power: 1,400ihp
Speed: 12½kt

Single screw three-island type ships with raking masts and funnel, they could carry about 50 first class passengers aft and up to a maximum of 360 emigrants in their spacious forward tween-deck. Speedwise they appear to have had a slight edge on their Tyne built counterparts, *Lutterworth* making 13¼kt on loaded trials whilst *Leicester* returned an average of 13kt of 17 August. Their engines were built by Earle's and their bunker capacity was 125 tons of coal which they consumed at a rate of some 26cwt an hour.

With the delivery of *Leicester*, the last of the four, the MS&L's building programme was for the time complete, and a daily service to Hamburg became a reality. On 16 February 1901 *Lutterworth* grounded in the River Elbe and was not refloated until 12 days later. On 15 August the following year, again in the Elbe, she was in collision with the German schooner *Emma* and subsequent repairs cost the Company £500. A third incident took place in the same river in the final week of 1908 when she was hit whilst at anchor in poor visibility by the German liner *Kaiserin August Victoria*, receiving damage to her bows.

Both ships were reboilered by J.T. Eltringham in 1912 and by this time it is probable they had been switched to other routes following the delivery of the new 'Dewsbury' class steamers.

On 12 October 1914, shortly after the outbreak of World War 1, they were requisitioned as naval store carriers and whilst acting in this capacity *Leicester* (Y8.23) was mined and sunk 2½ miles southeast of Folkestone Pier on 12 February 1916 with the loss of 17 lives. Just over a month later *Lutterworth* (Y8.24), which had been released by the Admiralty

Lutterworth, and her sister *Leicester,* were the Earle's-built equivalents of *Nottingham* and *Staveley.* Very similar in design but with slightly longer foc'sles, they could be distinguished by their horizontal-topped funnels. Shell doors in the two well-decks eased cargo handling. *Laurence Dunn Collection*

the previous October, was attacked by a submarine 21 miles north of Cap d'Antifer in the English Channel but luckily the torpedo missed her.

At the end of hostilities *Lutterworth* proceeded to Grimsby for reconditioning before starting a period of repatriation duties between Rotterdam and Harwich. She returned to normal service once more, mainly on the Rotterdam and Antwerp routes, but with passenger capacity reduced to 12. On 6 January 1928 whilst inbound from the latter port she sustained slight damage to her starboard quarter after being hit by the Grimsby trawler *Dahlia II*.

After over 40 years in railway service she was sold in 1932 for a sum of £2,500. Her new owners – The British & Irish Steam Packet Co – employed her on the Irish Sea for only a short while without change of name and she went to T.W. Ward for breaking at Preston in March 1933.

City of Leeds, City of Bradford

On 1 August 1897 with its main line to London, Marylebone nearing completion the MS&L rather grandly retitled itself the Great Central Railway. In 1903 after a gap of some 12 years the newly constituted Company ordered its first steel Continental passenger steamers from Earle's Shipbuilding Co Ltd, itself recently reorganised following rescue from insolvency by Thomas Wilson & Son. *City of Leeds,* the first of two new sisters, was launched on 8 June by the Lady Mayoress of Leeds, followed on 23 July by *City of Bradford,* whose sponsor was Mrs Robinson, wife of the Company's chief mechaical engineer. During speed trials on the Withernsea mile on 29 September the *City of Bradford* achieved an average of 14¼ kt and this was followed by a six-hour full power trial.

The new ships were basically larger and improved versions of *Lutterworth:*

Length: 256ft 6in
Breadth: 34ft 4in
Depth/draught: 18ft 6in/17ft 7in
Gross tonnage: 1,341
Machinery: 3-cylinder triple expansion
Boilers: 2se, 180lb/sq in
Power: 2,000nhp
Speed: 13kt (service)

They were built to standards in excess of Lloyds 100 A1 requirements and in accordance with the latest Board of Trade and German emigrant laws. Their steel hulls contained the now familiar pattern of foc'sle, bridge and poop, but conservatism prevailed when it came to passenger accommodation which was still situated aft, albeit in luxurious state-rooms for about 50 leading off a large saloon which seated 41 on revolving chairs. A separate ladies' saloon was provided whilst a house on the poop contained the gentlemen's smoking room. Emigrant accommodation for some 250 persons was arranged in the forward tween-deck though this number was later increased to 440 by the adoption of portable berths.

A substantial amount of cargo could be carried in the three holds which were fitted with fixed tween-decks fore and aft, and in addition horse stalling was provided under the bridge. For cargo handling there were two steam cranes and several derricks driven by steam winches, whilst steam also provided the motive power for the steering gear, capstan and windlass. Bunker capacity was 148 tons of coal and the boilers consumed about 34cwt an hour at full speed.

City of Bradford made her maiden voyage to Rotterdam, but later in the same year she made an unusual voyage to ports in Norway, Sweden and the

Baltic in order to keep alive certain of the Railway Company's steamship powers. Four years later on 27 July she collided with the Newcastle steamer *Hartley* in the Elbe, receiving damage which cost over £1,800 to make good.

When World War 1 broke out both sisters were in the vicinity of Germany. Not being fitted with wireless they could not be warned and were intercepted by German patrols at the mouth of the Elbe and taken to Hamburg, their unlucky crews being interned at Ruhleben. *City of Leeds* was soon taken to Friedrichsort near Kiel where she became a minelayer depot ship and in 1915 her sister was converted into a floating workshop and renamed *Donau*. The following year she became a mother ship for a coastal flotilla whilst *City of Leeds* began acting as a submarine depot ship. In October 1917 *Donau* took part in the German capture of Oesel Island off Riga.

With the war over both ships were returned to the GCR in January 1919, *City of Leeds* going to the Tyne for a refit and her sister to Immingham. It could have been at this time or possibly later that their bridge wings were fitted with cabs and the after end of their superstructure plated in. Their funnel cowls were also removed at a later stage and passenger accommodation reduced to 12 with subsequent reduction in life-boats.

Although they passed to the control of the LNER in 1923 they retained their GCR funnel colours and remained on the Grimsby–Continental services until 1935 when the formation of Associated Humber Lines rendered them surplus. *City of Leeds* was sold to Hughes Bolckow for £6,250 the following year and was broken up at Blyth, but *City of Bradford* went for further trading to the Near East Shipping Co, Istanbul for £5,500. She left the Humber in September 1936, bearing the name *Hanne*, and thereafter traded mainly in the Mediterranean until sunk by aircraft southeast of Malta on 22 February 1942.

Wrexham

It was rather unusual practice for Railway companies with their special requirements to buy in second-hand ships, but this was the case with the GCR's next Continental ship.

In 1902 the Finnish Nord Co of Helsingfors had ordered three steel passenger/cargo ships from Sir Raylton Dixon & Co Ltd's Cleveland Dockyard at Middlesbrough with the intention of running a weekly service between the Tyne and Finland under a Finnish government subsidy. *Nord I* and *Nord II* were launched on 4 October and 1 December and their sister *Nord III* early in 1903. Due to a local dispute however they had to be towed to Finland for completion.

All three ships were specially strengthened forward to protect their hulls against ice damage.

Length: 250ft 0in oa/239ft 10in bp
Breadth: 35ft 4in
Depth: 20ft 9in
Gross tonnage: 1,414
Machinery: 3-cylinder triple expansion
Boilers: 3se, 180lb/sq in
Power: 217nhp
Speed: 12kt

Quite advanced for their day the neat-looking 'Nords' were three-island type ships with one full-length deck and a spar deck and their hulls were subdivided by five watertight bulkheads. First class

Purchased from the unsuccessful Nord Company of Finland in 1905, the smart little *Wrexham* was originally one of three sisters designed for Finland–Newcastle passenger/cargo service. Reputedly one of the faster ships in the GCR fleet, she is depicted here by Dutch painter A.J. Jansen.
From 'Great Central' by George Dow

accommodation for 20 people was arranged amidships and included a smoke-room in the bridge deckhouse from which a staircase led to the dining-saloon one deck below. Berths for 30 second class passengers were provided in the poop and about 200 emigrants could be carried in the forward tween-deck. Cargo capacity was about 1,250 tons carried in three holds, and a refrigeration plant was provided for the carriage of butter and other dairy produce.

The new service was not a success due mainly to competition from Finland Line which was already well established in the Finland–UK (Hull) pasenger trade, and the three ships were disposed of. *Nord II* was purchased by the GCR on 8 March 1905 and was renamed *Wrexham* to commemorate the Company's acquisition of the Wrexham, Mold & Connah's Quay Railway at the beginning of that year. She was something of a bargain for her owners as a new ship would have cost about double her purchase price of £20,000; she was mainly employed on the Rotterdam and Antwerp services.

The coming of World War 1 brought a halt to normal services but after Germany had guaranteed Holland's neutral status *Wrexham* together with *Nottingham* and later *Staveley* were loaned to the GER which had resumed its Rotterdam service on 2 December 1914 with sailings from Tilbury instead of Harwich, which had been taken over by the Admiralty.

On 2 March 1915 under the command of Capt Fryatt who was later to gain notoriety with the *Brussels, Wrexham* was ordered to stop by an enemy submarine but thanks to the great efforts of her engineers she escaped after a chase of some 30 miles. Between 20 November 1916 and 18 October 1917 she was commissioned as an Admiralty armaments carrier, pennant No. Y2.177. Later still she was despatched to the White Sea where her ice-strengthening was put to good use, but on 19 June 1918 when outward bound from Murmansk she had the misfortune to strike a submerged uncharted rock off Chavanga near the mouth of the Yugina river and had to be abandoned two days later. Her owners later received substantial compensation for the ship and her cargo.

To complete the story it is worth noting that her former sisters (*Nord I* and *Nord II*) were disposed of to D.W. Deschler in 1905 becoming *Ohio IV* and *Ohio II*, but were sold a year later to Nippon Yusen Kabushiki Kaisha and put into Japanese coastal passenger/cargo service as *Hirosaki Maru* and *Kamikawa Maru*. The latter stranded and was lost in February 1919 but her sister continued until July 1936 when she was wrecked after a career of 34 years.

Marylebone, Immingham

In 1905 the forward thinking and ambitious directors of the GCR, spurred on perhaps by GER rivalry, decided to order two fast turbine steamers. Accordingly contracts were placed in November with Messrs Cammell Laird & Co, Birkenhead and Swan Hunter & Wigham Richardson Ltd on the Tyne, the cost of each being agreed at £73,600.

The ships were built of steel under the supervision of F.J. Trewent, the naval architect acting for the railway company, and *Marylebone* was launched at Birkenhead by Mrs Beazely, one of the director's wives, on 21 April 1906, the ship's name honouring the GCR's new London terminus. *Immingham* took her name from the Company's new dock complex then under construction just upstream from Grimsby, and her christening was performed by the general manager's wife Mrs Fay on 8 May. She was tried on 11 January the following year and averaged 18.3kt during a six-hour full power trial.

Length: 282ft 0in/271ft 0in bp
Breadth: 41ft 2in
Depth/draught: 21ft 6in/18ft 9in

Part of a bold GCR experiment to speed up its Rotterdam service, the 18kt twin screw turbine *Immingham* makes a fine picture on her trials early in 1907, but excessive wave-making points to a costly waste of power. The very deep black funnel tops were unusual.
Author's collection

Gross tonnage: 2,074/2,009
Machinery: 3 sets Parsons direct-drive steam
turbines
Boilers: 4se, 160lb/sq in
Power: 6,500ihp
Speed: 18kt

Their design introduced a twin-funnel profile to the
Company for the first and only time and their three-
island hulls were made to appear flush by the
adoption of high bulwarks in the two wells. A long
deckhouse with promenades was situated
amidships under the funnels and a smaller one aft
on the poop.

The Company's long outdated practice of placing
the first class accommodation in the rear of the ship
was finally abandoned and 60 passengers were
housed amidships, mainly in double state-rooms on
the main deck. Forward of these was the dining-
saloon whilst above on the bridge deck were three
special cabins and a further four state-rooms plus
smoke-room and bar. Twenty-four second class
passengers could be berthed under the small poop
and over 300 emigrants in the tween-decks where
the accommodation was well lit and ventilated in
accordance with German emigrant laws, and
included a galley, refreshment bar and hospital for
both sexes.

Cargo capacities were about 850 and 1,000 tons
respectively and cargo handling gear included the
by now standard steam cranes and silent winches.
The new ships were the first in North Sea service to
adopt the still novel turbine form of propulsion,
Marylebone's triple set being constructed by her
builder and *Immingham's* by the Wallsend Slipway
& Engineering Co. They operated on the direct
drive principle, power being supplied to three
bronze screws.

The new sisters were placed on the Rotterdam
service where their speed reduced the passage time
from about 17½ to 10½ hours. Sadly this bold
experiment did not find favour amongst the
travelling public and operating costs were high, so
that when the GER countered with its own faster

turbine ships over the next few years the
competiton proved too much for the GCR. Early in
1911 both ships were withdrawn and sent to Earle's
for re-engining. More conservative three-cylinder
triple expansion units driving only a single screw
were fitted, one boiler was removed and also the
forward funnel. The cost of these alterations
amounted to more than £38,000 and speed dropped
to a more stately 13kt on a coal consumption of
36cwt an hour.

The two ships ran in their new guise until the
outbreak of World War 1. *Immingham* was
requisitioned by the Admiralty in October 1914,
first as an accommodation ship and later as the store
carrier Y8.50. On 6 June 1915, whilst employed on
the 'errand boy' run between Imbros and Mudros
during the Gallipoli campaign, she collided with
GWR's *Reindeer* off Lemnos and was lost. Her
owners claimed £100,000 compensation for a
replacement but were only granted £45,000 by the
Admiralty.

Following the Armistice *Marylebone* was
chartered to the GER in February 1919 for its
temporary Tilbury–Antwerp service, but the
following year returned to her normal Grimsby
duties. In 1932 she was sold to Tramp Shipping
Development Co Ltd being renamed *Velos*. Later
her name was briefly changed to *Arafat* before
reverting to *Velos*, and as such she was disposed of
by Pandelis N. Macris to Italian shipbreakers early
in 1938.

Dewsbury, Accrington, Blackburn, Bury, Stockport

Following its unsuccessful flirtation with fast turbine steamers the GCR proceeded to echo on the North Sea what White Star Line had done on the Atlantic in that the company fell back on building ships of moderate speed with the emphasis on comfort and steady reliability. In August 1909 two new steamers were commissioned from Earle's Co Ltd for a fixed price of £41,500 each, an order for a further pair following three months later.

Dewsbury was launched by the general manager's eldest daughter on 14 April 1910. The ship's maiden voyage on 17 June was made from the Western Jetty of the GCR's new £2,600,000 dock complex at Immingham and she carried a large party of dignitaries to celebrate its inauguration. *Accrington,* the second ship, had entered the water some 10 days previously and she was followed in turn by *Blackburn* on 8 September and *Bury* on 3 November.

Unfortunately *Blackburn* was lost on her maiden voyage to Antwerp following collision with the coaster *Rook* off Sheringham on the morning of 8 December. She was hit on her port side amidships but took some five hours to sink allowing ample time for her 29 passengers and 28 crew to be rescued by the steamers *Aire* and *Geraldine*. Although both ships were later held to blame, *Blackburn's* master, mate and lookout all lost their jobs. A fifth sister was quickly ordered as a replacement, being named *Stockport* at her launching on 15 May 1911.

The elegant *Dewsbury* (1910) marked a return to leisurely reliability after the GCR's costly venture with speedy turbines. Quickly followed by three sisters – one of which, *Blackburn,* was lost on her maiden voyage thus necessitating a fifth ship – she was of similar hull design to *City of Leeds* but had a longer bridge deck and more extensive superstructure. Outliving her sisters she was finally broken up at Antwerp in her 50th year.
Author's collection

All five ships shared the following main particulars:

Length: 265ft 0in
Breadth: 36ft 0in
Depth/draught: 18ft 6in/17ft 10in
Gross tonnage: 1,630
Machinery: 3-cylinder triple expansion
Boilers: 2se, 180lb/sq in
Power: 2,000nhp
Speed: 13½kt

The basic design was an attractive one with a handsome sheer and tall raking funnel. The hull incorporated a raised foc'sle, long bridge deck and short poop with hidden after well in accordance with normal GCR prctice. First class accommodation was situated amidships with berths for 100 being provided in state-rooms along the bridge deck with additionally several four-berth cabins and one luxury state-room on the main deck. Public rooms included a full-width saloon on the main deck and gentlemen's smoking room and ladies' lounge on the bridge deck. Ten second class passengers could be berthed under the poop and some 300 emigrants, now described as third class passengers, in the fore and aft tween-decks.

The four remaining sisters had only been in service for about four years, mainly in the Hamburg trade, when World War 1 intervened. *Bury* was seized by the German authorities in Hamburg and her crew (including stewardesses) were interned at Ruhleben for the duration of the conflict. She was later used as an accommodation ship for naval pilots at Wilhelmshaven. *Dewsbury* maintained an irregular commercial service to the neutal Netherlands, being fitted with W/T in 1917, and at the end of the war was running between Fishguard and Rosslare. *Accrington* became an accommodation ship for POWs, afterwards helping to carry munitions to France, and finally she was commissioned as an Admiralty training ship at Portsmouth between 17 April 1917 and 29 November 1918. *Stockport's* movements are unclear but she too was fitted with W/T in 1918.

After the war *Accrington, Dewsbury* and *Stockport* were chartered to the GER for repatriation duties between Rotterdam and

Harwich, the former also sailing to Hull. In 1919 *Dewsbury* reopened the Hamburg service. *Bury*, after refitting and being equipped with radio at Swan Hunters, restarted the Rotterdam service. All four later reverted to the Hamburg route until 1935 when the formation of Associated Humber Lines brought a general rationalisation of Continental services from the Humber, *Bury* being transferred to the new concern.

Dewsbury was refitted in January 1936 with more first class berths and better appointed accommodation and was put on the Rotterdam service with *Melrose Abbey*. *Bury* traded mainly to Hamburg as before but *Stockport's* service varied and *Accrington* acted mainly as a reserve. With war again imminent *Dewsbury* made a last round voyage to Rotterdam in the first week of September 1939; *Bury* had arrived back at Grimsby from her final Hamburg trip on 25 August but later made two round trips to Rotterdam, the last one leaving Hull on the final day of January 1940. At about the same time *Dewsbury* was making the last of several trips to Zeebrugge before moving to the coal trade between the Bristol Channel and the Clyde and then to general coasting in 1941.

Towards the end of 1941 a dramatic change occurred when all four sisters were taken up by the Admiralty for conversion to convoy rescue ships. This involved the fitting of extra accommodation and hospitals as well as a large number of liferafts. Based on the Clyde they were originally intended to accompany convoys for a set number of miles across the Atlantic but very soon they were going the whole way across, performing invaluable work and saving many lives, often in atrocious conditions. That they survived at all is a tribute to the strength of their original construction but one ship, *Stockport*, after saving about 240 lives, mainly in Arctic convoys, was herself lost with all hands after being torpedoed by U.604 in the early hours of 23 February 1943 whilst en route for Iceland with survivors from *Eastern Trader*.

After the war *Dewsbury* was refitted and in 1945 returned to LNER service, but the following year a shortage of ships saw her on the Harwich–Antwerp run with *Accrington*. The remaining sister *Bury*, with modified accommodation, joined *Melrose Abbey* on the Hull–Rotterdam route on 1 February 1947.

In 1949 British Rail announced its intention of closing the Antwerp link and *Dewsbury* made her last departure from the Belgian port on 3 February 1950. *Accrington,* which had been running as a cargo ship, made her last trip from Antwerp on 6 January 1951. Laid up at Harwich she was sold not long after to Clayton & Davie Ltd for about £19,000, arriving at the Dunston scrapyard on 2 May.

Bury underwent more accommodation changes early in 1956 and her saloon and second classes were combined into a new first-class and her steerage was restyled third class. She remained thus sailing between April and October before making her final departure from Hull on 28 May 1958 after which she was replaced by the new motor ship *Bolton Abbey*. Soon afterwards she was sold to Dutch breakers at Nieuw Lekkerkerk and arrived in the New Waterway in tow of the tug *Airman* on 1 July.

Following the ending of the Antwerp service *Dewsbury* had made one round voyage to Rotterdam on 7 June 1950 but at the end of that year public demand saw her once more installed on the Antwerp run albeit carrying no more than 12 passengers on a weekly schedule. This final phase in the twilight years of her career lasted another eight years until in her 50th year she made her final exit from the Scheldt on the last day of January 1959. She was replaced by the motor cargo ships *Isle of Ely* and *Colchester* and was sold to the Brussels Shipbreaking Co, arriving at Antwerp on 10 March for demolition.

The longest lived of the five sisters (three of which had lasted over 40 years) and the last surviving Great Central passenger steamer, she had remained a coal burner to the end. She and her sisters had served with distinction in peace and two world wars – a tribute to the strength of the Great Central's ships – and as a group were certainly one of the most important ever to serve on the North Sea.

Wilson Line

Hull–Trondheim/Bergen/Oslo/Gothenburg/
    Hamburg, etc
1822–1836   Beckington, Wilson & Co
1836–1840   Wilson, Hudson & Co
1840–1850   Thomas Wilson & Co
1850–1916   Thomas Wilson Sons & Co
              (Ltd in 1891)
1916–1973   Ellerman's Wilson Line
Funnel colours: Red with black top

Thomas Wilson, a Yorkshire merchant, began his shipowning activities in 1825 when, in partnership with John Beckington and two others, he bought the 51-ton sailing vessel *Thomas & Ann*. He was appointed master and the success of the venture led to his acquiring the 100-ton schooner *Swift* in 1831. Beckington dropped out in about 1836 and the firm became known as Wilson Hudson & Co. In 1840 the two Hudson partners retired and Wilson brought in his eldest son, re-styling the firm Thomas Wilson Sons & Co. On 2 June in the same year the new company despatched its first steamer across the North Sea and a service to Gothenburg was initiated with a branch line to Kristiansand. Wilson obtained a small Norwegian postal contract but withdrew from the trade in 1842 on being refused an increased subsidy. Sailings were resumed in 1850 after Norway agreed to waive port and light dues.

In 1852 fear of competition led Wilson to sell his ships to the newly formed North of Europe Steam Navigation Co, but he was allowed to retain management. As before he prospered and six years later was able to buy back his ships when the new company failed. Shortly after this he set up a service from Hull to Kristiansand and Oslo in co-operation with the Norwegian firm Det Sondenfjeldske, the latter supplying the steamer *Ganger Rolf* and Wilson his *Scandinavian*. The two companies fell out and after a short freight war Wilson forced the Norwegian firm to abandon its Hull service in 1866. A year previous to this he had started a new link with Stavanger and Bergen based on the export of copper ore.

Thomas Wilson died in 1869 and the business was carried on by his sons. Passengers began to be carried on the Scandinavian services which prospered and in time new services were started to the Baltic, the Mediterranean, India and later North America. By 1878 the purchase of the seven ship fleet of Brownlow Marsdin & Co had swelled the Wilson Line's own fleet to no less than 52 ships and the company was well on its way to becoming the world's largest private shipowner. New ships were constantly being added, the majority of them coming from the Hull shipyard of Earle's Shipbuilding & Engineering Co.

Romeo

Early in 1880 Thos Wilson Sons & Co ordered a new passenger steamer from Earle's for their Gothenburg service. She was launched by Miss Dobson, the daughter of her prospective master, on 3 July and, after being fitted out and having her engines installed in the tidal dock, ran trials on 31 March 1881. During the course of four runs on the measured mile she averaged 13kt, and it took her 5½ minutes to turn a complete circle at full speed.

Length: 275ft 0in
Breadth: 34ft 7in
Depth: 19ft 10in
Gross tonnage: 1,840
Machinery: 2-cylinder compound
Boilers: 2de, 80lb/sq in
Power: 1,500ihp
Speed: 12½kt

Romeo was an iron-hulled steamer with a short top-gallant foc'sle and long combined bridge and poop topped by a long deckhouse and a single funnel placed well aft. As built she was fitted with three pole masts but her midships-mounted mainmast was later removed. Her first class accommodation provided about 40 berths in staterooms on either side of the ship abaft a large and well-fitted saloon. Second class passengers were carried aft in the poop with a smaller saloon and berthing arrangements for about 20, whilst a large number of emigrants (some sources give a figure of 1,000) could be housed in the tween-decks.

Thos Wilson's iron passenger steamer *Romeo* (1880) worked the Hull–Gothenburg service for nearly a quarter of a century before moving to the London–Riga run. As built she mounted a third mast amidships. Note the rather intricate deck railings which were a feature of early Wilson passenger ships. *M.W. Webster collection*

The accommodation was originally lit by means of a chemical process in the engine-room

The new ship was a great improvement on the *Rollo* and *Orlando,* both built by Earle's in 1870, which had operated the Gothenburg passenger service previously. In 1888 there was a scheduled departure early every Saturday morning in season and the sea passage occupied some 42 hours. Return sailings from the Swedish port, usually with many emigrants, started on Friday afternoons, and the first class return fare applying at the time was five guineas with an additional 6/6d a day for victualling.

By 1901 *Romeo* was sailing from Hull on alternate Saturdays with the newer *Ariosto* whilst the old *Orlando* and *Cameo* (1876) maintained a secondary service from Grimsby with weekly Tuesday afternoon departures in both directions. Some time later, possibly after the arrival of the new *Calypso* in 1904, *Romeo* was transferred to the Company's London–Riga service which she operated with the former Bailey & Leetham steamers *Jaffa* and *Zara*. She continued thus until the start of World War 1, latterly with a grey-painted hull, the only untoward incident during this part of her career occurring in May 1908 when she was damaged by ice in Riga.

During the war she was fitted with defensive armament but on 3 March 1918 in her 37th year she was torpedoed without warning seven miles south of the Mull of Galloway, sinking with the loss of her master and 14 crew members.

Juno (1882)

A new steamer for Thos Wilson & Sons' Continenal services was launched at Earle's shipbuilding yard by Mrs G. Godfrey on 24 March 1882. She was named *Juno* and was moved to the Albert Dock for the installation of her machinery by Messrs Amos & Smith. Her trials took place on 1 July and she reached a mean speed of 12½kt on the Withernsea mile. She was a single-deck iron steamer with the following dimensions and particulars.

Length: 250ft 0in
Breadth: 32ft 2½in
Depth: 16ft 6in
Gross tonnage: 1,302
Machinery: 2-cylinder compound
Boilers: 2se, 90lb/sq in
Power: 1,300ihp
Speed: 12kt

She was a three-masted ship with engines aft and her hull was built on the well-deck principle. Her first class accommodation amidships included a dining saloon, smoking room and promenade deck whilst sleeping arrangements were provided for 20 persons, with provision for an increase to 40 if required. A small cabin aft could berth about eight second class passengers and temporary fittings were placed in the tween-decks for some 200 emigrants, though this number could be increased if needed to a maximum of 400.

She was one of the last ships in the already numerous Wilson fleet to be fitted with an uneconomical compound engine and her deck machinery included a single steam crane in addition to derricks and winches.

She entered service in July 1882 and normally

operated on the Hull–Hamburg service. After only six years in the Wilson fleet she was sold to the Tyne Steam Shipping Co Ltd of Newcastle for a sum of £23,000. Reboilered in 1898, she became part of the newly formed Tyne-Tees Steam Shipping Co Ltd in 1904 but retained her original name and continued to trade in the main to Hamburg carrying both passengers and cargo. When World War 1 broke out in 1914 she was unfortunate enough to be in the German port and was detained by the authorities, later being abandoned by her owner to the North of England P & I Club.

The war over, she was returned to England on 27 December 1918 and passed briefly through the hands of brokers A. Lazarus before becoming the Portuguese *Afra* and later *Leca*. In 1921 she was bought by the US Shipping Board which allocated her to James R. Armstrong of Colon. She sailed under the Panamanian flag as *El Amigo* for only two years before changing hands again, being re-registered at Tampico, Mexico without change of name for the Hammond Oil Co.

In 1926 she was sold once more and commenced the final phase of her varied career, now under the Nicaraguan flag. Initially her owners were the American Fruit Co for whom she reverted to her original name. In about 1932 she became Gulf Coast Steamship Lines' *Edith F* and about a year later Galveston Foreign Traders' *Cecilia*. She was finally broken up in 1935 after 53 years of successful trading.

Eldorado (1885)

Requiring a new steamer for their service to the west coast of Norway, Thomas Wilson & Sons placed an order with Earle's Shipbuilding & Engineering Co early in 1885. Construction proceeded apace and the new vessel was launched on 2 April, being given the name *Eldorado* which had previously been held by a 3,300-ton twin-funnelled ship built for the Company's Indian service in 1873. The new steamer, which was much faster and more elegantly appointed than those preceding her, ran trials off the Humber in rather rough conditions on 16 May, obtaining an average of 14.43 kt on the measured mile at Withernsea.

Length: 235ft 0in
Breadth: 30ft 0in
Depth: 14ft 8in
Gross tonnage: 935
Machinery: 3-cylinder triple expansion
Boilers: 2 steel, 150lb/sq in
Power: 300nhp
Speed: 14kt

Eldorado was designed exclusively for passenger traffic, having very fine lines with a raised foc'sle and long combined bridge and poop. She was fitted with three pole masts which were schooner rigged, and her funnel and machinery were placed as far aft as possible. Her accommodation provided for the carriage of some 86 first class passengers at the forward end of the bridge deck, with additional arrangements for emigrants in the forward tween-decks.

She left Hull on her maiden voyage to Bergen on 26 May and quickly became popular during the busy summer season; however her services on this route lasted less than a year for early in 1886 she was sold to the Greek government. Renamed *Sfaktirea* she was used for some 20 years as a naval auxiliary before returning to commercial service as the *Mykali* of J. McDowall & Barbour's Hellenic Steam Navigation Co, this title later being altered to the Hellenic Co of Maritime Enterprises. Towards the end of the 1920s she passed briefly through the ownership of the Mandafouni Steamship Co before joining the Toyias fleet as the Syros-registered *Mykali Togia*. In 1931 she was absorbed into the newly formed Hellenic Coast Lines group and was finally broken up in Italy in 1933 after spending all but a few months of her long 49-year career in waters far removed from the North Sea.

The flush-decked *Eldorado* of 1886 differed from her earlier namesake in having only two masts. Wilson's crack passenger steamer on the Norway run for many years, her 15kt speed placed her amongst the fastest ships on the longer North Sea routes. In 1895 a new midship section was inserted and her funnel heightened. *Popperfoto*

Eldorado (1886)

Early in 1886 Wilson's placed an order with Earle's for a second *Eldorado* to replace the one the company had just sold to Greece. 'Number 300' was constructed very speedily being launched on 22 May and tried on 29 June, only 4½ months after being laid down, recording an average of 14.9kt on the Withernsea measured mile. She was larger than her predecessor but unlike that ship was built of iron.

Length: 249ft 7in
Breadth: 33ft 2½in
Depth: 16ft 7in
Gross tonnage: 1,382
Machinery: 3-cylinder triple expansion
Boilers: 2 steel, 150lb/sq in
Power: 2,080ihp
Speed: 15kt

Her design was based on the awning deck principle and incorporated a flush hull with a short funnel placed well aft and two schooner-rigged pole masts.

She was fitted with accommodation on the main and lower decks amidships for about 86 first class passengers. Sleeping arrangements were mainly in double cabins, plus eight single, eight three-berth and two six-berth cabins. Four of the double cabins were on the upper deck in a deckhouse which also housed a music saloon and a smoke room. The dining saloon was situated on the main deck and could take all 86 passengers at one sitting. A small number of second class passengers were carried aft with access via a small deckhouse. Special attention was paid to ventilation, and all passenger spaces and crews quarters were electrically lit as were the navigation lights.

The new ship sailed on her maiden voyage to Bergen on 6 July with a full complement of passengers and quickly became a favourite, befitting her reputation as a crack ship and one of the fastest on the North Sea. She left Hull during the season on Tuesday evenings, making a 27hr passage to Stavanger where a brief call was made before proceeding on the 9hr 'inland' route to Bergen. The return voyage started on Saturday. During the winter months she occasionally cruised further afield as on 24 January 1890 when she left Hull for Madeira, Nice, Malta, Constantinople and Odessa, returning home on 11 April.

In 1895 she was lengthened by some 17½ft, the new section being inserted amidships just forward of the bridge, and it is probable that her funnel was heightened by some 6ft at the same time. The alterations increased her passenger capacity to about 140 and raised her gross tonnage to 1,425.

In 1911 she was transferred to the Grimsby–Gothenburg run but in the second half of June she made two voyages to Oslo, standing in for *Eskimo* while the latter attended the Coronation Naval Review. She only carried second and third class passengers on the Gothenburg service, starting the 38hr outward passage on Saturday evenings and returning on Wednesday mornings.

The following winter she was withdrawn and fitted out as a cadet training ship before being moored in Hull's Railway Dock, close to Wilson's head office in Commercial Road. Two years later her hull was found to be unsound and she was sold in September 1913 to J. Cashmore for scrapping at Newport. A new shore-based training school continued to be known as RMS *Eldorado* in her memory.

Juno (1889)

On 10 July 1889 Earle's launched a new passenger cargo steamer for Wilson's Norwegian services. She was given the name *Juno* – which had become free following the sale of the earlier vessel of that name – and after fitting out in Hull underwent acceptance trials on 31 October.

Length: 215ft 6in
Breadth: 30ft 0in
Depth: 14ft 11in
Gross tonnage: 1,080
Machinery: 3-cylinder triple expansion
Boilers: 2 steel, 160lb/sq in
Power: 1,250ihp
Speed: 12kt

The new *Juno* was a steel awning deck type ship with a flush hull and a part cellular double bottom, whilst for added strength she was also fitted with a curved collision bulkhead. Originally schooner rigged she had two shortish pole masts and a single tall funnel with a minimum of rake.

Her first class accommodation was arranged amidships and included a dining-saloon, smoke-room and ladies' cabin as well as the usual sleeping arrangements, which could be readily extended for a number of additional passengers in the busy summer season. There was also a small but comfortrble cabin aft for a few second class passengers and the usual arrangements were made for emigrants in the tween-decks.

She was mainly employed in Wilson's Hull–Trondheim service, initially in company with *Hero* (1866), with a departure every Thursday in season and on alternate Thursdays for the rest of the year. The first class return fare was 11 guineas including food and the passage generally took between 65 and 70 hours.

After only 10 years in the Wilson fleet she was sold to the Bergen Line who refitted her at the Akers shipyard, Oslo and placed her in their Hamburg–Kristiansand–Vadso service under the new name of *Hera*. Her passenger capacity was now 100 but her certificate allowed this to be increased by deck passengers to 600 for the coastal part of the voyage.

In 1910 she was switched to the joint coastal express service between Bergen and Vadso and two years later underwent another major refit to bring her into line with newer tonnage and to further increase her berthing capacity. At the same time part of her midship superstructure was enclosed and she was fitted with a larger deckhouse aft with an open promenade deck above.

During the latter part of World War 1 she was chartered along with the other coastal express ships by the Norwegian Government in order to guarantee the service, but remained under Bergen Line management. She continued to sail throughout the 1920s although by this time she was the oldest ship in the coastal fleet. On the night of 17/18 March 1931, in her 42nd year, she was blown off course in a storm and ran aground between Honningsvaag and Hammerfest. Six people died in the wreck but due to the gallant efforts of crewman Einar Ramm – who swam ashore with a rope – 56 were saved.

Ariosto

In the period 1889–90 the Wilson Line took delivery of no less than 16 new ships amongst which were several passenger ships. The largest of these was given the new name, *Ariosto*, when launched by Earle's on 10 December 1889. On completion the following March she was placed in Wilson's Hull–Gothenburg service.

Length: 300ft 5in
Breadth: 38ft 0in
Depth: 20ft 0in
Gross tonnage: 2,376
Machinery: 3-cylinder triple expansion
Boilers: 2se, 160lb/sq in

Power: 2,600ihp
Speed: 14kt

Ariosto was the largest North Sea passenger steamer of her day and eclipsed her nine-year-old running partner *Romeo* by some 400 tons. Design-wise she was a well-proportioned flush-decker with a split superstructure amidships, two masts, and a medium-sized funnel mounted closer to the mainmast. Her electrically lit accommodation included sleeping arrangements on the main deck amidships for 53 first class passengers in two and three-berth cabins, above which was a large 56-seat saloon with adjacent ladies' room and smoking room. Second class accommodation aft provided for an additional 24 passengers but by far the greatest proportion of her accommodation, albeit of a somewhat rudimentary type, was for emigrants in the tween-decks. Gothenburg was a major emigrant port and over the years many thousands left there on the first stage of their one-way journey to the New World, lining the decks of steamers such as *Ariosto* which carried up to 1,000 at peak periods.

Initially she alternated with *Romeo* on a weekly basis sailing from Hull every other Saturday as soon as the tide allowed after the arrival of the mail train from London at 4.30am. Passengers could embark the night before if they so wished. From 1904 she was partnered by the new *Calypso*, and in 1909 received new boilers. Withdrawn in 1910 after 20 years of steady if rather uneventful service she was sold to Spanish owners La Roda Hermanos of Valencia who renamed her *Luis Vives*. Six years later she became a war loss when torpedoed off the Scilly Islands on 11 September 1916.

When built in 1890 for the Gothenburg service the 2,376-ton *Ariosto* was the largest passenger steamer on regular North Sea service. An improved *Romeo*, she carried many thousands of emigrants to Hull on the first stage of their one-way journey to the New World. *Author's collection*

An example of one of Wilson's intermediate passenger ships: the 1890-built *Tasso* pictured leaving Hull on one of her many voyages to Trondheim. Note the prominent donkey funnel, also the distinctive Company house flag of white pennant with red ball at the main truck.
M.W. Webster collection

Tasso

This new steamer for Thos Wilson's West Norway trade was launched by Earle's on 24 February 1890 after which she was towed to the Albert Dock for the installation of her machinery and boilers by Messrs Amos & Smith. The only previous holder of her name had been a 610-ton steamer built by Denny in 1852 as *Scandinavian* but rechristened *Tasso* in 1870 and eventually lost at Bergen in 1885.

Dimensionally *Tasso* was very similar to *Juno* of 1882.

Length: 250ft 0in
Breadth: 32ft 0in
Depth: 16ft 6in
Gross tonnage: 1,328
Machinery: 3-cylinder triple expansion
Boilers: 2
Power: 1,250ihp
Speed: 12½kt

She was a steel schooner-rigged ship with short raised foc'sle and combined bridge and poop stretching about two-thirds of her length. Her accommodation was designed to cater for 28 first class passengers amidships but this number was later increased to 44. Public rooms included the usual dining saloon and smoking room, and in addition a small cabin aft could sleep eight second class passengers, whilst the tween decks were fitted up for emigrants. All accommodation was lit by electricity.

Tasso entered service in May 1890 partnering *Juno* (1889) on the Trondheim route, with a departure in each direction every Thursday during the summer season and including calls at Aalesund and Kristiansund. She was reboilered in 1899 and two years later was lengthened by 20ft which increased her gross tonnage to 1,328 and her first class passenger capacity to 64. Later she ran in the year-round Hull–Bergen service with *Salmo*.

On 22 January 1911 she was badly damaged in a collision with the 18,000-ton Hamburg Amerika liner *President Lincoln* in poor visibility to the East of the Dover Strait. The liner escorted her to Dover where she arrived with three compartments flooded.

After being repaired she was sold to the Hull firm of W. Morphy & Son. Just before World War 1 she was sold again to the Achaia Steamship Co Ltd of Patras and renamed *Elefsis*, although Morphy remained as joint manager with Crowe & Stevens. After the war she changed hands yet again, her new owners being the Piraeus-based O.D. & G. Anghelatos, but it was as *Photios* that she foundered between Corsica and Elba on Christmas Day 1920 on a voyage from Marseilles to Alexandria.

Montebello

A new passenger steamer destined for Wilson's Oslo service was launched by Messrs Richardson Duck & Co at Stockton-on-Tees in the spring of 1890. She was named after the Duchess of Montebello and was towed round to Hull where her engines and boilers were fitted by Amos & Smith in Albert Dock. She then returned to the Tees for fitting out and on 11 June made the passage back from the Tees entrance to Spurn in a record six hours 48 minutes at a good 14kt, in spite of her propeller tips being about a foot out of the water.

Although not a great deal larger than the 15-year old *Angelo* and *Cameo* which had maintained the service hitherto she was a great improvement on them in all respects.

Length: 276ft 0in
Breadth: 35ft 0in
Depth: 15ft 6in
Gross tonnage: 1,735
Machinery: 3-cylinder triple expansion
Boilers: 2se, 160lb/sq in

The third passenger steamer delivered to the Wilson Line in 1890 – the 1,735-ton *Montebello* seen at speed in the Oslofjord. A product of the Stockton yard of Richardson Duck, she was later fitted with a taller funnel and accompanying donkey stack. *Author's collection*

Power: 1,500ihp
Speed: 13kt

She was a flush-hulled steamer of the spar deck type with an easy sheerline, a split superstructure, and a single funnel placed fairly well aft between two tall raking masts. Although smaller, her appearance was very similar to *Ariosto* built in the same year for Wilson's Gothenburg service.

As to passenger accommodation her main first class saloon which measured 38ft × 21ft was situated on the upper deck amidships beneath the hurricane deck. It was lit by daylight through a large skylight, whilst at night electric lamps were used at sea and oil lamps in port. There was a small smoke-room aft of the saloon, and on the main deck below was sleeping accommodation for some 70 passengers mainly in three-berth cabins. Second class accommodation for 20 persons was provided aft and the usual fittings and sanitary arrangements were made for up to 600 emigrants in the tween-decks. Her officers and engineers were housed on the upper deck around the engine casing with the remainder of the crew in the foc'sle.

Later in her career her accommodation was enlarged to cater for over 80 in first class with additional single and double berth staterooms, and at the same time her bathroom facilities were improved.

Initially she sailed opposite *Angelo* every other Friday for Kristiansand and Oslo, but by the time *Angelo* was replaced by *Oslo* in 1906 departures were on Saturday. The passage time to Kristiansand occupied about 32 hours with a further 12 hours onward to Oslo, five of which were in the sheltered waters of the fjord.

She became surplus to requirements in 1910 following the introduction of *Eskimo* and was sold that summer to Spain's Compania Valenciana. Renamed *Barcelo* she was placed in service between southern Spanish ports and the Canary Islands. Her owner became one of several Spanish coastal shipping companies absorbed into the newly formed Compania Trasmediterranea in 1917 and *Barcelo* continued to serve this company until 1929 when she was sold for scrap in her 40th year.

The name *Montebello* passed to a 4,400-ton cargo ship built by Earle's in 1911, but after she was torpedoed 320 miles west of Ushant on 21 June 1918 it was not used again.

Spero (1896); *Zero*

These two steamers were similar eough to be regarded as sister ships although they were products of different shipyards in 1896. *Spero* was launched by Messrs Archibald MacMillan & Co at Dumbarton in May and ran trials in stormy conditions on 4 July, achieving 12½kt. *Zero* followed more normal Wilson practice in being an Earle's product.

Both shared the following dimensions:

Length: 250ft 5in
Breadth: 30ft 2in
Depth: 15ft 8in
Gross tonnage: 1,132/1,143
Machinery: 3-cylinder triple expansion
Boilers: 2
Power: 1,180/1,430ihp
Speed: 12kt

Their design incorporated a short foc'sle and long combined bridge and poop separated by a longish well deck. Their superstructure amidships was split with the single funnel mounted on the after portion close to the short mainmast. Passenger accommodation included sleeping arrangements for 45 persons under the bridge in addition to a considerable number of emigrants. *Spero's* engines were supplied by Muir & Houston Ltd of Glasgow whilst *Zero's* were produced by her builders.

Both ships were originally employed in the emigrant trade, *Spero* often visiting Stettin, but later they served on North Sea routes. In the years

leading up to World War 1, *Spero* was trading fortnightly between Hull and Oslo on a supplementary second and third class service, whilst *Zero* was employed in the Copenhagen trade.

At the beginning of the war *Zero* was requisitioned as a frozen meat ship but was rejected as unsuitable after only a few days. *Spero* became a war loss when she was captured by a submarine on 2 November 1916 about 95 miles west-southwest of Helliso Lighthouse and then sunk by torpedo and gunfire.

Zero survived the war and continued as a cargo ship until laid up pending sale at the end of 1931. The following October she went to G. & W. Brunton for scrapping at Grangemouth.

Salmo

In the closing years of the 19th century when Earle's were experiencing considerable difficulties, Wilson's were forced to turn to other shipyards for new orders. Seven of these went to the Caledon Shipbuilding & Engineering Co, Dundee over a four-year period from 1897, but only one of them

was for a passenger steamer, the *Salmo,* which was launched on 17 February 1900. She was a neat little ship with a close family resemblance to *Montebello* and *Tasso* though her dimensions were nearer to the latter in her lengthened state, as can be seen from the following table of particulars:

Length: 265ft 0in
Breadth: 35ft 2½in
Depth: 16ft 2½in
Gross tonnage: 1,721
Machinery: 3-cylinder triple expansion
Boilers: 2
Power: 1,700ihp
Speed: 13kt

Unlike *Tasso* she had a flush hull and a more solid looking deckhouse beneath the bridge amidships. Later, solid bulwarks were added forward, reaching to a position just abreast of the foremast. She was originally credited with having accommodation for about 120 passengers in first and second classes but later figures give 64 in first and eight in second.

She was employed in the Norwegian trade, her usual run being a year-round, weekly one to Bergen via Stavanger on which she was later partnered by

Salmo, a Caledon product of 1900 for the Norwegian trade, was an improved, flush-decked version of *Tasso*. This view of her with 'salt-caked smokestack' was taken at Le Havre in January 1915 when she was acting as a World War 1 transport. *Author's collection*

Tasso. In 1911 she was replaced by *Aaro* and transferred to a supplementary second and third class service linking Grimsby with Oslo, outward departures being timed on Wednesday evening to give a Friday night arrival after a call at Kristiansand. A prompt return sailing on Saturday morning ensured an early Monday morning arrival back in the Humber. Immediately prior to World War 1 she was still based on Grimsby but was running once a week to Gothenburg on Saturdays, returning on Wednesday.

During the war she was mainly employed in coastal work and was later fitted with defensive armament. Her end came on 7 April 1917 when she was torpedoed without warning about 210 miles northwest of Fastnet Rock with the loss of two of her crew.

Una

Una. Author's collection

The small passenger steamer *Una* was built for Hull shipowner Bailey & Leetham Ltd by Messrs John Scott & Co, Kinghorn. She was launched virtually complete on 5 September 1899 by Miss Blair, daughter of the Dowager Duchess of Sutherland, and after loading at Burntisland performed her official trial only four days later, averaging 14kt. Following this successful outcome she steamed south to London to take up service in her owner's St Petersburg trade.

Length: 237ft 2½in
Breadth: 34ft 2½in
Depth/draught: 16ft 8in/18ft 5in
Gross tonnage: 1,406
Machinery: 3-cylinder triple expansion
Boilers: 2se, 180lb/sq in
Power: 1,426ihp
Speed: 13kt

She was built of steel with a short well deck hidden by high bulwarks in way of No 2 hatch and her two schooner-rigged masts were telescopic. Passenger accommodation included staterooms for 58 in first class on the main deck amidships, with a large oak-panelled saloon and ladies' room on the bridge deck.

In 1903, along with 22 other ships in Bailey & Leetham's fleet, *Una* was taken over by Wilson Line and exchanged her 'tombstone' funnel marking for the familiar red one with a black top. These additions made Wilsons the largest privately-owned fleet in the world.

Under Wilson ownership *Una* traded mainly to Copenhagen, operating out of either Hull or Newcastle in a joint service with DFDS, each company providing a sailing every other week. On 4 December 1909 she was sold to Jose Maria Maycas, La Roda Hermanos and others and was re-registered in Spain as *Vicente La Roda*. In the same year her owners became part of Compania Valenciana and this concern was in turn absorbed into Compania Trasmediterranea in 1917. The ship was sunk during the Spanish Civil War but later raised and after rebuilding in 1945 became Enrique Illueca's *Juan Illueca*. As such this remarkable ship sailed on until 3 June 1960 when in her 61st year she was wrecked in fog on Cape Penas whilst on passage from Bordeaux to Gijon.

Calypso (1904)

In 1903 Wilsons contracted for a larger new passenger steamer for their Gothenburg service from Earle's which they had just rescued from insolvency and now owned. The new ship was launched on 7 January 1904, becoming the second in the fleet to bear the name *Calypso*, which had previously been held by a long-lived 1865-built ship which had only gone for scrapping in Genoa at the end of 1902.

She was the largest North Sea passenger ship of her day and was the first two-funnelled one in her owner's short sea trades.

Length: 309ft 7in
Breadth: 42ft 8in
Depth: 23ft 9in
Gross tonnage: 2,876
Machinery: 3-cylinder triple expansion
Boilers: 3se, 180lb/sq in
Power: 2,800ihp
Speed: 14kt

Apart form her closely spaced cowl-topped funnels she differed from *Ariosto* in having a well-deck abaft the foc'sle in way of Nos 1 and 2 hatches, and her midship superstructure was noticeably more compact.

Her original passenger complement was 45 in first class, 46 in second class, and 200 in steerage with

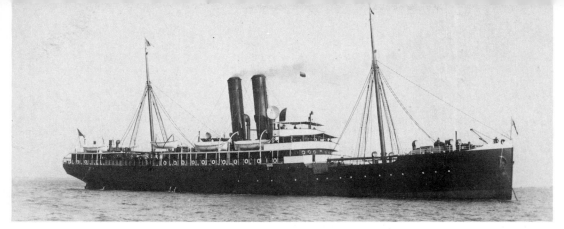

The stately *Calypso* of 1904 was Wilson's first two-funnelled North Sea passenger ship. Eclipsing *Ariosto*, her running partner on the Gothenburg service, by some 500 tons, she was hired as an AMC for a short while early in World War 1. *Author's collection*

additional facilities for the carriage of up to 580 emigrants in the tween-decks. Her three cargo holds were refrigerated for the carriage of fish, fruit and vegetables and her four hatches were each served by a single derrick. Total deadweight capacity was 2,192 tons.

She replaced *Romeo* on the regular weekly service from Hull to Gothenburg, taking alternate sailings every other Saturday from Riverside Quay with *Ariosto*. Return departure was timed at 1.00pm on Friday and the open sea passage took about 35 hours. A secondary service from Grimsby on Wednesdays was taken by the 1870-built *Orlando* or by *Rollo*.

During her short period of service with the new *Bayardo* in 1911/12, departures from Hull were altered to Thursday evenings. After the loss of the latter she was joined for a short while by *Spero* but thereafter appears to have run a weekly service on her own, leaving Hull on Tuesday evening and returning from Gothenburg late on Friday evening to arrive back in the Humber at about noon on Sunday.

On 17 May 1914 she stranded near Spurn Head on an inward sailing. Her passengers were taken off by the company's tug/tender *Presto* but she was successfully refloated without much damage the following day.

In the first November of World War 1 she was taken up by the Admiralty for conversion to an armed merchant cruiser. After refitting at Hull, where she was armed with eight 4.7in and two 3pdr guns, she joined the famous 10th Cruiser Squadron as HMS *Calyx* (M.86), her renaming being necessary to avoid confusion with the cruiser HMS *Calypso*. On northern patrols it soon became apparent that she was too small for the job and after

nearly foundering in heavy storms at the end of the year was paid off the following April; however, she was not returned to Wilson Line until 26 June.

She resumed North Sea service where her routeing varied, but on 11 July 1916 in the course of a voyage from London to Kristiansand and Oslo she was torpedoed and sunk with the loss of 30 lives, including that of her master.

Oslo

Early in 1906 Wilson Line placed an order with Earle's for a new passenger ship for their Oslo service which was then being maintained by the 16-year-old *Montebello* and the 32-year-old *Angelo*. She was launched on 9 April, her name *Oslo* being an unusual one as the Norwegian capital did not take on that name until 1927. Trials took place on the Withernsea mile on 19 May during which she achieved a mean speed of over 13½kt without resorting to forced draught.

Length: 290ft 0in
Breadth: 39ft 1in
Depth: 25ft 4in
Gross tonnage: 2,296
Machinery: 3-cylinder triple expansion
Boilers: 2se, 180lb/sq in
Power: 1,800ihp
Speed: 13kt

Oslo was an awning deck type steamer with a short raised foc'sle but apart from this and greater beam she was very much a modernised *Montebello*.

Her first class accommodation amidships included a spacious dining saloon above which was a library, smoking room and ladies' cabin. Well ventilated staterooms for 69 passengers, mainly singles and doubles, were situated on the main deck. Other accommodation included four-berth cabins for 32 second class passengers whilst 90 steerage were housed in six-berth cabins with

The Earle's-built *Oslo* joined *Montebello* in the Oslo passenger service in 1906. She was broadly similar to the earlier ship with the exception of a raised foc's'le, which provided extra accommodation as well as compensating for 'wetness' forward.
Col R.C. Gabriel collection

provision for a further 410 in the forward tween-decks.

Oslo sailed on her maiden voyage to Oslo on 25 May, replacing the aged 72-passenger *Angelo* which went to scrap. She in turn was replaced by the new *Eskimo* in 1910 and was transferred to the Bergen/ Trondheim service in place of *Tasso*. The following year she was joined by *Aaro* and the two maintained this seasonal service until the beginning of World War 1. The Hull–Bergen trip occupied about 48 hours with a 27hr open sea passage between Spurn and Stavanger and calls were made at Aalesund and Kristiansund en route to Trondheim, which was reached some 3½ days after leaving Hull.

Oslo continued trading to Norway during World War 1 and on 11 October 1915 she was chased by a submarine five miles southeast of Holy Island, but used her speed to make good her escape. She was later fitted with defensive armament but was torpedoed 15 miles east by north of the Outer Skerries, Shetland on 21 August 1917, sinking with the loss of three lives. The name *Oslo* was not used again in the Wilson fleet.

Aaro

A replacement for *Montebello* in Wilson's Oslo service began to take shape in Earle's shipyard in the early months of 1909. The new ship entered the water for the first time on 19 April, being christened *Aaro* after a small island south of Funen. She was an awning deck steamer with a short foc's'le, a cellular double bottom, and three holds with tween-decks forward for the carriage of either cargo or emigrants. Externally she was quite unlike any other Wilson steamer with an extensive two-deck superstructure amidships and two very tall masts, between which was strung the first wireless telegraphy aerial to be seen on the Humber.

Length: 300ft 0in
Breadth: 41ft 0in
Depth/draught: 20ft 0in/17ft 0in
Gross tonnage: 2,603
Machinery: 3-cylinder triple expansion
Boilers: 2se, 190lb/sq in
Power: 249nhp
Speed: 13½kt

Her main accommodation was amidships with single and double-berth staterooms for 104 first class passengers on the upper and main decks, whilst 40 second class passengers were housed in four-berth cabins. Both classes had their own saloons, that in first class seating over 100, and there

Aaro of 1909 was an improved *Oslo* with extra accommodation being substituted for the former midships hold. Note her exceptionally tall masts which carried the first W/T aerial fitted to a Humber ship. Note also how her status as a passenger ship was enhanced by the effective use of white paint. *Author's collection*

were also smoke rooms, lounges and a library. Third class accommodation, mainly for emigrants, was arranged under the foc'sle for 94 in six-berth cabins and a further 500 could be carried on the weather deck.

Aaro sailed on her maiden voyage from Riverside Quay at 6.30pm on Saturday 29 May 1909 and thereafter alternated every other Saturday with *Oslo*. On the morning of 20 January 1911 when inward bound from Oslo she collided with and sank the 1,082-ton Trondheim steamer *Richard* off Spurn, but was able to pick up all her crew before proceeding relatively undamaged to Hull. Later that year she replaced *Salmo* on the Bergen/Trondheim service on which she remained until November 1914.

On 1 August 1916, only six days after the capture of *Eskimo*, the seven-year old *Aaro* was torpedoed and sunk by a German submarine in the North Sea. Three lives were lost and the remainder of the crew were taken prisoner. Thus ended a disastrous three-week period for the Wilson Line during which it had lost no less than three of its largest and most prestigious North Sea passenger steamers, the third being *Calypso*. There can be little doubt that these losses contributed greatly to the Wilson family selling out to Ellerman late the same year.

The name *Aaro* was not used again until 1960 when a 12-passenger 2,468-ton motor ship was built for Ellerman Wilson's Danish services by Henry Robb at Leith. A handsome grey-hulled ship, she was sold in 1972 to the Maldives Shipping Co of Male and renamed *Maldive Trust*.

Eskimo

On 9 April 1910, barely a year after the launching of *Aaro*, another new passenger steamer for Wilson's Oslo trade slid down the Humberside ways of Earle's Co Ltd. As with the earlier ship her name *Eskimo* was a new one in the Wilson fleet. After fitting out she was sent out on an 8hr full power trial on 24 May during which she maintained an average speed of 17.3kt, thus becoming the Company's

fastest ship by a considerble margin. She was also the first North Sea passenger ship to exceed 3,000 tons.

Length: 331ft 2½in
Breadth: 45ft 2½in
Depth: 25ft 7in
Gross tonnage: 3,326
Machinery: 2 sets 4-cylinder quadruple expansion
Boilers: 4, 215lb/sq in
Power: 5,000ihp
Speed: 16kt

Her twin-funnelled three-deck design was quite unlike anything that had preceded her in the Norwegian trade and in fact owed more to the Gothenburg service *Calypso* of 1904. She had a raised foc'sle and a long raised bridge deck surrounded by solid bulwarks, stretching for more than half her length. Above this was a fine open promenade deck over 100ft in length. Her cowl-topped funnels were placed farther apart than *Calypso's*, but a lack of sheer gave her a somewhat stiffer overall appearance.

Passenger figures vary but it appears that she could carry a maximum of about 150 in first and 50 in second class in upper and main deck staterooms. Some 500 third class passengers (which was a polite way of describing emigrants) could be housed in four and six-berth cabins at the forward and aft ends of the main and lower decks. Public rooms included three separate dining saloons.

Eskimo replaced the four-year-old *Oslo* in the prestigious weekly Oslo service but in June 1911 was requisitioned by the Admiralty to help carry the official guests at the Coronation Naval Review, thereby missing her Saturday sailings from Hull on

Belching smoke from her twin stacks Wilson's crack steamer *Eskimo* (1910) speeds across the placid waters of the Humber estuary. Although no beauty due in the main to lack of sheer, her speed and comfort added greatly to the prestige of the Oslo service.
Laurence Dunn collection

17 and 24 which were taken by the old *Eldorado*. In normal service she left Riverside Quay at 6.30pm on Saturdays returning from the Norwegian port at 1.00pm on Wednesday to arrive back in the Humber in the early hours of Friday morning. Her speed cut down the open sea part of the voyage to about 22 hours and calls were made at Kristiansand in both directions.

World War 1 brought her short period of peacetime service to an end and on 19 November 1914 she was once again requisitioned by the Admiralty, though under less happy circumstances than before. After refitting as an armed merchant cruiser at Liverpool where she was equipped with four 6in and two 6pdr guns she commissioned as HMS *Eskimo* (M.75) into the 10th Cruiser Squadron. Although newer and larger than *Calypso* which accompanied her as HMS *Calyx* she nevertheless proved too small for the task of patrolling the Atlantic in all weathers and left the squadron with the latter in April 1915, being returned to her owners on 18 July.

She resumed her North Sea service and on 26 July 1916 only 16 days after her erstwhile consort *Calypso's* loss was herself captured by the German auxiliary cruiser *Möwe* off Risor, some 15 miles southeast of Arendal, in Norwegian territorial waters. It appears that the latter had followed her down the Oslo fjord posing as the neutral *Vineta* and then had suddenly speeded up, crossing her stern and opening fire at a range of about 200yd. After two hits *Eskimo* was stopped and boarded but while she was being taken to Swinemunde a fireman jumped overboard in the Danish Sound. He was rescued by a local yachtsman and taken to Helsingborg, later making his way home to England.

Eskimo became a netlayer under German naval control but was returned to Ellerman's Wilson Line after the war and arrived back in the Tyne on 19 January 1919. The company appears to have had no further use for her and she was sold to France in 1921 becoming a unit of the Compagnie de Navigation Paquet's fleet in the Mediterranean, without change of name. She traded as a cargo ship between the south coast of France and North Africa until 1930 when she was sold for scrap.

Bayardo

When the 1890-built *Ariosto* was 20 years old Wilson Line placed an order with Earle's for a large new passenger steamer to replace her on the Gothenburg service. The new building slid down the ways on the 29 May 1911 after being given the name *Bayardo*. (As with many of the Wilson names this one had no particular meaning and it would be interesting to learn just how they came to be chosen). Upon completion she proceeded on trials during which she averaged 15.33kt in the course of four runs on the measured mile of Withernsea.

In terms of tonnage and dimensions she just topped *Eskimo* built a year previously for the Oslo run and so became the 'Queen of the fleet' and the largest passenger steamer in regular North Sea service.

Length: 331ft 0in
Breadth: 47ft 0in
Depth/draught: 24ft 6in/16ft 9in
Gross tonnage: 3,570
Machinery: 3-cylinder triple expansion
Boilers: 3se, 180lb/sq in
Power: 3,600ihp
Speed: 15kt

Although she only had a single cowl-topped funnel amidships, her layout generally followed that of *Eskimo* with a raised foc'sle and bridge deck, but her upper promenade deck was covered with an awning. Due to her short career details of her passenger capacity do not come easily to hand but she could carry over 100 in first (or saloon) class.

She left Hull Riverside on her maiden voyage on 20 July 1911 and from then on alternated with *Calypso* every other Thursday at 6.30pm, arriving in Gothenburg early on Saturday morning. In the opposite direction she left the Swedish port at 10.00pm on Friday and arrived back at Hull at noon on Sunday.

Seven months later she left Gothenburg on 19 January 1912 on the return half of her 13th voyage with a number of passengers and a cargo of wood pulp, butter and several hundred cases of herrings.

A sad ending for Wilson's 'Queen of the Fleet', the Earle's-built *Bayardo* (1911), after only seven months on the Gothenburg run. At 3,570 tons gross she was the largest ship built for regular North Sea passenger service until the coming of Swedish Lloyd's sisters *Britannia* and *Suecia* in **1929.** *Author's collection*

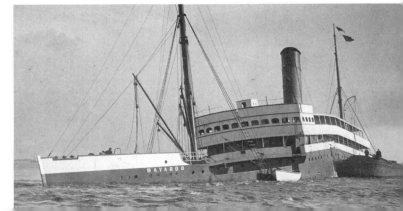

At about 7.00am on Sunday morning she was creeping up the fog shrouded Humber at reduced speed when she gounded on Middle Sands opposite Alexandra Dock. The strength of the flood pushed her well on to the bank but her stern remained afloat. Later as the tide fell she listed to port and broke her back.

All on board were taken off and the following day over 1,000 casks of butter and much of the rest of the cargo was off-loaded into lighters. At low water joiners from her builders were able to strip her of most of her valuable fittings.

The wreck settled very quickly and before long only the promenade deck and bridge remained visible, the bows having broken off and disappeared in the mud. Being quite immovable and a potential danger to navigation *Bayardo's* remains were later blown up – a sad end to the pride of the Wilson fleet.

Models of *Bayardo* and *Eskimo* can be seen in the Town Docks Museum, Hull.

Rollo

After World War 1 Ellerman's Wilson Line – as it had become known after its 1916 take-over by Sir John Ellerman – was faced with the task of finding suitable replacements for its lost passenger ships. The first acquisition in October 1920 was more of an internal transfer involving the Ellerman & Papayanni steamer *Italian* which had been built by Messrs Barclay Curle, Glasgow as *Fantee* back in 1899. At that time she and her sister *Sobo* were the finest ships in the Africa Steamship Co's West African trade combining shallow draught for river work and a respectable passenger capacity of 70 in first and 40 in second classes. Managed by Elder Dempster she continued in this trade (surviving a lengthy grounding at Sheebar, Sierra Leone in February 1913) until 1915 when she was sold to Ellerman.

Upon entering the Wilson fleet she was given the traditional name of *Rollo* which had previously been held by a popular passenger steamer built by

Rollo, the first of three second-hand steamers acquired in 1920 to replace war losses, was transferred from Ellerman and Papayanni Line though she had begun life as far back as 1899 as the West African trader *Fantee. Capt E. Sigwart collection*

Earle's in 1870 for the Norwegian trade and only scrapped in 1909. With postwar emigration to America again running at a high level she was refitted with this in mind and her accommodation was altered to cater for 256 in third class and only 61 in first class. Her tonnage and measurements, etc were by this time as follows:

Length: 345ft 0in
Breadth: 44ft 0in
Depth: 25ft 8in
Gross tonnage: 3,658
Machinery: 3-cylinder triple expansion
Boilers: 2se, 180lb/sq in
Power: 459nhp
Speed: 11½kt

In her new guise she was mainly employed in the Hull–Gothenburg service but also ran to Oslo and later Danzig. The introduction of reduced US immigrant quotas in 1923 reduced her passenger carrying activities and she was never a very successful ship, being laid up in Hull in July 1928. She remained in this state until the summer of 1932 when she was sold to Danish shipbreakers Petersen & Albeck and left in tow for Copenhagen on 29 September.

Orlando

The second postwar passenger ship purchased by Ellerman's Wilson in 1920 was the Harrison liner *Inanda* which had been by Hall Russell Aberdeen in August 1904 for John T. Rennie's direct service from the UK to Natal. She was a spar deck steamer and as built could carry just over 60 first class and 50

second class passengers. She had been absorbed into the Harrison fleet in May 1911 without change of name.

Length: 370ft 0in
Breadth: 46ft 2in
Depth: 18ft 6in
Gross tonnage: 4,233
Machinery: 3-cylinder triple expansion
Boilers: 6se, 180lb/sq in
Power: 525nhp
Speed: 11½kt

After her purchase by Ellerman's she was given the name *Orlando,* formerly borne by a 50 year old ship at that time still trading as the French *Algerie,* and destined to be wrecked at Chanea four years later.

Orlando was refitted at the same time as *Rollo* but had more than double her emigrant capacity at 594 persons, whilst her first class accommodation was reorganised to cater for 76 instead of the original 116. She looked good in Wilson colours and was initially used in the Hull–Danzig trade until replaced by the new *Tasso,* which was purpose built for this route in 1922. Afterwards she was employed in Wilson's North Sea services running out of Hull and London to Gothenburg and Oslo, but in the winter of 1927/28 she made a round voyage to South Africa on charter to Ellerman Bucknall. Her passenger capacity by this time was shown as 60 in first, 20 in second and 60 in third classes.

In 1929 she was laid up with *Rollo* in Hull and there she remained until July 1932 when she was towed round to the Bristol Channel for scrapping by T.W. Ward at Briton Ferry.

Calypso

On 4 November 1920 Ellerman's Wilson purchased a third passenger/cargo steamer, the former Woermann liner *Alexandra Woermann* which had been surrendered to the Shipping Controller in March 1919 and which had in the interval been under White Star management.

She had been launched originally as the Belgian *Bruxellesville* by Sir Raylton Dixon, Middlesbrough on 27 October 1897 and on

The elegant *Calypso* of 1898 ran to the Congo as *Bruxellesville* and later *Alexandra Woermann* before her acquisition in 1920. After serving on various routes she became a regular on the Hull–Oslo service and in 1933 started a new seasonal series of 10-day Scandinavian cruises from London which continued until her eventual demise late in 1936. *Author's collection*

completion the following year was put into service between Antwerp and the Congo under the ownership of the Woermann-controlled Soc Maritime du Congo. She was a well-proportioned ship with a well-deck forward and had comfortable accommodation for 100 first class passengers and about 60 in second class. Her cargo capacity totalled about 165,600cu ft and she was propelled at a maximum speed of 13kt by triple expansion engines supplied by T.E. Richardson of West Hartlepool.

In January 1901 she was transferred to full Woermann ownership and after being renamed *Alexandra Woermann* was placed in the Hamburg–German West Africa trade. During World War 1 she was used as a transport by the German navy and on 5 September 1918 ran down and sank the submarine UC.91.

After her purchase by Ellerman's Wilson she was renamed *Calypso* in memory of the former Gothenburg service steamer lost during the war. Her accommodation was altered to cater for three classes of passenger with respective berthing arrangements for 60, 20 and 60. After these alterations her tonnage and other particulars were as follows:

Length: 353ft 7in
Breadth: 44ft 2in
Depth/draught: 23ft 5in/22t 10in
Gross tonnage: 3,817
Machinery: 3-cylinder triple expansion
Boilers: 3se, 180lb/sq in
Power: 432nhp
Speed: 12kt

Early in her new career she made a round voyage to Bombay but then alternated between the Oslo, Gothenburg and Danzig services. From the mid-1920s she settled down to regular summer service between Hull and Oslo, laying up in the former port

during the winter. In 1933 she inaugurated a new series of seasonal 10-day cruises from Millwall Dock, London to Copenhagen (via Kiel) and Oslo, returning via Kristiansand. These were successful and continued until the autumn of 1936 when after a two-month lay up in Hull she was sold for scrap to Van Heyghen Freres and towed to Bruges, where she arrived on 24 November.

It is worth adding that in 1933 a similar series of cruises was run from Hull to Kristiansand and Oslo by the chartered Ellerman liner *City of Canterbury*. These were repeated in 1934 and 1935 by *City of Paris* and between 1936 and 1939 were performed by the specially modified *City of Nagpur*.

Spero (1922)

Due to all shipbuilding yards having full order books in the immediate post World War 1 years, it was not until 1922 that Ellerman's Wilson were able to take delivery of a new refrigerated passenger/cargo ship for their North Sea services. The second *Spero* was a product of the Dundee Shipbuilding Co Ltd and her launch took place on 9 August. She was intended for the Hull–Copenhagen service which had been run jointly with DFDS since 1903.

Length: 257ft 0in
Breadth: 37ft 0in
Depth/draught: 17ft 0in/18ft 3in
Gross tonnage: 1,589
Machinery: 3-cylinder triple expansion
Boilers: 2se, 225lb/sq in
Power: 169nhp
Speed: 13kt

Her design followed one favoured by Wilson Line for a number of cargo/passenger ships built for its Baltic services in 1906/07, which consisted of a short raised foc'sle which was made to appear as though it reached to the foremast by high-sided bulwarks around No 1 hatch, separated by a short well from a long combined bridge and poop. The superstructure was split around No 3 hatch, aft of which were a pair of kingposts and tall ventilators in front of the single tall funnel. The only apparent modern features were a cruiser stern and a more enclosed superstructure.

Her accommodation was designed to cater for 30 first class passengers with a further 24 in third class. Her deadweight capacity was 1,665 tons and cargo handling by means of a combination of steam winches and 10 derricks was supposed to be good enough to obviate the need for shore cranes.

The initial months of her career were spent on the Oslo service and on 24 March 1923 she grounded (fortunately not seriously) at Arendal. Soon afterward she took up her intended Hull–Copenhagen run on which she was to remain for the whole of her career with the exception of World War 2.

Her usual inward cargoes consisted of bacon, eggs and butter and these were off-loaded at Riverside Quay after which she bunkered before moving to Railway Dock to load. She sailed on Friday night to make way for her DFDS running partner *Hroar* which arrived the following day to repeat the process. Passenger fares for 1939 including food were £5.10s for a first class single and £2.15s for third class.

She survived World War 2, during which she was usually employed on coastal duties, and returned to her Copenhagen station in 1946, though her passenger capacity was thenceforward limited to 12. Her loading berth in Hull had also been changed and was now 28 Shed in the William Wright Dock.

Latterly she was laid up for long periods and only came out for occasional relief voyages during the winter months. She was finally withdrawn and laid up in October 1958, being by then easily the oldest unit in the Ellerman's Wilson fleet. The following summer she was sold to Belgian breakers for £10 per gross ton and was towed to Antwerp where she arrived on 24 September to await demolition at Lillebroek.

Borodino

In 1948 Ellerman's Wilson Line ordered a new refrigerated passenger/cargo ship from the Ailsa Shipbuilding Co, Troon, whose yard had delivered the sisters *Dago* and *Domino* to the company in the previous year. She was the first of her type to be built since *Spero* in 1922, passenger services having been maintained in the meantime by a number of

The smart-looking Ailsa-built *Borodino* entered Ellerman Wilson's Hull–Copenhagen service in the summer of 1950. The last of a long line of passenger steamers, her days were numbered when the passenger/car ferry *Spero* entered service in 1966 and she went to Belgian breakers the following year. *Author's collection*

second-hand passenger steamers or chartered Ellerman liners and from the mid-1930s by a succession of new 12 passenger cargo ships.

The new ship was also destined to be the only one of her type to be built by her owner after World War 2 and she was christened *Borodino* on Feburary 1950 by Mrs G.W. Bayley, the wife of one of the company's directors. The name *Borodino* had been used twice before in the Wilson fleet, once in 1880 for a 1,264-ton ship which was scrapped at Falmouth in 1909 and again in 1911 for a 2,004-ton passenger cargo steamer for the Baltic trade which had ended her days as a blockship at Zeebrugge in 1940.

The new *Borodino* was delivered by Ailsa on 13 June after performing trials on the Skelmorlie mile.

Length: 312ft 1in oa/295ft 4in bp
Breadth: 48ft 4in
Depth/draught: 25ft 4in/18ft 0in
Gross tonnage: 3,206
Machinery: 3-cylinder triple expansion and LP turbine
Boilers: 2 oil-fired se, 225lb/sq in
Power: 318nhp
Speed: 13½kt

She was an attractive little ship with red and black funnel, white bulwarks and superstructure and light grey hull in place of the traditional Wilson green. Her hull contained two complete decks and had a short raised foc'sle with a raking stem and cruiser stern. Her five cargo holds, three forward and two aft of the machinery, could carry a total bale capacity of 103,522 cu ft of which about three-quarters was insulated for the carriage of dairy products. Handling arrangements comprised 10 derricks and cargo winches.

She could carry 36 passengers in first class in comfortable accommodation amidships, mainly in single or double cabins on the bridge and upper decks. In addition there were six extra large cabins, two on the boat deck and the rest on the bridge deck, which had two beds and their own bathrooms. Further sleeping arrangements for about 20 third class passengers were provided aft in No 5 hold upper tween-deck. For the comfort of passengers

the cabins were mechanically ventilated with filtered air and each had a telephone. Public rooms included a first class lounge and bar on the bridge deck forward and below this a 42-seat dining saloon, both with large windows. The crew numbered 52.

Main propulsion was provided by means of a triple expansion engine exhausting into a Bauer Wauch low pressure turbine driving a single screw.

Her schedule called for a fortnightly return trip to Copenhagen, generally leaving Hull on a Friday and returning via Aarhus the following week. Alternate sailings were taken by a DFDS ship in accordance with the time-honoured agreement.

In the summer of 1953 she steamed south for a few days to represent her owners officially at the Coronation Naval Review at Spithead which took place on 15 June.

The fare structure existing in about 1960 was £20 for a single passage in the summer reducing to £14 during the winter months and round voyage trips had become quite popular with travellers from the Midlands. In 1965 she was switched to the London–Copenhagen/Aarhus run, changing places with the 1960-built 2,468-ton *Aaro* which only had accommodation for 12 passengers. This new run involved a 9/10-day round voyage, much the same as before, and departures were still every other Friday.

Fares for the summer of 1966 had risen to £26.10s for a single passage and would-be passengers were either tending to fly or else take one of the fast new car ferries being offered on other North Sea routes. By now her old-fashioned engines were making her expensive to run and at the end of the year she made one last round trip, arriving back in London on 2 January. After a few days discharging she returned to Hull and was laid up pending sale. No trading buyer came forward and in July 1967 she was sold to Van Heyghen Freres SA for breaking at Bruges where she arrived in tow on 18 August, with work commencing the following month.

She was the last of a long line of 'conventional' passenger/cargo ships in the Wilson fleet which had been a conspicuous feature of North Sea travel for over 150 years.

64

The Wilson's & North Eastern Railway Shipping Co

Hull–Hamburg/Antwerp/Ghent/Dunkirk
1906–1922   Managed by NER
1923–1947   Managed by LNER
1948–1957   Managed by BTC
Funnel colours: Red with black top separated by
                narrow white band

Length: 256ft 0in
Breadth: 36ft 2in
Depth: 15ft 0in
Gross tonnage: 1,076
Machinery: 3-cylinder triple expansion
Boilers: 2se, 180lb/sq in
Power: 373nhp
Speed: 15kt

Darlington

In March 1906 Thos Wilson Sons & Co agreed to hand over the day-to-day running of their established Hamburg, Antwerp, Ghent and Dunkirk services to the North Eastern Railway Co. The latter already held powers to operate ships to these ports but up till then had only owned a variety of harbour and service craft. A new jointly-owned company was set up and entitled The Wilson's & North Eastern Railway Shipping Co and the following Wilson steamers were transferred to it: *Cito* (1899), *Dynamo* (1884) and *Juno* (1900) on 17 March; *Bruno* (1892) and *Hero* (1895) on 24 March of that year. Most of these were able to carry 12 passengers and later they were joined by two more Wilson ships, the 1898-built sisters *Otto* and *Truro* which in addition to their 12 could also carry a number of steerage passengers.

The first new ships to be built for the company were the sisters *Hull* and *York* which appeared from the Caledon Shipyard, Dundee in 1907. Of 1,132 gross tons they were similar to *Juno* but had longer foc'sles extending to the foremast. They remained in the fleet till sold in 1937 but for the last two years came under the management of Associated Humber Lines. Their new owners Soc Algerienne de Nav puor L'Afrique du Nord renamed them *Ville de Djidjelli* and *Ville de Bougie* respectively and placed them under Charles Schiaffino management where they remained until scrapped in the 1950s.

On 5 July 1910 Earle's Co launched the *Darlington*, a similar but more powerful version of the earlier pair, and after fitting out she performed her trials on 29 June, attaining about 16kt. Her dimensions were almost identical to the earlier ships and were as follows:

Design-wise she was a four-hatch ship with No 2 placed in a short well-deck aft of the foc'sle and No 3 between a tall bridge and even taller funnel. Her accommodation for 16 first-class passengers was arranged under the bridge though a later 1911-built consort *Harrogate* could apparently only carry 12. She was generally employed on the Antwerp run, her Hull terminal, as with most of the Humber passenger services, being Riverside Quay.

Harrogate foundered off the Norwegian coast on 20 February 1918 but *Darlington* resumed her normal service after World War 1 although by this time only carrying 12 passengers. On 13 February 1926 in thick fog in the Scheldt she was in collision with the LNER passenger steamer *Antwerp*, which resulted in both ships grounding with severe damage. Otherwise her career continued uneventfully till October 1935, when being surplus she was transferred to Ellerman's Wilson Line and given the name *Castro*.

After only two years under Wilson colours she was sold to Billmeir's Stanhope Steamship Co and renamed *Stanrock*, but changed hands again almost immediately becoming the *Lydia* and then in 1938 the *Ocu* of E. Godillot, Colon. Renamed *Ilowa* in the same year she became the *Sona* of Margit SS Co, Colon in 1939 and finally met her fate in Greek waters at the hands of the Luftwaffe in April 1941 at Adamas bay, Milos.

The Wilsons and NER Shipping Co continued until 1957 and its two remaining cargo ships, *Selby* and *Harrogate*, built at Aberdeen and Leith in 1922 and 1925 respectively, were broken up a year later.

Hull & Netherlands Steamship Co

Hull–Amsterdam/Rotterdam
1894–1957   Hull & Netherlands Steamship Co
1957–1972   Associated Humber Lines Ltd
Funnel colours: Buff with black top until 1935,
    when red band added with black letters AHL
    superimposed

Swift (1884)

Early steamer services out of Hull were operated by
the St George Steam Packet Co, but by 1849 the
Hull Steam Packet Co was running services to
Antwerp, Copenhagen and St Petersburg with
several paddle steamers. Over the years further
steamers were built or acquired, many of them
being given bird names which had been a feature of
the St George company.
On 1 March 1894 Messrs H.H. Hutchinson and
C.L. Ringrose together with a number of other
shareholders formed a new amalgamated company
which was registered as the Hull & Netherlands
Steamship Co Ltd with a paid up capital of
£210,000. One of the ships it took over was the *Swift*
which had been built for Hutchinson 10 years
previously by the Sunderland Shipbuilding Co with
engines from the Hull workshops of E. Wales. She
had been launched on 26 April by Mrs Hutchinson.

Length: 210ft 0in
Breadth: 28ft 5in
Depth: 12ft 9in
Gross tonnage: 671
Machinery: 3-cylinder triple expansion
Boilers: 2 steel, 40lb/sq in
Power: 177nhp
Speed: 13kt

Swift had a raised foc'sle and a long raised quarter
deck; contemporary reports described her as having
a large amount of accommodation amidships with
promenade deck and all the latest appliances for the
comfort and safety of the passengers. Her deck gear
included three powerful steam winches from Clarke
Chapman and steam steering gear was supplied by
the local firm of Amos & Smith.

She was engaged in the Hull–Rotterdam trade of
the new company for about seven years before
being sold early in 1902 to the General Steam
Navigation Co. She traded out of London without
change of name until 1911 when she was purchased
by the Bank of Athens. Renamed *Osmanie* she
traded in the Mediterranean for many years under
the management of A. Gaetano & Co which
company later became her full owner. After 39
years afloat she was eventually broken up in 1933.

Sea Gull

Sea Gull was the newest steamer taken over by the
Hull & Netherlands SS Co at its inception. She had
been built at Glasgow by Messrs Murdoch &
Murray some two years previously for W. & C.L.
Ringrose, and was one of the very few ships in the
Company to come from west coast builders. She
had been christened *Sea Gull,* a name used twice
before, in May 1892, but unlike the earlier ships she
was built of steel.

Length: 225ft 9in
Breadth: 32ft 6in
Depth: 14ft 0in
Gross tonnage: 817
Machinery: 3-cylinder triple expansion
Boilers: 2 steel, 170lb/sq in
Power: 258nhp
Speed: 14kt

Somewhat larger and slightly faster than *Swift,* she
nevertheless conformed to the latter's basic design
having one continuous deck and a well-deck
forward. Details of her passenger accommodation
have gone unrecorded but it can be assumed that a
number of first class passengers were carried
amidships.
Her triple expansion machinery was constructed
by the well-known Glasgow firm of Kincaid & Co
and steam was supplied by two single boilers
working at 170 lb/sq in.
Following replacement by more modern tonnage
she became a reserve ship and was sold in March
1911 to the Constantinople based Hilal Steam

Navigation Co, being renamed *Millet*. Her new career in Middle Eastern waters came to an end in May 1915 when she was sunk off Eregli by gunfire from the Russian fleet.

Swallow, Swan, Swift/Selby Abbey (1902)

The first new ships ordered by the Hull & Netherlands SS Co after its incorporation were the sisters *Swallow* and *Swan* which were constructed by the local firm of Earle's in 1899. *Swallow* was launched on 18 September and *Swan* about a month later on 17 October. Both ships entered service on the company's Rotterdam service before the year was out.

Length: 240ft 0in
Breadth: 33ft 0in
Depth: 15ft 1in
Gross tonnage: 1,004
Machinery: 3-cylinder triple expansion
Boilers: 2, 160lb/sq in (*Swift* 3, 180lb/sq in)
Power: 1,500ihp *(Swift* 3,000 ihp)
Speed: 12kt (*Swift* 14kt)

The new steamers had steel hulls with a short foc'sle and long raised quarterdeck, with the bridge placed over the machinery and boiler space amidships. A double bottom was incorporated in the main and after holds for water ballast tanks which were also fitted in the forward and aft peaks.

Accommodation was provided for a total of 22 passengers, 12 in a first class cabin under the quarterdeck aft, which had its entrance and staircase in a steel house on deck, and 10 second class in comfortable under-deck accommodation forward. The crew was housed in the foc'sle with the captain on the bridge and officers and engineers at the after end of the bridge deckhouse.

Cargo handling gear consisted of extra long derricks driven by four powerful steam winches, and provision was made for the stalling of 40 horses under the bridge.

When the two sisters had been in service for about 2½ years a third steamer was ordered from Earle's, possibly as a replacement for her owners' old steamer *European* (1850, 538gt), which had been wrecked off the Dutch coast in September 1900. The new ship became the second to bear the name *Swift* when she was launched by Lady Marjorie Wilson on 28 October 1902. The ship's dimensions were the same as *Swallow* and *Swan* but she was given more powerful engines and an extra boiler to give her a 2kt speed advantage. Her first class accommodation for 12 was placed under the bridge amidships with a dining saloon of polished hardwood, and 10 second class passengers could be berthed in a deckhouse aft.

In 1908 *Swift* was renamed *Selby Abbey* to bring her into line with the four newly completed 'Abbey' steamers, but some three years later whilst approaching the Hook in a snow squall on 12 January she ran at full speed on to the Inderribben Sands. The wind was a strong northerly at the time and her four passengers and some crew were taken off by a steam lifeboat, the remainder of the crew following them later. The next day the wind moderated and the crew returned. Cargo lightening operations were put in hand and she was refloated on 16 and towed to Hull. Bottom damage and propeller repairs cost about £5,000, almost a fifth of

her value, in addition to a £1,500 salvage award. At the subsequent enquiry the captain was held to blame and his certificate suspended for three months.

The two earlier ships had by now become surplus and *Swan* was sold in 1910 to Stoom Maats Friesland who renamed her *Minister Tak Van Poortvliet* whilst *Swallow* went to the Bank of Rome a year later becoming *Roma*. The former was torpedoed by UB.10 20 miles north of Ijmuiden on 24 April 1917 on a voyage from Hull to Harlingen, but *Roma* continued under Italian ownership for many years becoming the Palermo registered *Tobruk* of Soc di Nav Italia in about 1923. Some three years later her owners were Soc Italian di Nav Florio and her final years were spent in the Tirrenia fleet before being scrapped in 1934.

At the end of December 1912 *Selby Abbey* became the 10,000th ship to enter the port of Rotterdam that year and it is worth noting that the passenger fare at the time was the equivalent of 12 florins. She was sold to Gerhard & Hay of Windau in 1913 and renamed *Triton* but was sunk as a blockship at the beginning of World War 1. She was raised and used as a survey ship by the German navy until 1916 but remained in govenment hands until 1921. Between 1924 and 1927 she traded as *Triton 1* for two Hamburg companies before becoming *Falke* of Kauffahrt AG, Altona. As such she played an important but unsuccessful part in the abortive 1929 revolution in Venezuela, landing General Delgado who was later killed.

After her escapade she was acquired by E. Vormauer and renamed *Ilse Vormauer* but trading was difficult in the Caribbean and in 1932 she became the Cuban owned *Yunque* of Cia Naviera de Baracoa. At one stage she was involved in gun-running for Cuban revolutionaries and was chased by a Cuban gunboat but managed to escape and hide in the Bahamas. Presumably the authorities eventually caught up with her as she became the Cuban naval transport *Colombia* in about 1935. The long career of this remarkable little ship finally came to an end when she stranded in 1944.

Whitby Abbey, Rievaulx Abbey, Jervaulx Abbey, Kirkham Abbey

In 1907 the Hull & Netherlands SS Co embarked on a major fleet replacement programme and four new ships were ordered, two from the local yard of Earle's and two from Wm Gray & Co Ltd, West Hartlepool. They were all named after local abbeys and Earle's launched *Whitby Abbey* on 5 December and Gray's *Rievaulx Abbey* two days before Christmas. Gray's second ship, *Jervaulx Abbey*, was christened just about a month later on 20 January and the final steamer, *Kirkham Abbey*, entered the waters of the Humber on 4 February. Trials in each case consisted of 200-mile runs at full speed, the Gray-built ships performing their's during delivery from Hartlepool to Hull, and all four recorded averages of about 15½kt.

The new ships were built of steel to Lloyd's 100 A1 classification.

Length: 265ft 0in/255ft 4in bp
Breadth: 33ft 7in
Depth/draught: 15ft 5in/15ft 9in
Gross tonnage: 1,166 (Earle's)/1,188 (Gray)
Machinery: 3-cylinder triple expansion
Boilers: 3se, 185lb/sq in
Power: 3,400ihp
Speed: 15kt (contract)

They were basically longer versions of *Selby Abbey* but with a more enclosed superstructure amidships.

Whitby Abbey, **first of four larger and faster steamers built for Hull & Netherlands' Rotterdam service in 1908. A product of Wm Gray's West Hartlepool Yard with sister** *Jervaulx Abbey,* **her design continued the theme of earlier ships but with an enlarged superstructure to cater for up to 120 passengers.** *Author's collection*

Accommodation was considerably enlarged and catered for 48 in first class amidships in the case of the Earle's-built ships and 44 in the other pair. All four sisters could carry 28 second class passengers in the poop and 44 steerage under deck forward.

Their deadweight capacity was just under 1,000 tons and their three holds were served by seven derricks driven by five steam winches. Engines for all four ships were supplied by the Central Marine Engineering Co Ltd, West Hartlepool, with boilers employing forced draught, and their bunkers could hold about 120 tons of coal which was consumed at a rate of 48cwt/hr.

Their entry into service in the summer of 1908 enabled the Company, in which a controlling interest had just been acquired by the North Eastern Railway, to operate a daily service to Rotterdam.

Several minor accidents befell them including a collision between *Whitby Abbey* and the trawler *Princess Louise* in the Humber in fog on 27 January 1909, whilst on 12 July 1914 *Jervaulx Abbey* sank the Grimsby trawler *Monimia* off Spurn but rescued all her crew.

The four sisters were only destined to serve together for six years before World War 1 brought disruption to the service and with it separation. *Rievaulx Abbey* was hired by the Admiralty as a store carrier between 13 March and 29 May 1915 and on 27 August was again taken up as the armaments carrier Y2.56. Just over a year later on 3 September 1916 she hit a mine northeast of the Rosse Spit buoy in the Humber and was lost along with two of her crew. Some reports suggest that *Whitby Abbey* was used as an Armed Boarding Steamer and Fleet Sweeper during the Gallipoli campaign.

Kirkham Abbey appears to have had the most 'exciting' war, twice escaping before finally being sunk. On the first occasion on 14 February 1915 she was pursued by a submarine for some 20 miles, using her speed to escape, and later on 27 February 1918 was the object of an unsuccessful bombing attack off the Hook of Holland. Her end came exactly five months later when she was torpedoed two miles northeast of Winterton with the loss of eight lives.

The two surviving sisters returned to their former peacetime service in 1920 and in 1929 were joined by the new and larger *Melrose Abbey*. Following the rationalisation of Humber shipping services in 1935 under the banner of Associated Humber Lines the ageing sisters became surplus and were disposed of a year later. *Whitby Abbey* went for scrap but her sister was sold to the Ching Kee Steam Navigation Co Ltd of Chefoo for £9,500 through the intervention of Townsend Bros (Shipping) Ltd. She was renamed *Houlee* and made the long voyage out to China arriving at Darien in June 1936. After a few years in coastal service she became a war loss.

Melrose Abbey (1929)

In the late 1920s the Hull & Netherlands SS Co, which had passed to LNER control in 1923, ordered a new passenger/cargo ship from Earle's, the Company's first after a gap of 20 years. The new ship was given the name *Melrose Abbey* at her launch on 28 February 1929, and, after completing trials on 23 April, entered service on the Company's traditional Hull–Rotterdam route. She was substantially larger than the pre-World War 1 sisters and her dimensions were as follows:

Length: 292ft 6in oa/281ft 4in bp
Breadth: 38ft 3in
Depth/draught: 18ft 3in/15ft 4in load
Gross tonnage: 1908
Machinery: 3-cylinder triple expansion
Boilers: 3se, 220lb/sq in
Power: 2,800ihp
Speed: 14kt

Her design echoed the changes that had taken place in naval architecture during the preceding 20 years. Gone were the old long raised quarterdeck and tall funnel and in their place were substituted a flush-decked hull and shortish funnel mounted on a long midship accommodation block. The latter housed 84 first class passengers in two and three-berth cabins, including two de-luxe cabins, and the accent was placed on good, solid comfort. In addition about 38 steerage passengers could be accommodated in the after tween-deck.

The new ship was a coal burner with a bunker capacity of some 180 tons, and her boilers, which operated with forced draught, consumed about a ton an hour at an economic 13kt, rising to 1½ tons at 14½kt.

In 1935 she passed to the newly-formed Associated Humber Lines, adding a red band with the letters AHL to her buff funnel. After the sale of her erstwhile partners the following year she was joined by the former GCR *Dewsbury* and continued thus until the start of World War 2. From June 1940 she was employed in wartime convoys around the UK coast and in 1941 was the first of several short sea passenger ships taken up by the Admiralty for conversion to convoy rescue ships. She served with North Atlantic and Gibraltar convoys and between May 1942 and November 1944 steamed about 100,000 miles in the course of 17 round voyages, performing a little publicised but nevertheless invaluable task.

During a postwar refit early in 1946 – which raised her gross tonnage by 16 tons – her accommodation was altered to cater for a total of 116 passengers in saloon and third classes. She re-entered the Rotterdam service on 14 March, running one trip a week until joined by *Bury* the following January. A further refit in 1948 raised her tonnage to 1,941 and in 1955/56 her accommodation was reclassified as first and second class, respective capacities being then 92 and 24.

In April 1958 she was renamed *Melrose Abbey II* in order to release her name for one of the new motor ships then under construction. She continued alongside the new *Bolton Abbey* from June until the following January when she was replaced by her new namesake. After a short lay-up in Hull she was sold in April 1959 to Typaldos Lines and made her way out to Piraeus. There she underwent a major conversion, her former holds being fitted with passenger accommodation, and a much enlarged and somewhat unprepossessing superstructure added, which increased her gross tonnage to 2,069. Under her new name of *Kriti* (Crete) she was now able to carry some 350 people with 180 in first class, 130 in tourist and the remainder in dormitory. Her routes varied but she was employed at first on weekly cruises around the Aegean, later running between Piraeus and the Adriatic port of Brindisi.

Following the *Heraklion* disaster in December 1966 she was laid up near Piraeus, along with other

Melrose Abbey of 1929, the only Hull & Netherlands ship built between the wars, marked a complete break with earlier design, the only recognisable feature being the rather unusual funnel cowl incorporated in the 1908-built ships. In 1935 she adopted the new Associated Humber Lines' colours by adding a red band under her black funnel top with the letters AHL superimposed in black. *Col R.C. Gabriel collection*

Typaldos ships, and there she remained, becoming increasingly delapidated, until 1984 when she was broken up locally in her 53rd year. The last and largest of the Hull & Netherlands' ships, she was remarkable in that she remained a coal-burner throughout her working life.

Bolton Abbey, Melrose Abbey (1959)

In 1954 Associated Humber Lines embarked on a major postwar replacement programme and by 1959 10 new motor vessels had been added to the fleet. Only two of these carried more than 12 passengers, the sisters *Bolton Abbey* and *Melrose Abbey* for the Rotterdam service. They were constructed by the small Lowestoft yard of Brooke Marine which launched *Bolton Abbey* on 11 December 1957 and her sister on 16 October the following year. Although about the same overall length as the 1929-built *Melrose Abbey* they were some 6ft broader in beam, the details of their dimensions and outfit being as follows:

Length: 293ft 4in oa/285ft 0in bp
Breadth: 45ft 1in
Depth/draught: 14ft 3in (to 2nd deck)/14ft 0in
Gross tonnage: 2,741/2
Machinery: 2 8-cylinder geared Ruston & Hornsby diesels
Power: 1,806bhp
Speed: 15½kt

The new ships represented a complete departure from traditional North Sea design with their two forward-placed cargo holds and superstructure aft over the machinery spaces. Comfortable family type accommodation was provided for 80 passengers in 12 single and 33 double cabins (including one de-luxe) on the upper and poop decks.

Their cargo capacity totalled about 116,500cu ft and they could carry about 45 large British Rail-type containers below deck. Additionally their tween-decks could be adjusted to carry palletised cargo. Their engines were the largest built at the time by Rustons and operated through reverse reduction gearing at a maximum of about 190rpm.

They entered service on 4 June 1958 and 17 January 1959 respectively, reducing the crossing time by four hours to approximately 14½ hours. Their schedule allowed for three sailings a week in both directions with departures on Monday, Wednesday and Saturday evenings increasing to five in the height of summer and reducing to Wednesdays and Saturdays only in winter. Fares including meals were £7.50 for a single cabin and £1 less for a double, each reducing by £1.50 in winter.

Early in 1962 in the course of their annual overhauls eight single cabins were converted to doubles, thereby increasing their passenger capacity to 88. Some two years later long-term plans were made to shift the emphasis of the Company's operations from conventional cargo to unit loads. Conversion plans for the two sisters including the addition of a new 52ft midships hold and the removal of all cargo handling gear were put forward and approved. *Melrose Abbey* was sent to Smith's Dock in November 1967 where she was dry-docked and cut amidships. The new section was inserted and after only 30 working days she was re-delivered to her owners on 14 December. Work on her sister started the following day and was completed in the same amount of time. As a result of these alterations the gross tonnage of both ships was increased by 528 tons and they could now carry over 60 containers.

To assist with the new cargo handling arrangements new berths had been prepared and *Melrose Abbey* made her last departure from Riverside Quay to Parkhaven, Rotterdam on 29 January 1968, transferring after discharge to a new berth in the Prinses Beatrixhaven. Her sister opened the new Hull terminal at 'A' jetty Alexandra Dock with her 31 January sailing.

In 1968/9 AHL offered one-day bulb-field tours with their spring sailings and these proved very popular; however, their overall operations were showing a loss and this had reached such proportions by November 1971 that the Rotterdam service was withdrawn and the two ships put on the sale list.

The following summer they were sold to the Carras subsidiary Chion Shipping Co and left Hull for Piraeus on 4 July bearing the new names *Ionia Express* and *Aegeon Express*. The latter was converted back to a geared cargo ship and from about 1974 traded for the one-ship company Aegeon Express SA between northwest European ports and either the Mediterranean or West Africa. She was laid up at Chalkis in July 1978 and met her final short voyage to Piraeus for scrapping on 2 August 1980.

Her sister remained in Carras hands for only a short while, being quicky resold to Offshore Diving & Financial Inc, Panama, which renamed her *Capalonga*. In 1974 she was converted to an offshore diving support ship by the Boele shipyard at Bolnes. This involved the fitting of a gantry on the starboard side of her well deck for a submersible and the erection of a large helicopter deck at the aft end of her superstructure. At the same time she was equipped for pipeline burial and repair.

After working in the Mediterranean and North Sea for about three years under the management of Sub Sea Oil Services she returned to Holland in 1977 for further conversion work. This lasted some four months and was undertaken by the Amsterdam Drydock Co. She emerged with a full dynamic positioning system consisting of four Schottel propellers, stability bulges, raised bridge and foc'sle, and a second gantry and Perry PC.8 submersible on her port side. In addition she was equipped with four gas turbine-driven fire monitors on her foc'sle.

Following this extensive alteration she returned to the North Sea where she was employed in the Shell/Esso Brent and Auk oil fields. Five years later her usefulness was at an end and she was sold to Micoperi SpA which commenced demolition work at the Adriatic port of Ortona in autumn 1983.

The Lowestoft built *Bolton Abbey* (1959) was the first engines-aft passenger ship to appear on the North Sea for over 60 years. A twin-screw motor vessel, she maintained AHL's Hull—Rotterdam service with her 1959-built sister *Melrose Abbey*.
Laurence Dunn

Lancashire & Yorkshire Railway Co

Goole/Hull–Antwerp/Zeebrugge, etc
1902–1921   Lancashire & Yorkshire Railway Co
1922   London & North Western Railway Co
1923–1947   London, Midland Scottish Railway Co
Funnel colours: Buff with red band under black top

Length: 260ft 0in
Breadth: 35ft 8in
Depth: 15ft 0in
Gross tonnage: 1,204
Machinery: 2 sets, 3-cylinder triple expansion
Boilers: 2
Power: 296nhp
Speed: 16½kt

Mellifont

The Lancashire & Yorkshire Railway Co first entered the shipowning business in 1870 when it obtained joint parliamentary powers with the London & North Western Railway Co to run steamer services from the Lancashire port of Fleetwood to Belfast and Londonderry. By the time both companies had enhanced these services with new paddle steamers and later during the 1890s with new twin screw steamers, the L&YR decided to go into shipping on its own account and in 1902 obtained further powers to acquire the Drogheda Steam Packet Co with its four paddle steamers, and to run services from Fleetwood and Liverpool to Drogheda.

No time was lost in ordering two modern twin-screw sister ships, *Colleen Bawn* and *Mellifont*, which were delivered by Vickers, Sons & Maxim Ltd, Barrow in 1903. Their entry into service between Liverpool and Drogheda (Fleetwood was never used) brought about a great improvement and allowed two of the old paddlers to be withdrawn.

Their steel hulls, which had a straight stem and deep counter stern, gave the appearance of being flush decked, but high-sided bulwarks containing outward swinging doors hid two short wells immediately forward and aft of the partly enclosed midship deck-house. Their masts and funnel had appreciable rake but the latter had a horizontal top and was painted in the newly adopted livery of black with a deep yellow band. Comfortable accommodation was provided amidships for 70 first class passengers with rather more simple facilities for 83 in steerage aft.

In January 1905 the L&YR extended its shipowning activities to the East coast by taking over the 19-ship fleet of the Goole Steam Shipping Co which ran a large number of Continental services employing smart little steamers such as the 15kt *Wharfe* (1890, 914 gross tons), though none of these carried more than a handful of passengers. Shortly after this the railway company transferred *Mellifont* to Goole and she took on the local company's funnel colours of buff with a red band and black top. On 29 May she carried a party of directors and

Following its acquisition of the Goole Steam Shipping Co in January 1905 the L&YR transferred the 1903-built Liverpool–Drogheda passenger steamer *Mellifont* to Goole registry. Seen in the Humber in the former Company's 'soot, blood and suet' colours, she traded regularly to Antwerp until 1912. *Col R.C. Gabriel collection*

officials to Zeebrugge to inspect the new canal and harbour works but otherwise was mainly employed in the Antwerp trade. She remained in North Sea service for over six years and during this time alterations were made to her bridge and the two ventilators just forward of it were heightened.

In 1912 she returned to the Drogheda run to replace the two remaining paddle steamers and thereafter continued in her old colours once more to maintain a regular service with her sister. In 1922 she passed to the ownership of the LNWR which had taken over the L&YR and the following year became an LMS ship after the regrouping of the railways.

In 1928 the running of the Drogheda route was entrusted to the British & Irish Steam Packet Co and *Mellifont* and her sister were transferred to Holyhead. The former was used as a reserve cargo and livestock carrier on the Dublin and Greenore routes and after outliving her sister by two years went to the breakers in her 30th year in 1933.

Duke of Clarence

In the spring of 1906 the L&YR became sole owners of the Irish Sea passenger steamer *Duke of Clarence*, which up till then had been shared with the LNWR, and moved her from Fleetwood to the Humber where she was placed under Goole registration in line with the railway company's recently acquired East Coast fleet. After being repainted with a buff funnel, red band and black top she was placed on a new seasonal passenger/cargo service linking Hull with the newly completed Belgian port of Zeebrugge.

She had originally been ordered by the two railway companies in 1891 as the first of several fast twin-screw steamers to replace the paddle steamers on their joint Fleetwood–Belfast service. It was originally intended to call her *Birkenhead* but she was completed by Laird Bros as *Duke of Clarence* in 1892. Her entry into service enabled the overnight service to be accelerated and her successful design

set the pattern for a further four 'Dukes' over the next 10 years.

As with so many of the short sea ships of her time she conformed to a three-island design with short 'hidden' well-decks at either end of her long midships deck-house.

Length: 312ft 6in
Breadth: 36ft 2½in
Depth: 15ft 10in
Gross tonnage: 1,458
Machinery: 2 sets, 3-cylinder triple expansion
Power: 4,000ihp
Speed: 19kt

At first her summer schedule was an undemanding one of two overnight sailings a week in each direction, leaving Hull's new but only partially completed Riverside Quay at 6pm on Wednesday and Saturday and returning from Zeebrugge at 7pm on Thursday and Monday. The voyage normally occupied about 13 hours. After her first season she was reboilered by her builders and the following summer sailings were increased to three times a week after the North Eastern Railway had accepted an invitation to take a share in the service.

During the winter months she returned to the Irish Sea, being employed on the Liverpool–Drogheda service until 1912 after which she was generally laid up in Fleetwood. It became the practice to offer her positioning voyages as coastal cruises and these became very popular. In the spring she would sail up the west coast of Scotland to Stromness, passing through Scapa Flow and calling at Aberdeen on her way down the east coast

The jointly-owned L&NWR/L&YR Fleetwood-Belfast passenger steamer *Duke of Clarence* (1892) became the sole property of the latter Company in 1906 and was transferred to the East Coast where she inaugurated a seasonal service linking Hull with the new port of Zeebrugge. Her speed and regularity earned her the nickname 'Greyhound of the Humber'.
Author's collection

to Hull. In the autumn she returned to Fleetwood via the south coast as far as the Isle of Wight thereafter making a call at St Helier, Jersey before rounding Lands End and proceeding up the Irish Sea.

The Zeebrugge service was suspended during World War 1 and she was taken up by the Admiralty on 6 November 1915 and converted into an Armed Boarding Steamer with one 4in and one 12pdr gun. Her pennant numbers varied, being MI.14 at first then MI.04 and later MI.03, but she was generally employed on the Northern Patrol for the remainder of hostilities. She was not released until 11 February 1920 when she returned to her builders for a refit after which she was laid up for about two months before resuming her Zeebrugge service on 15 May.

In 1922 her owner was taken over by the LNWR and a year later she passed into the LMS fleet after which the tri-weekly Zeebrugge service was advertised as the LMS & LNER Joint Express Continental Service. In the late 1920s her spring and autumn cruises were reinstated and once again became popular, but she was getting on in years and was withdrawn at the end of the 1929 season. The following May the 38-year old favourite and Humberside's swiftest ship was sold to T.W. Ward for breaking up at Barrow.

Duke of Connaught

In 1930 the LMS transferred its Irish Sea passenger steamer *Duke of Connaught* to Hull where she took over the seasonal Zeebrugge service in place of her erstwhile consort *Duke of Clarence*.

She had been the fourth of the twin-screw 'Dukes' built for the joint L&YR and LNWR Fleetwood–Belfast overnight service, having been launched by John Brown & Co, Clydebank on 20 August 1902 and tried between Greenock and Cumbrae on 15 October. Although a little larger and faster than the earlier ships her design was an obvious development of them.

Length: 315ft 0in
Breadth: 38ft 2in
Depth: 16ft 8in
Gross tonnage: 1,680
Machinery: 2 sets, 4-cylinder triple expansion
Boilers: 4se
Power: 340nhp
Speed: 20kt

She had more extensive passenger accommodation than the earlier 'Dukes', and this was spread over the main, upper and promenade decks and included berths for 490 first class passengers amidships and about the same number in steerage aft. Her first class dining saloon extended across the full width of the upper deck and there was a smoking room on the promenade deck above. Officers and engineers had their cabins in a house on the poop whilst the crew was berthed in the foc's'le.

She remained on her normal Irish Sea service throughout World War 1, surviving a brush with an enemy submarine on 22 October 1918 when she used her speed and a round or two from her defensive armament to make good her escape. Immediately after the war she was loaned to the City of Dublin Steam Packet Co for Holyhead–Kingstown service, but was returned in 1921 and sent to the Vickers yard at Barrow for refitting and reboilering with four Babcock & Wilcox water-tube boilers.

The L&YR dropped from her joint ownership in 1922 after being swallowed up by its other partner, the LNWR, which was itself absorbed into the LMS the following year. This new company adopted the old Goole funnel colours of buff, red and black, but public indignation soon forced the company to revert to the former LNWR's buff with a black top.

Under LMS ownership *Duke of Connaught* was mainly used on Heysham–Isle of Man service until her move to Hull in 1930 following a refit to her accommodation. She completed only three seasons on the Zeebrugge run before being withdrawn, and was sold to Dutch breakers in 1934.

Duke of Connaught was a 1902 John Brown derivative of the Laird-built Duke of Clarence. She took over the Zeebrugge service in the spring of 1930 following the latter's withdrawal.
Author's collection

West Hartlepool Steam Navigation Co

West Hartlepool–Hamburg
1856– 1982 West Hartlepool Steam Navigation Co
    (Ltd from 1899)
Funnel colours: 1856 – Buff with black top
  1899 – Black 'G' added

Kaiser

The West Hartlepool Steam Navigation Co was first formed in 1856 by Ralph Ward Jackson, the recognised founder of the town of West Hartlepool, and who was at that time the chairman of the West Hartlepool Harbour & Railway Co. The latter controlled the new venture which incorporated the West Hartlepool Steam Shipping Co of 1853, which itself had grown out of the 1849-registered West Hartlepool Shipping Co. The new company's ships were employed in the coal trade but there was also a twice-weekly service to Hamburg and a seasonal one to St Petersburg.

On learning in 1862 that the Harbour Co's articles did not allow ships to be run, the fleet was sold locally and after several further changes a combination of local interests formed a new limited company in 1899.

Kaiser came from local builders Wm Gray in 1880, being launched in June and running loaded trials to Whitby on 31 July at an average of 11kt.

Length: 220ft 0in
Breadth: 28ft 6in
Depth: 16ft 2in
Gross tonnage: 816
Machinery: 2-cylinder compound
Boilers: 2se, 85lb/sq in
Power: 130nhp
Speed: 11kt

She was an iron steamer and her hull had a short raised foc'sle 28ft in length and a rather longer poop of 48ft. Her compound engines were the product of another local firm, T. Richardson & Sons, and she was licensed to carry a total of 350 passengers.

Her 24-year career on the Hamburg service came to an end on 25 July 1904 when she was wrecked off Ravenscar, homeward bound with general cargo.

Empress

In 1889 Wm Gray constructed a second passenger steamer to the order of C.M. Webster for the West Hartlepool Steam Navigation Co's Hamburg service. She was named *Empress* on 29 June and trials were completed on 22 August; both events being the object of much local interest. She was an appreciable advance on the earlier *Kaiser* as can be seen from her dimensions.

Length: 260ft 0in
Breadth: 31ft 6in
Depth: 15ft 4in
Gross tonnage: 990
Machinery: 3-cylinder triple expansion
Boilers: 2de, 160lb/sq in
Power: 1,500ihp
Speed: 14kt (service)

Built of mild steel she was a three-island ship and first class passenger accommodation was arranged aft in the poop with comfortable staterooms leading off either side of a long dining saloon.

Main propulsion was by means of a triple expansion unit from her builders' Central Engine Works which on loaded trials between Hartlepool and Whitby produced some 1,700ihp at 90rpm for a speed of about 15kt.

Empress sailed on her maiden voyage to Hamburg on 24 August and thenceforward she and *Kaiser* with some older ships maintained a regular twice weekly connection, sailing from West Hartlepool on Wednesday and Saturday evenings and returning from the Elbe on Tuesdays and Fridays. The single saloon class fare in 1898 was £1.10s inclusive of meals.

Her career with the Company was a comparatively short one due perhaps to her being too ambitious for the service and also too expensive to run. She was sold in 1899 to the Russian-owned Chinese Eastern Railway and was renamed *Ningoote*. Two years later this was altered to *Ninguta* and in 1904 she was sunk during the siege of Port Arthur. The Hamburg service ceased for ever with the coming of World War 1.

Tyne Steam Shipping Co

Newcastle–Hamburg/Rotterdam, etc
1864–1904   Tyne Steam Shipping Co
1904–1976   Tyne-Tees Steam Shipping Co
Funnel colours: Black with red over white bands

Grenadier

The Tyne Steam Shipping Co was formed at Newcastle in 1864 by an amalgamation of a number of local firms already engaged in the coastal and North Sea trades. This move generated new business and brought about lower costs. The main service of the new company was undoubtedly that between the Tyne and London on which a large number of passengers were carried, but the ships on the continental routes to Hamburg, Amsterdam, Rotterdam, Antwerp, Ghent and Dunkirk also carried passengers. The latter service was quickly dropped, but a new one to Copenhagen was started in 1874 for which the Company's largest steamer to date, *Royal Dane* of 1,282 gross tons, was built a year later. Danish competition proved too strong however and the Tyne Co pulled out in 1877, moving *Royal Dane* to the London service.

Perhaps the best known ship in the Company's Continental trades before 1880 was the 1873-built *John Ormston*, a raised quarterdeck steamer of 971 tons which set new standards in the short sea trade.

Her partners were mainly elderly, lengthened ships. In 1888 the six-year old cargo passenger steamer *Juno* (qv) was acquired from the Wilson Line and in 1894 a new ship was ordered from Wigham Richardson & Co, Low Walker to replace the 1865-built *Grenadier* lost in a collision in the North Sea on 1 August.

The new ship (which cost about £22,000) was launched on 25 April 1895, perpetuating the name *Grenadier*, and she underwent trials on 7 June, reaching about 14 kt.

Length: 240ft 0in
Breadth: 30ft 0in
Depth: 17ft 0in
Gross tonnage: 1,004
Machinery: 3-cylinder triple expansion
Boilers: 1se, 160lb/sq in
Power: 165nhp
Speed: 13½kt

Grenadier **was built by Wigham Richardson in 1895 for the Tyne Steam Shipping Co's Rotterdam service, her three-masted design being similar to the Company's successful London service passenger ships of the period. She is shown after stranding on the Frisian coast in July 1908, a precarious position from which she was later salvaged.** *W. Haentjens, Alkmaar collection*

The workmanlike *Sir William Stephenson* of 1906 was the first passenger ship built following the formation of the Tyne-Tees Steam Shipping Co in 1903. Her design was a development of Tyne Steam Shipping's trend-setting Continental steamer *John Ormston* of 1873. *Laurence Dunn collection*

Her three-masted, engines-aft design followed that already adopted for some of the Company's previous ships, notably the *Tynesider* on the London run, and it incorporated a short well-deck separating the foc'sle from a long raised quarter-deck. She could accommodate 56 passengers in first class on the main and saloon decks with comfortable staterooms, a large oak-panelled saloon and separate ladies' and smoking rooms. In addition, two rooms were provided under the foc'sle for 16 second class passengers, and for general comfort steam heating and electric lighting were fitted throughout.

After a period of eight years in the Rotterdam trade – which involved a weekly Tuesday departure from the Tyne – she was transferred to the ownership of the Tyne-Tees Steam Shipping Co, a new concern brought about by the merging of her original owners with the Tees Union Shipping Co, Furness Withy & Co's coastal service, and the Free Trade Wharf Co.

Following the merger *Grenadier* continued to serve Rotterdam and also on occasion Hamburg. On 21 July 1908 whilst homeward bound from Cuxhaven she stranded between the islands of Langeoog and Spiegeroog, her 12 passengers being taken off. She remained fast for several days, eventually being refloated on 29 after lightening, but not before heavy seas had removed her rudder and screw. She was taken to Hamburg on 1 August and four days later left for West Hartlepool in tow of the tug *Atlas* for dry-docking and repairs.

After some nine years further trading she became a war loss on 23 February 1917, torpedoed without warning six miles east-northeast of the Shipwash light vessel with the loss of her master and seven crew members.

Sir William Stephenson

Towards the end of 1905 Tyne-Tees Steam Shipping ordered a new steamer for their Continental services. Launched at Yarrow by Palmer's Shipbuilding Co on 7 April 1906 she was named *Sir William Stephenson*. Trials were run just over two months later on 8 June after which she proceeded to Newcastle to load for her maiden voyage.

She differed from previous Tyne-Tees passenger steamers in having her engines amidships.

Length: 270ft 0in
Breadth: 36ft 6in
Depth: 16ft 6in
Gross tonnage: 1,540
Machinery: 3-cylinder triple expansion
Boilers: 2, 180lb/sq in
Power: 292nhp
Speed: 13½kt

Her design incorporated a short raised foc'sle separated from a long combined bridge and poop by a well-deck hidden by high bulwarks. Amidships a 100ft long deck-house contained accommodation for some 60 first and 50 second class passengers, whilst her three holds could carry about 1,300 tons of cargo handled by a mix of derricks and four steam cranes. Her propelling machinery was supplied by Richardson Westgarth and her boilers employed forced draught.

She gave a considerable boost to her owners' Continental trade which became increasingly important before World War 1, with early morning arrivals in the Tyne on Mondays and Thursdays bringing fresh farm and dairy produce for northern markets.

Also employed from time to time in the London service she was southbound on 29 August 1915 when she struck a mine off the Cockle light vessel, two crew members losing their lives in the explosion. She was later towed to Yarmouth Roads where she sank, thus ending a rather short nine-year career.

Alnwick

The neat little Swan Hunter-built *Alnwick* of 1929 was the last passenger steamer built for Tyne-Tees. Berthing about 75 passengers she was designed for Rotterdam service but later ran in the coastal trade to London before being sold to Fred Olsen in 1935.
Laurence Dunn

After World War 1 the Tyne-Tees Steam Shipping Co embarked on a replacement programme to make good its many war losses. This involved the building of two new ships for the London service in 1923, the well-known *Bernicia* and *Hadrian* which were amongst the finest in the coastal passenger trade. Some four years later an order was placed with Swan Hunter, Wigham Richardson for a slightly smaller ship for the Tyne–Rotterdam service.

Alnwick was launched at the Neptune yard, Walker-on-Tyne on 6 March 1929 by Miss Violet Chipchase Roberts (a grand-daughter of shipowner R.M. Hudson) and after only five weeeks fitting out was tried on 12 April, obtaining over 14kt on the measured mile.

Length: 254ft 0in
Breadth: 38ft 8in
Depth/draught: 16ft 8in mld
Gross tonnage: 1,400
Machinery: 3-cylinder triple expansion
Boilers: 2se, 215lb/sq in
Power: 2,530ihp
Speed: 13kt

In appearance she was a neat little ship with raised foc'sle and bridge deck and although by this time raked bows and cruiser sterns were becoming generally more prevalent, she retained the old fashioned straight stem and counter stern. Her rather unusual masting arrangement consisted of a foremast in the normal position between Nos 1 and 2 hatches forward but her mainmast was placed on the end of her bridge deck and was supplemented by a short single kingpost aft. A standard size funnel bearing the Company's white and red bands was mounted behind a built up bridge on a single deck superstructure amidships.

Accommodation was arranged on and below the bridge deck for 50 first class passengers and about half that number in second class, though later sources show the latter as being increased to around 50. As to cargo she could carry around 1,400 tons in her holds with each of her four hatches being served by a single derrick and winch.

Shortly after her delivery she was one of the first ships to berth at the newly extended Newcastle Quay after it had been vacated by the ships of both Bergen and Olsen Lines in favour of North Shields.

The depression years were the final nail in the coffin of the London passenger service which had already been seriously eroded by the long-distance motor coach. After *Bernicia* and *Hadrian* had been laid up in 1932 *Alnwick* was transferred to take their place but this phase lasted for only a short while. She was sold in 1935 to Fred Olsen, renamed *Bali* and after a short refit placed on the Oslo–Rotterdam service which included a call at Kristiansand. Her partner on this route (which terminated at Lekkade in the Dutch port) was the former Antwerp steamer *Biarritz*, and there were departures every Friday in each directon.

She survived World War 2 and in 1945 was transferred to Olsen's main Oslo–Newcastle route to help offset the loss of *Black Prince* and *Black Watch*. She sailed alternately with the former Antwerp motor vessel *Bretagne*, calling at Kristiansand en route. Replaced early in 1951 by the new *Blenheim*, she completed one final season (May to October) on the weekly Antwerp service with *Brabant* before being sold the following year to the Burmese Shipping Board. Renamed *Pyidawtha* she made the long voyage out to Burma where she was placed on coastal passenger/cargo services out of Rangoon.

This final phase of her career lasted only about three years for on 6 May 1955 she grounded on North Shoal rock whilst entering Kyaukpyu in the course of a voyage from Rangoon to Akyat. She took on a 33° list to starboard, all her holds later becoming flooded, and after unsuccessful salvage attempts was abandoned as a total loss.

Leith, Hull & Hamburg
Steam Packet Co

Leith–Hamburg/Copenhagen/Kristiansand
1836–1852 Hull & Leith Steam Packet Co
1852–1940 Leith, Hull & Hamburg(h) Steam
           Packet Co
1940–1977 Currie Line Ltd
Funnel colours: Black with white band

Length: 254ft 6in
Breadth: 33ft 2½in
Depth: 17ft 10in mld
Gross tonnage: 1,366/5
Machinery: 2-cylinder compound
Boilers: 2se, 60lb/sq in
Power: 175nhp
Speed: 12kt

Breslau, Coblenz

The Leith, Hull & Hamburg Steam Packet Co owed its origin to the 1836 merger between the Hull & Leith Shipping Co of about 1800 and the Leith & Hamburgh Shipping Co formed around 1816. At first the new concern was known as the Hull & Leith Steam Packet Co and operated a coastal service between those two ports, but after a regular service to Hamburg was started by the new steamer *Best Bower* in 1852 the name of the company was altered, though the old form of Hamburgh persisted for a few years.

In 1862 James Currie (the brother of Donald Currie, whose exploits in opening up the Cape route with his Castle Line were later to make him a household name), joined the Company and through his energies built up the fleet to 20 ships over the same number of years.

In 1882 two new steamers were ordered from the Greenock yard of Robert Steele & Co. They were intended for the Hamburg passenger/cargo trade and were given suitably germanic names, *Breslau* being launched on 22 December 1882 and her sister *Coblenz* on 20 February the following year.

The new steamers were rigged as three-masted schooners with a single funnel placed between the main and mizzen. Their steel two-decked hulls incorporated a very long foc'sle stretching for more than half their length, aft of which was a short bridge deck and even shorter poop. Their passenger layout was unusual for the time, with 56 first class berths situated forward of the bridge, 170 second class in the poop and a number of steerage in the tween-deck. The ship's officers had their cabins amidships under the bridge.

The two sisters maintained a regular schedule departing Leith for Hamburg on Wednesdays and Saturdays, and were accompanied at first by older steamers such as the 1872-built 1,077-ton *Prague* which made a fortnightly call at Bremerhaven. They were already over 30 years old when World War 1 forced them to trade elsewhere, and on 14 January 1916 *Breslau* hit a mine six miles northwest of Boulogne and had to be beached, though she was later salvaged. About 1½ years later *Coblenz* was attacked by a submarine in the Atlantic but the torpedo missed. The submarine then resorted to gunfire and obtained hits which resulted in the

The seemingly old fashioned Leith, Hull and Hamburg steamer *Breslau* of 1883 lasted with her sister *Coblenz* for nearly 50 years. Built for the Hamburg service they moved to the Copenhagen run from 1919 until new tonnage appeared in 1928. An unusual feature of their design was a very long foc'sle extending to the mizenmast whilst their first class accommodation was forward of the bridge.
EN. Taylor collection

death of one crewman, but the ship used her own gun to good effect and escaped.

After the war the ships were transferred to the Leith–Copenhagen service in place of the *Rona* and *Thorsa* which had both been lost, continuing thus until 1928 when the arrival of two new 12-passenger sisters *Hengist* and *Horsa* allowed them to return to their original Hamburg trade. Not long afterwards however economic depression plus their great age sent them to the scrapyard, *Breslau* going to J.A. White at North Queensferry in 1932 and her sister to G.W. Brunton at Grangemouth in the same year.

Rona, Thorsa

Shortly after taking delivery of two new Hamburg steamers the Leith Hull & Hamburg Co continued its replacement programme by ordering a further pair of ships for the Leith–Copenhagen/Christiansand service. The builders were Barclay Curle, Whiteinch and the first ship, *Rona*, was launched on 29 April 1884. She entered service in June after attaining over 13kt on trials, which took place in the Firth of Forth on 24 of that month. Her sister *Thorsa* had entered the water on 12 June and she reached the same speed when tried just over a month later.

The two sisters were slightly smaller than their counterparts on the Hamburg service.

Length: 240ft 0in
Breadth: 32ft 2in
Depth: 15ft 5in
Gross tonnage: 1,294/93 (later 1,312/19)
Machinery: 2-cylinder compound
Boilers: 2se, 66lb/sq in
Power: 200nhp
Speed: 12kt

They were steel ships with two full decks and a part awning deck and their raised bridge deck extended for 54ft. Their passenger accommodation provided sleeping arrangements for 46 in first class, mainly in two-berth staterooms, with the remainder being housed in the saloon and ladies' cabin. Provision was also made for an unspecified number of second class passengers and the usual arrangements were made for emigrants in the tween-decks. Apart from cargo they were also fitted with stalling for the carriage of horses and cattle.

In service the sisters sailed on Thursdays in each direction with the homeward ship making a call at Christiansand on Friday. Cabin fares applying in about 1906 were three guineas for a single journey and five guineas for a return including meals.

World War 1 brought inevitable disruption to the service and *Rona* was a long way from her accustomed waters when she was captured by a German submarine on 16 June 1916 about 90 miles west of Cape Falcone, Sardinia. After the crew had been allowed to take to the boats she was sunk by gunfire.

Her sister *Thorsa* survived until 2 May 1918 when she too succumbed to a U-boat, being torpedoed without warning three miles north-northwest of Pendeen Lighthouse, happily without loss of life. She was the last of the Company's 20 war losses amounting to more than half its fleet. Although

Rona (1884), seen here at her Copenhagen berth, and *Thorsa* maintained a weekly service from Leith with an intermediate call at Kristiansand. Note the grey painted hull denoting the carriage of perishable foodstuffs, thereby deserving berthing priority.
Col R.C. Gabriel collection

their ends were dramatic and far apart the two ships had put in 30 years of useful service across the North Sea.

After World War 1 the Copenhagen service was resumed by the former Hamburg steamers *Breslau* and *Coblenz* until 1928 when they were replaced by the new 980-ton sisters *Hengist* and *Horsa* which carried only 12 passengers.

Weimar

Passenger traffic on the Leith Hull & Hamburg Co's service to the latter port continued to increase during the 1880s and a larger passenger steamer was ordered from the local yard of Ramage & Ferguson. She was named *Weimar* by Miss Elsa Currie on 21 December 1889, the name being in keeping with the 'German town' style of nomenclature already adopted for the Hamburg service ships. Though about the same length as her predecessors *Breslau* and *Coblenz* she was a little broader in the beam and her gross tonnage showed an increase of about 200 tons. Her relevant particulars were as follows:

Length: 254ft 0in
Breadth: 34ft 1in
Depth: 16ft 6in
Gross tonnage: 1,590
Machinery: 3-cylinder triple expansion
Boilers: 2se, 165lb/sq in
Power: 1,285ihp/288nhp
Speed: 12kt

Although only a two-masted ship she nevertheless reflected a similarity in design to the earlier ships with engines placed well aft. She had a 54ft long raised bridge deck over the machinery spaces and a short raised poop deck aft, whilst the navigating bridge rested on a separate deck-house set about a third of her length back from the bow.

Her passenger capacity was about the same as her predecessors' with berths being provided for 56 in first class passengers and about 170 emigrants in the tween-decks.

She could carry about 1,700 tons of cargo in her four holds, which were served by four steam cranes and two derricks. Her engines consumed about 25 tons of coal a day and during trials on 17 February 1890 undertaken in poor weather on the Gullane mile they gave the ship a speed of 13¼kt. Her bunker capacity at 144 tons was less than in her forbears as a result of her tripled engines' greater efficiency.

Weimar made her maiden voyage in February 1890 just before a period of depression in the shipping industry, but this soon passed and she settled down to regular if uneventful service with *Breslau*, *Coblenz* and the 1903-built *Vienna*. The twice weekly departures were scheduled from Leith on Wednesdays and Saturdays, returning from Hamburg on Mondays and Fridays, and in 1906 the first class single fare including provisons was £2.10s, rising to four guineas for a return.

She survived World War 1 unscathed and returned to the Hamburg run until 1933 when after a long career of 43 years she was sold to the Stockton Shipbreaking Co for demolition.

The Leith-built *Weimar* of 1889 was an improved, beamier version of *Breslau* with engines still placed aft. War years apart, she spent the whole of her 43-year career on the Hamburg run. *Author's collection*

Vienna

Appropriately enough the first passenger steamer to be constructed to the order of James Currie for his Leith, Hull & Hamburg Steam Packet Co in the 20th century marked a complete break from the old split superstructure, engines threequarters aft, design which had reached its culmination in the *Weimar*. The new ship was launched by the owner's wife at Ramage & Ferguson's Leith shipyard on 29 January 1903, her name *Vienna* echoing an earlier Currie ship which had foundered with all hands near the Dogger Bank on 2 December 1867. Fitting out occupied some four months and she performed trials in the Forth on 25 May, attaining a mean speed of 14.85kt in the course of several runs on the measured mile.

She was a neat little ship with engines amidships, and had the following main particulars.

Length: 280ft 4in
Breadth: 37ft 2½in
Depth: 19ft 10in to main deck
Gross tonnage: 1,912
Machinery: 3-cylinder triple expansion
Boilers: 2se, 180lb/sq in
Power: 3,000ihp
Speed: 14kt

She had a flush-decked hull with solid bulwarks forward and along the midships deck-house, and her single centrally placed funnel between two tall masts gave her a nicely balanced profile.

She was designed to carry 50 first class passengers in large and airy staterooms on the main deck reached by corridors leading aft from the dining saloon which was luxuriously appointed with oak

Carrying 50 first class passengers the smart little *Vienna* of 1903 was Currie's crack Hamburg steamer before World War 1. A great advance on previous ships, she was seized at the outbreak of hostilities and was later lost when acting as the German raider *Meteor*.
Laurence Dunn collection

panelling and velvet upholstery. On the bridge deck above was a large panelled smoking room reached by an internal stairway and also an entrance hall and a music room. Electric lighting and steam heating added to passenger comfort.

Her four holds provided substantial cargo capacity and each was served by a pair of derricks driven by steam winches. All in all she was a great advance on the previous ships employed in the Hamburg trade, both in size and speed, and she did much to popularise the service in the 11 years before World War 1 brought it to a halt.

She had the misfortune to be in Hamburg when hostilities were announced and was detained by the German authorities on 4 August 1914. The following year she went to the German navy and was converted into the armed auxiliary raider *Meteor*, entering service on 6 May. One of her duties was to lay minefields off the Moray Firth and whilst so engaged she surprised and sank the armed boarding steamer *The Ramsey*, a former IoMSP packet, on 8 August. The following day she was approached by three Royal Navy cruisers and was scuttled by her crew to avoid capture – a sad end to a fine ship that might otherwise have seen many more years of useful postwar service alongside her former consorts.

Gibson Line

Leith/Grangemouth–Antwerp/Rotterdam
1797–   George Gibson & Co Ltd
         W.S. & J.M. Burger
Funnel colours: Black, but passenger ships
         occasionally buff before 1914

Mascotte

The Leith based firm of George Gibson & Co Ltd
was formed in 1797 and initially it ran schooners in
the Rotterdam trade. It was not until 1850 that the
Company acquired its first steamer, *Balmoral*, from
Wm Denny & Bros, Dumbarton, but by 1890 it had
built or purchased another 19 ships and had started
additional services from Leith and Grangemouth to
Antwerp in 1864, Amsterdam in 1877, Dunkirk in
1878, and Ghent in 1880.

Passengers were carried mainly on the
Rotterdam and Antwerp routes, and a year after
the acquisition of the 1865-built *Anglia* from the
Dundee Perth & London Shipping Co a new
steamer was ordered in 1885 for the former from the
Leith yard of Ramage & Ferguson. She was
launched by Miss Gibson on 15 January and ran
trials on the Aberlely mile on 19 February,
attaining an average speed of 13kt. Upon
completion she was transferred to the ownership of
W.J. and J.A. Burger, Gibson's Dutch agents, and
placed in the Leith–Rotterdam trade.

Length: 249ft 8in
Breadth: 30ft 9in
Depth: 16ft 4in
Gross tonnage: 1,094
Machinery: 2-cylinder compound
Boilers: 2se, Scotch, 90lb/sq in
Power: 208nhp
Speed: 12½kt

Mascotte could carry about 50 passengers:
accommodation was arranged aft in the poop and
consisted of eight mainly four-berth staterooms
grouped round a saloon with a further 12 berths in a
handsome right aft. For cargo handling she was
fitted with two 2¾-ton steam cranes situated
between Nos 2 and 3 hatches and her deadweight
capacity was about 1,130 tons including 208 tons of
bunkers.

In 1907 along with *Nigel* and *Amulet* (1876,
1018gt) she returned to Gibson ownership and
continued to trade successfully until she became a
war loss when mined 6½ miles southeast of
Southwold on 3 September 1916. One crew
member lost his life but her owner later recovered
£12,369 from war insurance.

Durward (1892)/ Quentin, Durward (1895)

When the Antwerp trade began to gain in
importance, Geo Gibson ordered in January 1892 a
smart new passenger/cargo steamer from A. & J.
Inglis, Glasgow, the predecessors of Alexander
Stephen & Sons. The new ship, No 342, was named
Durward on 28 June by Miss Somerville, the
daughter of one of the directors, a name which
incidentally was in keeping with Gibson's generally
accepted practice of naming its ships after a Sir
Walter Scott theme. Launched with her engines
already in place and tried some two weeks later,
Durward's speed earned a premium for her builder.
She was also away to sea loaded only five months
and 23 days after the initial placing of the order.

Durward was the largest ship in the Gibson fleet
and the first passenger ship built for the company
since *Mascotte*, though in the interim the second-
hand *Britannia* had been acquired from the Dundee
Perth & London Shipping Co.

Length: 259ft 9in
Breadth: 32ft 6in
Depth/draught: 17ft 5½in/16ft 2in
Gross tonnage: 1,274
Machinery: 3-cylinder triple expansion
Boilers: 2se, 170lb/sq in
Power: 2,000ihp
Speed: 13kt

She was an iron three-island steamer and her hull was subdivided by five watertight bulkheads and incorporated three hatches in a long well forward of the bridge deck with a short hatch between the latter and the poop. A single raked funnel and two schooner-rigged pole masts completed a pleasing appearance.

Her total passenger capacity was just under 90 persons, 50 of whom were berthed in first class staterooms leading off a 30-seat dining saloon under the poop. Access was by means of a deck-house above, which also contained an oak-panelled smoking room. In addition 16 beds were provided forward for second class passengers with a number of portable berths for steerage in the alleyways.

Part of Gibson's trade included the export of old horses for the Continental meat trade and *Durward* was fitted with stalling in the alleyways. Cargo handling arrangements included derricks and two

A contemporary painting of George Gibson & Co's passenger steamer Durward *(1892). An Inglis product, she was renamed* Quentin *in 1895 to allow her name to pass to a new sister.* Geo Gibson & Co

steam cranes between Nos 2 and 3 hatches (a third was added at No 4 hatch in 1898) and her total deadweight capacity including bunkers was about 1,260 tons.

In service her schedule consisted of a Tuesday departure from Leith direct for Antwerp and she returned from the Belgian port on Saturday evening to give a Monday morning arrival back in her home port.

Early in 1895 she was renamed *Quentin* to free her name for a sister ship being built at Linthouse by Alexander Stephen. The new *Durward* was launched on 11 January and underwent trials on 19 February during which she attained a maximum speed of 14.8kt on the measured mile. As a result of minor differences her gross tonnage at 1,304 was slightly greater than the earlier ship's. Only about a month after her delivery she grounded in the Scheldt but refloated three hours later without damage.

The graceful Durward *of 1895 sails up the Scheldt to Antwerp. Similar to her earlier namesake, but with a taller funnel, she spent the first 12 years of her career under Dutch flag. This was a recognised Gibson practice in conjunction with the Company's Dutch agents Burger & Co which continued until 1907, though the parent company retained control.* Col R.C. Gabriel collection

Later on in 1895 she was transferred (for operational reasons) to the ownership of W.S. & J.M. Burger of Rotterdam who were also Gibson's agents in Antwerp. On 12 January 1900 she arrived in Leith with a broken stem following a collision with the Liverpool collier *Congress* early on the previous morning off the North Hasbrough light vessel. In the autumn of 1904 she made a record passage of 24 hours 40 minutes beating that of 25 hours 10 minutes set by *Britannia* on a Rotterdam–Leith voyage in March 1903, and both considerably bettered the normal passage time of 30 hours. In 1907 she returned to Gibson ownership.

World War 1 brought a modified service between the Forth and Rotterdam under neutral flag and *Quentin* was requisitioned to serve on the London–Rotterdam mail service. *Durward* also traded to Rotterdam and on 21 January 1915 she was torpedoed by the submarine U.19 about 22 miles northwest of the Maas light vessel. She did not sink immediately but lacked sufficient speed to escape and was captured and sunk by explosive charges. The submarine then towed the boats to the vicinity of the lightship.

After the Armistice *Quentin* was chartered by the Great Eastern Railway to reopen its Parkeston–Rotterdam link before reverting to Gibson's. Thereafter she only carried 12 passengers and in February 1927 was sold to J.J. Donelly of Dublin for £4,750. She changed hands again the following year, becoming the Belgian flag *Erin* of Cie Maritime L'Alliance SA, Antwerp, but traded for no more than a year before going to the breakers.

Ronan

Some two years after taking delivery of the second *Durward*, Gibson's ordered a further steamer from the local yard of Ramage & Ferguson. *Ronan* entered the waters of Leith harbour on 10 September 1897 and performed her loaded trials on the Aberledy mile the following March, attaining 13¼kt, after which she left immediately for Rotterdam on her maiden voyage, making a fast passage of 30 hours to the Hook.

Length: 259ft 0in
Breadth: 33ft 9in
Depth/draught: 18ft 9in/16ft 4in
Gross tonnage: 1,198
Machinery: 3-cylinder triple expansion
Boilers: 2se, 170lb/sq in
Power: 232nhp
Speed: 12½kt

She was a steel steamer with a raised foc'sle and combined bridge and poop-decks and her hull was fitted with bilge keels and a double bottom fore and

aft for water ballast. She was primarily a cargo ship but was fitted with five first class staterooms aft with 14 fixed berths and six sofa-beds. A few additional beds were arranged forward for a number of second class passengers, and her crew numbered 22.

Cargo was carried in four holds which were served by three derricks and a single crane situated on the port side between Nos 3 and 4 hatches. Additionally she was provided with stalling for 30 horses.

In April 1907 after trading in the main to Rotterdam she opened a new direct service between Leith and Boulogne, presumably without passengers as her certificate was allowed to lapse early the following year. World War 1 saw her employed between Hull and Rotterdam and she survived hostilities without incident, returning to Gibson's service as a 10-passenger cargo ship until 1935 when she was sold for scrap after a useful career of 37 years.

Nigel, Peveril

In 1903/04 the Grangemouth & Greenock Dockyard Co, Grangemouth built two large sister ships for Gibson's continental passenger/cargo service. The first of these, the *Nigel*, was launched on 11 April 1903 by Miss Gibson, but on completion the ship was transferred to W.S. & J.A. Burger, joining *Durward* under Dutch flag. A sister ship was ordered in September at a first cost of £36,250 and entered the water as *Peveril* on 4 April the following year. She reached 14½-kt on light trials and during her official loaded trials on 11 June exceeded her guaranteed speed of 13 kt by about half a knot.

The two ships were identical except for minor internal differences, and shared the following main characteristics:

Length: 275ft 0in oa/260ft 2in bp
Breadth: 35ft 0in
Depth: 18ft 6in
Gross tonnage: 1,400/1,459
Machinery: 3-cylinder triple expansion
Boilers: 2se, 180lb/sq in
Power: 2,500ihp
Speed: 13kt

They were built to a three-island design which was basically a development of *Durward's*, but an absence of rake to masts and funnel gave them rather a stiff appearance when compared with the grace of the former. This was compounded by the placing of a pair of rather ugly kingposts at the break of the foc'sle and on the poop.

Their plush accommodation was lit electrically and steam heated, and unlike previous practice it was situated amidships with a full width saloon at the forward end of the main deck seating about 50 in the case of *Nigel* and 44 in *Peveril*, the difference being due to extra cabins in the latter. The first class staterooms were aft of the saloon on either side of the engine casing with one double and seven four-berth cabins in *Nigel*, whilst her sister had a double and 10 four-berth ones. Both had an additional 20 berths in the saloon and eight apiece in ladies' and

smoke-rooms in a small deck-house above. Provision was also made for a small number of second class passengers and emigrants and their total capacity according to a certificate was about 190.

The main propelling machinery for both ships was supplied by S. & H. Morton of Leith and deck machinery included two steam cranes and six

Above:
On 8 November 1904, five months after her delivery, *Peveril* opened the new Imperial Dock, Leith. Yellow funnels were adopted for the passenger ships at Dutch insistence but Gibson's was never happy with this, and they later reverted to their normal black.
Geo Gibson & Co

Below:
A painting of *Nigel* (1903), the first of two Grangemouth-built sisters which were the largest passenger carriers in the Gibson fleet. Her two well decks were concealed by high bulwarks and she operated under Dutch colours until 1907. *Geo Gibson & Co*

derricks. Stalling for 20 horses was provided under the poop.

The carriage of passengers was a seasonal business as far as Gibson's was concerned and summer tours were widely advertised in the Scottish press.

On 8 November 1904 *Peveril* officially opened the new £75,000 Imperial Dock in Leith. *Nigel* reverted to Gibson ownership in 1907 and in August 1909 had to be dry-docked in Leith for bottom damage repairs as a result of a grounding.

World War 1 claimed both ships. *Nigel* was mined off Boulogne on 12 November 1915 with the loss of five lives, but £45,000 was recovered by Gibson's from her war risk insurance. *Peveril* meanwhile had been commissioned as a decoy ship on 18 February 1915 and served under the various names of *Puma*, *Q36* and *Stephenson* until 21 April. She was taken up again on 17 February 1917 but was sunk by a German submarine outside the Straits of Gibraltar on 6 November.

Eildon

On 4 September 1905, just over a year after the delivery of *Peveril*, another new steamer for Gibson's went down the ways of Alexander Stephen & Co at Linthouse. Named *Eildon* (pronounced *Eeldon*) she ran light load trials on the Skelmorlie mile on 19 October during which she averaged 12¾kt in the course of four runs. Broadly similar to the Grangemouth-built sisters but with less extensive passenger accommodation for 165 persons she could be distinguished by her lower well-deck bulwarks which made the task of cargo handling easier.

Length: 260ft 0in
Breadth: 34ft 1¼in

Depth/draught: 18ft 7½in/14ft 5in light
Gross tonnage: 1,329
Machinery: 3-cylinder triple expansion
Boilers: 2se, 180lb/sq in
Power: 1,800ihp
Speed: 13kt

The forward part of her bridge deck was fitted up for the carriage of a maximum of 28 first class passengers in four four-berth staterooms with a further six beds being provided in both the ladies' cabin and smoking room. The remainder of the bridge deck was bulkheaded for 56 emigrants in the alleyways with beds for a further 54 under the poop. Second class accommodation was provided one deck beneath first class and her crew numbered 24. Her deadweight capacity was just over 1,500 tons and incuded bunkers of 172 tons. The usual arrangements were made for the carriage of horses, and stalling for 44 was provided in the alleyways and poop.

Eildon ran mainly in the Grangemouth–Antwerp trade and in 1913 she was fitted with extra temporary accommodation for the summer months, comprising eight large double staterooms and two roomy four-berth cabins. These alterations brought her more into line with the other passenger steamers but it proved impossible to enlarge her smokeroom situated next to the chartroom immediately below the open bridge.

Her loss during World War 1 was not due to enemy action for she was wrecked near Brest on 4 May 1915, her owners recovering £20,295 from insurers.

The Clyde-built *Eildon* (1905) carried fewer passengers than *Nigel* and *Peveril* but was broadly similar with lower bulwarks in the well-decks to facilitate cargo handling. Note the open bridge favoured by her owners for many years to keep watch officers alert!
Geo Gibson & Co

Rankine Line

Grangemouth–Amsterdam/Rotterdam
1863–1903   James Rankine & Son
1903–1920   James Rankine Ltd
Funnel colours: Black with white band

Dundee

The origin of shipowner James Rankine & Son can be traced back to the appointment in November 1837 of James Rankine as master of the schooner *Glasgow Merchant* which was engaged in the Glasgow–Rotterdam trade. Some five years later he became part owner of the schooner *Glasgow*, purchasing his first wholly owned ship, the schooner *Port Dundas*, in 1848.

In 1854 increased trade and the desire to obtain a quicker connection with Holland led Rankine to place the new steamer *Therese* (which he managed on behalf of her owner Tennant & Co) on a new service linking Grangemouth with Rotterdam. The use of the east coast port virtually halved the distance travelled from Glasgow yet it was conveniently connected to the latter by the 35 mile Forth & Clyde Canal along which goods could be transported by lighter directly to or from the ships.

Sailings from Glasgow ceased in 1861 when the last surviving sailing ship, the original *Glasgow*, was lost in Dundrum Bay, N Ireland. At the same time a working agreement was signed with Geo Gibson & Co to avoid unnecessary duplication of sailings from the Forth to Holland.

Throughout its early existence James Rankine & Son maintained a close working link with its Dutch agent D. Burger & Zoon, which had become a shipowner in 1856; however, the former had absorbed the Dutch Company's interest in the Grangemouth trade by the late 1860s allowing the Dutch Company to concentrate on its Rotterdam–Norway service although it continued to hold shares in Rankine's ships.

It was not until 1890 that James Rankine Jnr, who had taken over the management of the firm on the death of his father in 1866, ordered his first passenger steamer. *Dundee* was a product of J. Scott & Co, Kinghorn, which launched her with

engines in place on 2 August and sent her on trial only four days later when she achieved a speed of 13kt. She was the Company's largest ship, also its first to be built of steel and to employ reciprocating engines.

Length: 223ft 9in
Breadth: 29ft 0in
Depth: 16ft 1in mld
Gross tonnage: 839
Machinery: 3-cylinder triple expansion
Boilers: 2, 165lb/sq in
Power: 200nhp
Speed: 12kt

A steel single deck steamer with raised foc'sle, bridge and poop she had two masts and a single funnel amidships, whilst her cargo handling arrangements included three steam winches and three cranes. She could carry 50 passengers in first class accommodation under the poop with provision for a large number of second class in the foc'sle.

Being a lone steamer she at first maintained a weekly schedule between the Forth and the New Waterway but the success of the new passenger service was such that a second ship was ordered in 1893 to increase sailings to twice weekly.

Dundee's comparatively short career came to an end on 26 January 1896 when she was wrecked on Flamborough Head on an outward voyage to Rotterdam.

Glasgow

Some four years after its inception Rankine's passenger service was augmented by the addition of a new steamer from W.B. Thompson's shipyard at Dundee. Originally destined to be named *Stirling* she in fact entered the waters of the Tay as the owner's third *Glasgow* on 6 January 1894 – the previous bearer of this name, a 24-year old iron cargo ship, having been disposed of in 1893.

Some 200 tons larger than *Dundee* the new ship set the pattern for subsequent passenger new-building.

James Rankine & Son's second Continental passenger steamer to bear the name *Glasgow* was built by Thompson's of Dundee in 1894. Seen here at Rotterdam in World War 1 dazzle paint, she set the pattern for subsequent ships with the proximity of funnel and mainmast being a distinctive feature.
Laurence Dunn collection

Length: 248ft 9in oa/240ft 0in bp
Breadth: 32ft 0in
Depth/draught: 14ft 5in/16ft 0in
Gross tonnage: 1,068
Machinery: 3-cylinder triple expansion
Boilers: 2se, 170lb/sq in
Power: 228nhp
Speed: 13kt

She was a steel two-deck ship with foc'sle, bridge and poop-decks separated by two wells hidden to the outside observer by high bulwarks. Her tall masts and thin, single funnel had a pronounced rake and imparted a certain grace to her otherwise rather insubstantial looks. Passenger capacities were 48 in 'cabin' or first class and 68 in third class. As to propulsion her main engine was a tripled unit from the builder's Lilybank Works and deck machinery included three steam cranes and two steam winches.

After completing trials on 28 February *Glasgow* joined *Dundee* in the Rotterdam service allowing passenger sailings to be increased to two a week.

Her career continued without major incident for some 17 years but in the autumn of 1911 she was involved in a serious mishap. Having left Rotterdam for Dundee on 30 September she was encountering heavy weather when, about 15 miles from the Galloper light vessel, she was swept by a large sea which carried away her steering gear, leaving her drifting. Help was soon at hand in the shape of the Cardiff steamer *Hatfield,* inbound from Huelva with a cargo of ore, but whilst the latter was trying to pass a tow she was struck heavily by *Glasgow's* pitching stem and so badly holed that she sank within seven minutes, taking with her all but one of her 19 crew. *Glasgow* was now further damaged with a twisted stem and flooded forepeak but she was eventually towed to a position off

Dover by the *Clan MacDonald,* being finally brought into the Naval harbour by the German tug *Albatros.*

She was soon repaired and back in service, coming through World War 1 unscathed, but on 1 January 1920 she was taken over by George Gibson & Co Ltd along with two other surviving Rankine Line ships. Stripped of her passenger accommodation she served her new owner until 1925 when in her 31st year she was sold to the Carron Co of Grangemouth. Renamed *Carron* she ran in the Forth-London trade until 1940 when she was taken up by the Admiralty as a potential blockship and after being stripped of her fittings was finally sunk at Scapa Flow on 3 March.

Rotterdam

In March 1896, just over a month after the loss of *Dundee,* James Rankine & Son ordered a replacement passenger steamer from Gourlay Bros of Dundee in order to restore the twice weekly service to Rotterdam as soon as possible. The new ship was launched on 11 August taking the name *Rotterdam* from another of the Company's ships, an iron cargo steamer of 485 tons dating from 1874 which was renamed *Dundee.* Trials took place on 9 September with a morning trip to Arbroath followed by several runs over the measured mile in the afternoon during which she averaged 14kt.

Length: 250ft 0in
Breadth: 32ft 0in
Depth/draught: 17ft 0in mld/164ft 1in
Gross tonnage: 1,092
Machinery: 3-cylinder triple expansion
Boilers: 2
Power: 203nhp
Speed: 13kt

Apart from her greater length which gave her an extra hold the two-deck *Rotterdam* was very similar to *Glasgow,* following the by now familiar three-island layout with high well-deck bulwarks and a tall raking funnel placed somewhat closer to the mainmast. Her passenger accommodation catered

Gourlay-built in 1896 to replace the lost *Dundee,* the 1,092 gross *Rotterdam* was a more robust development of *Glasgow.* Note the open bulwark doors in the well-decks which eased the task of loading or discharge by deck cranes.
Col R.C. Gabriel collection

for 44 in first class and 67 in steerage, whilst her four holds, served by a mix of three steam cranes, three derricks, and a like number of winches, could take about 1,000 tons of cargo.

Her career paralleled that of *Glasgow* until 1924 when she was sold to the Limerick Steamship Co Ltd, taking the name *Clounanna.* As such she traded in her new owners' west coast of Ireland–northern Continental ports service for about five years before going for scrapping at Alloa in 1929.

Ballycotton

On 4 October 1899 James Rankine & Son acquired the steamer *Ballycotton* from the Clyde Shipping Co Ltd in order to start up a new passenger service

between Grangemouth and Amsterdam. This steamer had been launched back in December 1880 by W. Simons & Co, Renfrew for coastal passenger cargo service between Glasgow and Cork.

She was an iron two-deck ship, dimensionally somewhat smaller than those employed by Rankine on the Rotterdam service, being more akin to the *Dundee* of 1890.

Length: 225ft 0in
Breadth: 30ft 5in
Depth: 15ft 7in
Gross tonnage: 888
Machinery: 2-cylinder compound
Power: 200nhp
Speed: 12kt

Her design incorporated a foc'sle and combined bridge and poop separated by a well-deck disguised by high bulwarks which contained two sets of doors on either beam to facilitate the handling of cargo. She had two masts with tall fiddled topmasts and a short funnel placed on a deck-house just aft of the midships position. There were two lifeboats on either side of the stack and a working boat to starboard of a small deck-house aft.

Her new owners retained the name *Ballycotton* but her career with them was tragically short for she was wrecked on Emblestone Rock near Newton, Northumberland on 15 February 1900 whilst on a return voyage from Amsterdam to Leith. Passenger sailings to the Dutch port were suspended (cargo only being carried by the 1877-built steamer *Grangemouth*) until later in the year when the purchase of another second-hand passenger steamer allowed them to be resumed.

Glanmire

Following the loss of *Ballycotton*, James Rankine & Son – which had been controlled by a former partner Thomas MacGill since the death of James Rankine Jnr in 1897 – were forced to find a suitable passenger ship to reinstate the now lapsed Amsterdam service. The Company's choice fell on the City of Cork Steam Packet Co's *Glanmire* which was duly purchased on 4 April. This steamer had been built like her lost predecessor by W.B. Thompson & Co Ltd, Dundee in 1888, though the latter had since become known as the Caledon Shipbuilding & Engineering Co. She was designed to be interchangeable on the Irish company's various services, and her dimensions and particulars were as follows:

Length: 242ft 2½in
Breadth: 33ft 2½in
Depth: 15ft 4in
Gross tonnage: 1,150
Machinery: 3-cylinder triple expansion
Boilers: 2se, 150lb/sq in
Power: 282nhp
Speed: 13kt

She was an iron two-decked ship with raised foc'sle, bridge and poop, topped by two steel masts and a single funnel amidships. Sixty-six first or 'cabin' class passengers were carried aft and 37 steerage passengers under the foc'sle, and a major part of her main deck was fitted out for the carriage of livestock. Her powerful tripled machinery from Thompson's Tay foundry had produced a speed of 13.7kt during trials on 29 December 1888, making her more of an equal in speed and size to Rankine's *Rotterdam*.

She re-opened the Amsterdam passenger service in time for the 1900 summer season and continued to maintain it thereafter with weekly departures for the next 12 years. Her end came at about 6.20am on 25 July 1912 when, inward bound for Leith and in thick fog, she struck the rocks just southeast of St Abb's Head lighthouse. She sank half an hour later in 20 fathoms, her 15 passengers and 22 crew reaching safety in two boats. Her insured value at the time of loss was £20,000 and it is ironic that her final resting place was only some 30 miles north of that of her predecessor on the Amsterdam service.

Amsterdam (acquired 1903)

On 11 March 1903 James Rankine & Son acquired their third second-hand passenger steamer within a period of four years. She was William Sloan & Co's *Avon*, completed by Cunliffe & Dunlop, Port Glasgow in February 1878 for service between the Clyde and Bristol. She was a smaller ship than the previous purchases and her particulars as built were as follows:

Length: 219ft 10in
Breadth: 29ft 1in
Depth: 15ft 4in
Gross tonnage: 749
Machinery: 2-cylinder compound
Power: 150nhp
Speed: 11kt

In July 1888 her owners sent her to D.J. Dunlop for a major refit, in the course of which she received new boilers and a more economical triple expansion engine developing some 169nhp.

After her purchase by Rankines she was re-christened *Amsterdam* – a name previously held by a 549-ton cargo steamer which had inaugurated the Grangemouth–Amsterdam service upon completion in August 1878. She survived a grounding on the Farne Islands in May 1881 and was disposed of to the Ayr Steamship Co in 1901.

In the spring of 1903 *Amsterdam* joined *Glanmire* in the passenger/cargo service to the Dutch city from which she took her name; her passenger complement being quoted as 46 first class and 41 steerage. Later the same year, in August, the MacGill family re-registered the firm as a limited company under the title Rankine Line Ltd.

In the final year of World War 1 *Amsterdam* became the Company's only war loss, torpedoed without warning on 24 February about three miles southeast of Coquet Island with the loss of four lives.

Grangemouth

The next passenger steamer built for Rankine Line was the Company's largest yet but she was also destined to be the last. She was constructed by the Grangemouth & Greenock Dockyard Co and her christening was performed by Miss Annie MacGill on 3 February 1908. After fitting out in Grangemouth the ship underwent trials in the Firth of Forth attaining a maximum speed of around 16kt.

The elegant 15kt *Grangemouth* was the last and largest of the Rankine pasenger steamers. A 1908 product of Grangemouth & Greenock Dockyard, she differed from *Rotterdam* in having the forward part of her deck-house plated in plus a small chart-house on her bridge.
Geo Gibson & Co

In essence her design by the Company's superintendent William Filshie was a development of the earlier *Rotterdam,* though she was larger all round as can be seen from the following table of her relevant particulars.

Length: 275ft 2in
Breadth: 36ft 0in
Depth/draught: 17ft 0in/18ft 0in
Gross tonnage: 1,419
Machinery: 3-cylinder triple expansion
Boilers: 3
Power: 3,000ihp/310nhp
Speed: 15kt

Dimensions apart the only obvious external differences between *Grangemouth* and the earlier ship were her more enclosed deck-house at the forward end of the bridge deck and the addition of a small charthouse on the bridge. Her passenger complement (as with many of these early North Sea steamers) was not recorded in the shipping press but it would appear that she could accommodate about 26 in first class amidships with provision for a number of emigrants in the poop. Her triple

expansion engines constructed by Messrs Dunsmuir & Jackson, Glasgow were considerably more powerful than those installed in earlier Rankine steamers, and her four holds could carry about 1,300 tons cargo with the by now usual handling arrangements of three steam cranes and three derricks.

After only six years in the Rotterdam trade World War 1 brought disruption, and on 5 January 1915 *Grangemouth* was taken up by the Admiralty for conversion to an Armed Boarding Steamer. Fitted with a single 4in and a 12pdr gun she continued thus, mainly on northern patrol under successive pennant numbers M.22 and MI.08, until her release on 1 April 1919. On 1 January 1920 she was transferred to Gibson ownership along with her surviving Rankine consorts *Glasgow* and *Rotterdam,* plus the cargo steamer *Bowling.* Her new owner removed one of her boilers to give her a more economical speed of 12kt on 25 tons of coal a day, and at the same time her passenger capacity was reduced to 12.

After a further 19 years in Gibson's Continental trade she collided with another steamer on 21 March 1939, northeast of Spurn Head on a voyage from Antwerp to the Tees. She was taken in tow but foundered the following day about 15 miles form the Humber light vessel, her loss ending the final link with the old Rankine Line passenger service which had lasted for about a quarter of a century prior to World War 1. Rankine's colours disappeared for ever in November of the same year when the *Bowling* disappeared with all hands in the course of a voyage from Leith to Antwerp.

ALA

Dunkirk–Tilbury/Folkestone
1927– Societe Anonyme de Navigation
        'Angleterre–Lorraine–Alsace'
Funnel colours: Black

On 29 October 1926 an agreement was reached in France to form a new company to operate an overnight cross-Channel service between Dunkirk and Tilbury. The firm was registered on 23 February 1927 as the Societe Anonyme de Navigation Alsace–Lorrain–Angleterre, or ALA for short, and the Rothschild-owned Societe Anonyme de Gerance et d'Armement (SAGA) was given a controlling interest.

Early in April the new board decided to purchase three passenger steamers from the LMS' Irish Sea services with delivery on successive days at the end of the month. On 1 March 1928 a management agreement was signed with LMS and two weeks later a fourth steamer was acquired.

In October 1931 mounting losses forced a board decision to close the service and terminate its agreement with LMS, but after some discussion the Southern Railway stepped in with a new agreement allowing ALA to use Folkestone as its English terminal, the transfer being effected the following year.

In 1933 SAGA relinquished a large part of its holding, allowing the SR to obtain financial control and plans were laid to replace the three remaining steamers with new train ferries. These were completed on the Tyne in 1934/35 but because of delays with the new ferry dock at Dover did not enter service until October 1936. The old steamers, which had nearly been sold to South Africa a year before, were disposed of, two going for scrap and one being sold to Greece.

ALA remained in existence purchasing the train ferry *Twickenham Ferry* from the SR for £150,000. After a long career of 38 years this ship went to Spanish breakers in May 1974 and the following year her replacement *St Eloi* took up service to continue the ALA connection to the present day.

Lorrain

Built: 1908 by Vickers Sons & Maxim Ltd, Barrow
Length: 299ft 6in
Breadth: 40ft 2½in
Depth: 14ft 9in
Gross tonnage: 1,569
Machinery: 2 sets 4-cylinder triple expansion
Boilers: 2de and 2se, 180lb/sq in
Power: 6,300ihp
Speed: 20kt
Hull: Three-island type, 2 decks
Passengers: About 1,000 (first class and third class aft)
History: Built as *Rathmore* for LNWR Holyhead–

Except for her black funnels *Lorrain,* seen arriving at Dunkirk from Southend Pier in the summer of 1930, looked much as she had done in her previous career as the Holyhead–Greenore steamer *Rathmore.* The first of three ships purchased by ALA from the LMS in 1927, she became surplus in 1932 after the transfer of the UK terminal from Tilbury to Folkestone consequent upon agreement with the SR which superceded an earlier management agreement with the LMS.
Author's collection

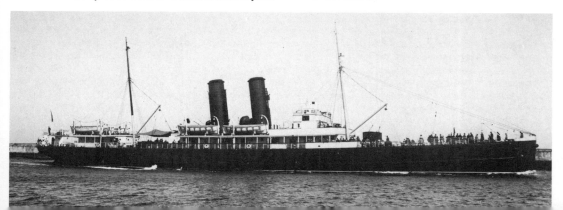

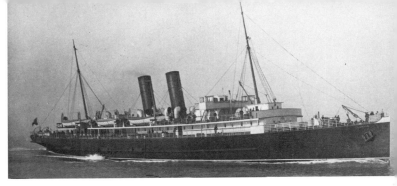

ALA's turbine-driven *Flamand* was originally the Heysham–Belfast steamer *Londonderry*. When built for the Midland Railway in 1904 she had her bridge at the forward end of the superstructure and cowl funnel tops. Her early service was marred by several accidents.
Author's collection

Greenore service. Launched 3 March 1908, trials 1 July (21½kt). Acquired from LMS 27 April 1927 and renamed *Lorrain*. July 1930 inaugurated thrice-weekly day excursion trips Dunkirk–Southend but service short-lived because of poor weather. September 1932 sold to Belgian breakers for 182,000 francs.

Flamand

Built: 1904 by Wm Denny & Bros, Dumbarton
Length: 330ft 7in
Breadth: 42ft 1in
Depth/draught: 17ft 1in/14ft 8in
Gross tonnage: 2,086
Machinery: 1 HP and 2 LP Parsons turbines
Boilers: 2de and 1se, 150lb/sq in
Power: 9,500shp
Speed: 21kt
Hull: Three-island type, 2 decks
Passengers: 174 first, 76 third (as built)

The triple-screw turbine *Picard* was acquired in 1928 some 10 months after her sister *Alsacien* from the LMS Fleetwood–Belfast service. Apart from minor alterations in the bridge area and removal of cargo derricks and funnel cowls the ships remained much as built, but an unusual feature, not visible in this picture, was recessed anchors. When ALA's service, never a financial success, was abandoned in 1936 in favour of a new train ferry service from Dover, *Picard* was sold to Greece for further trading and her sister scrapped. *Author's collection*

History: Built as *Londonderry* for Midland Railway• Heysham–Belfast service. Launched 29 April, trials end of June (max 22.39kt). Acquired from LMS 28 April 1927 and renamed *Flamand*. Withdrawn October 1936 and sold to German shipbreakers.

Alsacien, Picard

Built: 1909 by Wm Denny & Bros, Dumbarton
Length: 340ft 0in oa/330ft 8in bp
Breadth: 41ft 0in
Depth/draught: 17ft 1in and 16ft 2½in/15ft 6in
Gross tonnage: 2,052
Machinery: 1 HP and 2 LP Parsons turbines
Boilers: 5se, 157lb/sq in
Power: 9,000shp
Speed: 20½kt (contract)
Hull: Three-island type, 2 decks, bow rudder
Passengers: 241 first, 37 third (as built)
History: Built as *Duke of Cornwall/Duke of Argyll* for LNWR Fleetwood–Belfast service. Launched 9 March/6 May, trials mid-May/end of June (22¼kt). *Duke of Argyll* acquired from LMS 29 April 1927; renamed *Alsacien*. Sister acquired 15 March 1928, renamed *Picard*. 1935 prospective sale to South Africa fell through. October 1936 withdrawn; *Alsacien* sold to German breakers (with *Flamand*) for £14,000. November 1936 *Picard* sold to Skenderia Shipping Co for £7,900; renamed *Heliopolis* – Eastern Mediterranean service until broken up 1939/40.

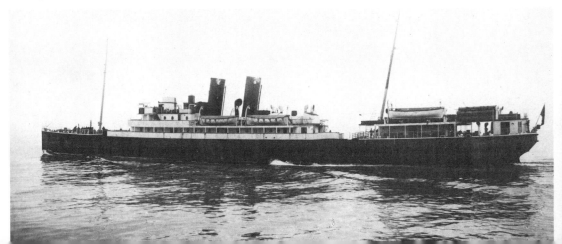

Zeeland Line

Flushing–Queenborough/Folkestone (after 1911);
 Hook of Holland–Harwich (after 1927)
1875– Zeeland Stoomvaart Maatchappij
 (Koninklijke Nederlandsche Postvaart NV)
Funnel colours: 1875 buff with narrow red, white
 and blue bands
 1878 buff with narrow black top
 1887 buff with normal black top
 1895 buff with narrow black top
 1906 buff with normal black top (deep black top
 before World War 1)
 1915 buff with narrow red, white and blue bands
 1920 black top added

Stoomvaart Maats Zeeland (Zeeland Steamship Co) was formed on 10 June 1875, largely due to the encouragement of Prins Hendrik of the Netherlands. On 26 July an overnight service was established between Flushing and Sheerness with three second-hand paddle steamers but it had to be suspended on 14 November because of several accidents and poor time-keeping.

Service was resumed on 15 May 1876 using the new Queenborough Pier as English terminal and a Dutch government mail contract was obtained, but the pier was destroyed by fire on 15 May 1882, necessitating a temporary move to Dover.

On 1 June 1887 a new day service was inaugurated with three large paddlers from Fairfields and the night service received three even

larger ships in 1893 to counter competition from the GER's twin-screw *Amsterdam* trio. Both services had to move to Dover again in 1897 when bad weather damaged the Queenborough railway branch and three years later the pier again burned down, forcing a move to Port Victoria on the opposite bank of the Medway.

The night service received a major boost in 1910 with the introduction of three new twin-screw steamers from Fairfields and the remaining paddlers were moved to the day service. Draught problems in the Medway approaches however occasioned the transfer of the new ships to Dover in May 1911, at the same time shortening the route from about 112 to 92 miles. Two of the new ships were lost in World War 1, their replacements being the first of their type to be built in a Dutch shipyard.

The next move came at the beginning of 1927 when Zeeland – following agreement with the LNER – transferred its UK terminal to Harwich (Parkeston Quay). Two new motorships commenced a day service just before World War 2 but hostilities destroyed Zeeland's Flushing terminal so that a postwar night service had to be resumed from the Hook of Holland instead. In 1949, a seasonal daytime service was re-established between Flushing and Folkestone, but it lapsed three years later.

Koningin Wilhelmina, Zeeland's last conventional passenger ship, entered service in 1960 but only eight years later was relegated to relief sailings on the arrival of the car ferry *Koningin Juliana*.

Prinses Marie and **Prinses Elisabeth** were Zeeland's first purpose-built steamers and the first of many to come from John Elder & Co (later Fairfields). Designed for the Flushing–Queenborough night service they were a great improvement on the second-hand ships which they replaced. Note the very narrow black funnel tops adopted by their owners at that time, also the black paddle boxes.
F.G.E. Moll collection

Prinses Marie, Prinses Elisabeth

Built: 1878 by John Elder & Co, Glasgow
Length: 278ft 2½in
Breadth: 35ft 1in/34ft 8in
Depth: 16ft 1in
Gross tonnage: 1,652
Machinery: 2-cylinder compound oscillating
Power: 3,000ihp
Speed: 16kt
Hull: Iron, flush deck
Passengers: 240 berths (including c150 first class)
History: Launched 24 October/10 December 1877; entered service 28 March/5 April 1878. Flushing–Queenborough night service. 1889 reboiled by builder (*Prinses Marie* 17.2 kt on trials). 1896 *Prinses Marie* chartered by Albert Ballin for one season on Elbe–Heligoland service; renamed *Prinzess Marie* (white hull). 1898 both sold – *Prinzess Marie* to Stettiner DG, renamed *Germania*; *Prinses Elisabeth* to G.O. Wallenberg, Stockholm (Svea Line), renamed *Svea* in 1901, Stettin–Stockholm joint service. December 1902 *Germania* broken up. 1909 *Svea* withdrawn; broken up at Stettin 1910.

Prins Hendrik (1880), Willem Prins van Oranje

Built: 1880/1883 by John Elder & Co, Glasgow
Length: 278ft 8in/278ft 10in
Breadth: 35ft 0in
Depth: 16ft 5in
Gross tonnage: 1,573
Machinery: 2-cylinder compound oscillating
Boilers: 75lb/sq in
Power: 3,000ihp
Speed: 16kt (*Willem Prins van Oranje* 18.2kt at 4,628ihp on trial)
Hull: Iron, flush deck
Passengers: 240 berths (including 150 first class)
History: *Prins Hendrik* ordered to cope with extra traffic after 1880 start of London–Berlin through service via Flushing. Delivered 11 May 1880, entered service June. *Willem Prins van Oranje* entered service 12 July 1883 – Flushing–Queenborough night service. Reboiled 1889 and 1896 by builders. 1895 *Prins Hendrik* laid up Flushing; 1902 broken up Bremen by Gebr Specht. *Willem Prins van Oranje* reserve ship; 1908 broken up by Hendrik Ido Ambacht, near Dordrecht.

Duitschland/Zeeland, Engeland, Nederland

Built: 1887 by Fairfield Shipbuilding & Engineering Co. Govan
Length: 286ft 6in
Breadth: 35ft 4in
Depth: 16ft 6in
Gross tonnage: 1,653/1,648/1,660
Machinery: 2-cylinder compound oscillating
Boilers: 4se, 80lb/sq in
Power: 4,600ihp
Speed: 17kt
Hull: Steel, flush deck
Passengers: About 1,000
History: Launched 25 November 1886/23

Willem Prins van Oranje of 1883 was the last of four similar iron ships to enter Zeeland's overnight service to the Medway. Credited with a speed of 18kt she is pictured here lying in reserve in her homeport during the final years of her career.
F.G.E. Moll collection

A fine view of *Engeland,* one of three sisters delivered to Zeeland by Elder & Co in 1887 following overtures by the Dutch and German governments for an additional daytime service. As built they had shorter funnels with narrow black tops but were distinguishable from the earlier ships by their solid bulwarks forward.
World Ship Society

December 1886/1 March 1887. Trial speed c19¼kt. Designed for a new day service inaugurated 1 June 1887. 1910 *Engeland* and *Nederland* replaced by new screw steamers and sold to Hendrik Ido Ambacht for scrap, former not broken up till 1911. *Duitschland* renamed *Zeeland* during World War 1 to emphasise Dutch neutrality; 1918 became hopsital ship for repatriating wounded PoWs between Rotterdam and Boston, Lincs. November 1922 sold to Diederichsen, Bremen for scrap.

Koningin Wilhelmina, Koningin Regentes, Prins Hendrik (1895)

Built: 1896 by Fairfield Shipbuilding & Engineering Co. Govan
Length: 320ft 0in
Breadth: 35ft 9in

Depth: 16ft 0in
Gross tonnage: 1,947
Machinery: 3-cylinder triple-expansion diagonal
Boilers: 6se, 170lb/sq in
Power: 9,000ihp
Speed: 21kt
Hull: Steel, flush deck
Passengers: 244 berths
History: Launched 27 May, 9 July, 22 August 1895. Night service. Reboilered November 1901, July 1903, December 1904. 1910 replaced on night service by new triple-screw steamers and converted for day service, continuing to run into Queenborough till World War 1 when service transferred to Tilbury. *Koningin Wilhelmina* sunk 31 July 1916 near North Hinder light vessel by mine laid by submarine UC1, three crew lost. *Prins Hendrik* escorted into Zeebrugge by torpedo boats 23 September 1916, later released. 10 November 1916 *Koningin Regentes* captured by submarine UB.19 west of North Hinder L/V and taken to Zeebrugge, later to Ostend. 17 December released in Zeebrugge after which regular service abandoned. 1918 *Koningin Regentes* hospital ship for transfer of wounded PoWs; 6 June torpedoed and sunk 21 miles from East Leman L/V while bound for Rotterdam from Boston, Lincs – seven lost. 31 January 1919 *Prins Hendrik* inaugurated day service Flushing–Gravesend; soon transferred to Folkestone night service as reserve. November 1922 sold to Diederichsen, Bremen for scrap.

Built to counter competition from GER's *Amsterdam* trio, *Koningin Regentes* and her two sisters of 1895 were logical developments of the 1887-built ships. Their taller funnels gave them a more imposing appearance and they were amongst the largest of their type, ranking equal in size to their contemporaries in the Belgian Government and IOMSP fleets. *Koningin Regentes* is depicted in hospital ship colours in 1918 shortly before her loss.
Author's collection

Prinses Juliana (1909), Oranje Nassau, Mecklenburg (1909)

Built: 1909 by Fairfield Shipbuilding &
    Engineering Co. Govan
Length: 364ft 0in/350ft 0in bp
Breadth: 45ft 4in
Depth/draught: 25ft 10in to upper deck/12ft 6in
Gross tonnage: 2,885
Machinery: 2 sets, 4-cylinder triple expansion
Boilers: 4de, 190lb/sq in
Power: 10,000ihp
Speed: 22kt (*Oranje Nassau* 23.7kt, six hour trial)
Hull: Raised foc'sle, counter stern, three decks
Passengers: 246 first class berths, 110 second
History: April 1910 entered service on Flushing–
Queenborough night run. May 1911 transferred to
Folkestone because of draught limitations in the
Medway. 1913 record passenger figures because of
shorter crossing and new through rail connections
from Flushing. 1 February 1916 *Prinses Juliana* hit
mine laid by submarine UC.5 near Sunk L/V; 2
February beached near Felixstowe in half

submerged condition; night 28/29 March broke in
two in storm, total loss. 27 February 1916
Mecklenburg sunk by mine from submarine UC.7
southeast of Galloper L/V when bound for Flushing
from Tilbury; service suspended. *Oranje Nassau*
laid up; 23 June 1919 resumed night service to
Folkestone; 1922 day service. 1927 transferred to
Harwich, 1932 reboilered. Early World War 2
thrice-weekly service to Tilbury. May 1940 escaped
to UK; became depot ship for Royal Dutch Navy in
various ports. 1946 released; partnered LNER
Prague in thrice-weekly night service Hook–
Harwich; 1947 day service. 1948 converted to oil-
firing. 1949 chartered by Batavier Line for
Rotterdam–Tilbury service. 1952 resumed Hook–
Harwich day service. Summer 1954 sold Hendrik
Ido Ambacht for scrap.

Prinses Juliana (1920), Mecklenburg (1922)

Built: 1920/1922 by Kon Maats de Schelde,
    Flushing
Length: 350ft 5in
Breadth: 42ft 8in
Depth/draught: 23ft 10in/12ft 7in
Gross tonnage: 2,907
Machinery: 2 sets, 4-cylinder triple expansion
Boilers: 4de, 180lb/sq in
Power: 9,330ihp
Speed: 22kt
Hull: Raised foc'sle, counter stern, three decks
Passengers: 266 first class berths, 110 second
History: 15 August 1920 *Prinses Juliana* first night
crossing Flushing–Folkestone. July 1922
Mecklenburg completed; new daytime service
inaugurated. January 1927 both transferred to
Harwich; boat deck extended and promenade
decks fitted with glazed screens. 29 June 1935

**Combining elegance with high speed, Zeeland's first
screw-driven steamer, *Prinses Juliana,* was
photographed on trials in the Clyde during the autumn of
1909. She and her two sisters were built on Dutch
Government insistence whilst re-negotiating the 10-
yearly mail contract in 1908 and were Zeeland's answer
to the new GER turbine ships. Propelled by triple screw
reciprocating machinery balanced on the Yarrow–
Schlick–Tweedy system to minimise vibration on the
overnight crossing, their greater draught forced a
change of English terminal from the Medway to
Folkestone in April 1911. *Oranje Nassau* survived both
World Wars in her 45-year career.** *Author's collection*

Built to replace their war lost namesakes, *Prinses Juliana* (1920) and *Mecklenburg* (1922) were the first ships of their type to come from a Dutch shipyard. Constructed from the same plans as the earlier sisters but outwardly distinguishable by their lack of external steam pipes, they retained reciprocating machinery at a time when nearly all like ships were propelled by turbines. *Mecklenburg* ran for a while after World War 2 without her mainmast which had been removed during hostilities. Later fitted with a repositioned stump mainmast she is shown passing Dover in August 1951 whilst on summer service between Flushing and Folkestone. *Laurence Dunn*

Prinses Juliana damaged in collision with DFDS m/v *Esbjerg* off Harwich, out of service till 11 August. 21 November 1937 *Prinses Juliana* grounded in fog 15 miles southwest of Flushing; refloated. September 1939 both laid up in Flushing. 12 May 1940 *Prinses Juliana* bombed by German aircraft whilst taking troops from Flushing to Ijmuiden; breached Terheyden Bank but later broke in two. *Mecklenburg* escaped to UK; became Royal Dutch navy accommodation ship. 1943 converted to assault landing ship for Normandy landing. 1946 converted to oil-firing. 14 June 1947 entered Hook–Harwich day service. 7 July 1949 revived Flushing–Folkestone day service (twice weekly in summer); 8 September 1952 last sailing. Became relief ship Hook–Harwich. 25 October 1959 withdrawn; May 1960 sold to Van Heyghen Freres SA, Ghent for scrap.

Koningin Emma, Prinses Beatrix

Built: 1939 by Kon Maats de Schelde, Flushing
Length: 380ft 0in oa/359ft 7in bp
Breadth: 47ft 2½in
Depth/draught: 28ft to upper deck/13ft 6½in
Machinery: 2 sets, 10-cylinder de Schelde/Sulzer
Power: 12,650bhp
Speed: 23kt
Hull: Long raised foc'sle, cruiser stern
Passengers: 1,800 (+ 25 cars); 1,600 post World War 2

The 22kt grey-hulled *Koningin Emma* and her sister *Prinses Beatrix* were Zeeland Line's first motor ships, being delivered by de Schelde just before the outbreak of World War 2. They were Holland's answer to the fast Belgian motor packets and introduced an entirely new profile to the southern North Sea with their single mast and funnel together with unusual boat arrangement. *Author's collection*

History: Launched by Queen Wilhelmina 14 January 1939, by Prince Bernhard 25 March 1939. Entered service 4 June/3rd July but both laid up September because of World War 2. May 1940 escaped to UK and assisted in evacuation of France, then trooping to Iceland. August 1940 requisitioned by Admiralty for conversion to LSI(M) – new bridge and funnel, six LCAs, two LCMs in 30-ton davits, 22 officers/350 troops plus 227 crew. *Koningin Emma* renamed *Queen Emma*. Served on Lofoten Raid March 1941; West Africa; Dieppe Raid August 1942; North African, Sicilian and Italian landings 1943; Normandy landing June 1944; Far East 1945 (Japanese forces surrender aboard *Queen Emma* in Penang). April 1946 released in Far East and assisted evacuation of Dutch civilians from Java. 1947 returned to builders for major refit; new funnel, masts and passenger spaces. Spring 1948 Harwich–Hook service. *Koningin Emma* chartered by W.H. Muller for Rotterdam–Tilbury service 15 June–30 September 1948. 1960 improvements to reduce noise level, *Koningin Emma* in reserve. Summer 1968 replaced by car ferries. *Prinses Beatrix* withdrawn August, *Koningin Emma* last trip 17 October. Laid up at Flushing; sold in December to Jos de Smedt, Antwerp for scrap.

Koningin Wilhelmina (1960)

Built: 1960 by De Merwede, Hardinxveld
Length: 361ft 10in
Breadth: 53ft 4in

Zeeland's only postwar conventional passenger ship, the 1960-built *Koningin Wilhelmina,* had a unique appearance with her streamlined bridge front – somewhat reminiscent of SNCF's *Cote d'Azur* and *Lisieux* – and an extraordinary long, low funnel placed well aft. Special attention was paid to the reduction of noise and vibration levels and she was fitted with stabilisers, but the coming of the specialised car ferry led to her early withdrawal. Happily she remains in service today, little altered, as the Greek *Panagia Tinoy,* one of the last survivors of her breed. *Author*

Depth: 31ft 2½in
Gross tonnage: 6,228
Machinery: 2 x 12-cylinder MAN diesels
Power: 15,600bhp
Speed: 23kt
Hull: Long raised foc'sle
Passengers: 1,600 (700 in first class) plus 30–40 cars (side doors)
History: Launched by Queen Juliana 5 June 1959; replaced *Mecklenburg* in day Harwich–Hook service 7 February 1960. First Zeeland ship with stabilisers. 1968 downgraded to extra summer and relief sailings following arrival of new car ferry *Koningin Juliana*. Poor garage space led to long periods of lay up in 1970s, occasionally chartered for inauguration of North Sea gas platform. 1976 fitted with electric bow thrust. 1978 replaced by car ferry *Prinses Beatrix,* last sailing from Parkeston on 28 June. Laid up at Flushing. 1979 sold to Ventouris Group, Piraeus; renamed *Captain Constantinos.* Piraeus–Syros, Tenos, Mykonos service (daily). 1981 renamed *Panagia Tinoy* (Holy Mother of Tenos). Still in service.

Batavier Line

Rotterdam–London
1823–1895 Netherlands Steamship Co
1895–1920 Netherlands Cargo & Passenger
    Steamship Co
1895–1927 Wm H Muller & Co's General
    Steamship Co
1895–1971 Wm H Muller & Co
Funnel colours: Originally white with black top,
    later changed to yellow with black top
From 1903 black with white 'M' on broad red band
    between two narrow white bands.

On 12 April 1830, following unsuccessful attempts to start a Rotterdam–Hamburg service and later one between Antwerp and London, NV Nederlandsche Stoomboot Maats (NSM) inaugurated a Rotterdam–London link – the first regular foreign-owned service to trade into London – with the 300-ton wooden paddle steamer *De Batavier* (1829). The service prospered and over the years two more paddlers and four screw-driven steamers were added, all built of iron in the Company's own shipyard, the last being the 760-ton *Fijenoord* of 1879.

In 1895 NSM decided to concentrate entirely on shipbuilding and accordingly sold the London service with its ships and goodwill to Messrs Wm H Muller & Co, with the proviso that it should continue under the 'Batavier Line' banner. Mullers formed a new company, the Netherlands Cargo & Passenger Steamship Co, and quickly ordered two new steel ships from Gourlays Bros of Dundee,

enabling a daily service (excluding Sundays) to be started to Custom House Quay on 1 April 1899.

Further pairs of ships were added in 1903 and 1921 – to replace war losses – and on 15 June 1922 a new terminal, Batavier Pier, was inaugurated at the SECR's West Street station, Gravesend. World War 2 left only one ship, *Batavier II*, in commission and she continued alone until withdrawn in April 1958, thereby closing the 128-year old passenger link.

Batavier II (1897), *Batavier III* (1897)

Built: 1897 by Gourlay Bros, Dundee
Length: 244ft 0in
Breadth: 33ft 6in
Depth: 14ft 6in
Gross tonnage: 1,136
Machinery: 4-cylinder triple expansion

Batavier III, depicted at speed in Southampton Water by local photographer F.G.O. Stuart, and her sister *Batavier II*, were the first steamers built for Wm H. Muller following the latter's acquisition of the assets and goodwill of the Batavier Line from the Netherlands Steamship Co in 1895. Well-proportioned ships and typical short sea traders of their day, they retained their NSM funnel colours until 1903 when a change was made to Muller livery. Later lengthened they also had their boats raised one deck and a new pair fitted aft, whilst a crane replaced the forward derrick. *Popperfoto*

Batavier V, and sister *Batavier IV* of 1903 were the second pair of ships to be built by Gourlays at Dundee. Some 15ft longer than the earlier ships, they differed structurally in having a well-deck at No 3 hatch instead of at No 2 and solid bulwarks forward, whilst cargo gear consisted entirely of steam cranes. After World War 2 service as a headquarters ship at Tobermory *Batavier IV* ended her exceptionally long career as a static Dutch naval training ship at Den Helder in the early 1970s.
World Ship Society

Boilers: 2se, 170 lb/sq in
Power: 2,000 ihp
Speed: 14 kt
Hull: Foc'sle and combined bridge and poop; steel, two decks
Passengers: 44 first class, 27 second, up to 250 steerage
History: Launched 17 August/14 September 1897; trials 5 October/13 November (13½/14½kt). 1907 fitted with wireless. 1909/10 lengthened by 16ft and reboilered by Wilton's, Rotterdam. 24 September 1916 *Batavier II* captured by submarine UB6 and taken to Zeebrugge: July despatched to Germany as prize but attacked 27th by HM Submarine E55 with gunfire one mile north of Molengat Buoy, Texel; abandoned and later sunk. Early 1919 *Batavier III* resumed thrice-weekly service with *Batavier IV* and *Batavier VI*; promenade deck partly enclosed c1930. 1939 sold to L.P. Sclavounos, renamed *El Sonador* (Panamanian flag). 18 February 1940 torpedoed and sunk by U.61 east of Shetland Islands.

Batavier IV, Batavier V (1903)

Built: 1903 by Gourlay Bros, Dundee
Length: 260ft 2½in
Breadth: 35ft 1in
Depth/draught: 16ft 6in/15in 6in
Gross tonnage: 1,568
Machinery: 3-cylinder triple expansion by Hutson & Sons
Boilers: 2se
Power: 2,300 ihp
Speed: 14½kt
Hull: Combined foc'sle and bridge deck with poop steel; 2 decks
Passengers: 75 first, 28 second, up to 325 steerage
History: Launched 17 October/28 November 1902;

delivered 1903. 8 December 1909 *Batavier IV* ran aground in New Waterway after collision with fishing boat, which sank. 18 March 1915 *Batavier V* captured and taken to Zeebrugge; released. 16 May 1916 mined near Inner Gabbard L/V and sank, four lost. *Batavier IV* promenade deck partly enclosed c1930. May/June 1940 assisted evacuation of France and Channel Islands. Converted to training ship HMS *Eastern Isles*. From 14 September 1940 became HQ ship of ASW Escort Training Group at Tobermory; renamed HMS *Western Isles* 1941. February 1946 released and taken to Rotterdam. De-engined for role as static ASW training base KNS *Zeearend* (Sea Eagle) in Waalhaven; moved to Den Helder early 1960s. Replaced by shorebase and scrapped early 1970s.

Batavier VI

Built: 1903 by Mackie & Thomson, Glasgow
Length: 240ft 4in
Breadth: 35ft 6in
Depth/draught: 14ft 2½in/15ft
Gross tonnage: 1,181
Machinery: 3-cylinder triple expansion by Hutson & Sons
Boilers: 2se
Power: 169nhp
Speed: 12kt
Hull: Combined foc'sle and bridge with poop; 2 decks and awning deck
Passengers: 24 (Later 68 first, 43 second)
History: Launched 12 February 1903. Relief ship for London service. November 1915 captured and taken to Zeebrugge; released. 1918 refitted with extra passenger accommodation. 1919 London service. November 1928 sold to M.H. Bland & Co, Gibraltar for £14,000; renamed *Gibel Zerjon* – Gibraltar–Tangier/Casablanca passenger (360 max)/cargo service. Escaped capture by Republican warship off Melilla because of timely

arrival of RN warships, and laid up for duration of Spanish Civil War, but served three-month Red Cross charter September 1937 to move refugees from Valencia to Marseilles. June 1939 sold to Soc Courtage & Transport; renamed *Florida* (Panamanian flag). 1940 sold to Cia Diana de Vapores SA, Panama. 2 June 1940 beached near Cape Spartel in sinking condition; salvage attempts failed and became a total loss.

Batavier II (1921), *Batavier V* (1921)

Built: 1921 by Wilton Engineering & Slipway Co, Rotterdam
Length: 260ft 0in
Breadth: 35ft 0in
Depth/draught: 15ft 6in/16ft 6in
Gross tonnage: 1,573
Machinery: 3-cylinder triple expansion
Boilers: 2 Scotch (coal or oil)
Power: 2,250ihp
Speed: 15kt
Hull: Combined foc'sle and bridge with poop; 2 decks
Passengers: 98 first, 53 second
History: Launched 1920/21. Promenade decks partly enclosed c1930, first class accommodation reduced to c70. May 1940 *Batavier V* seized by German forces in Rotterdam; used to supply Channel Islands. Early November 1941 sunk by RN MTB west of Cap Gris Nez when bound Antwerp–Guernsey. 21 May 1940 *Batavier II* evacuated 350 troops Boulogne–Falmouth, later trips Cherbourg–Milford Haven and Brest–Falmouth. Accommodation ship for Dutch naval cadets at Falmouth. Late July 1940 moved to Portsmouth for crew of KNS *Jakob van Heemskerk* during conversion; mainmast removed; given grey livery with white funnel top. April 1941 released; UK

Dutch built to replace war losses in 1921, *Batavier II* and *Batavier V*, were virtual repeats of the 1903 sisters with full-height steam pipes around the funnel and Welin instead of quadrant davits. *Batavier V*, seen passing Erith in 1933, became a war loss in German hands but, her sister resumed London sailings alone after the war, at first without a mainmast but later with a new short one added. Her withdrawal in April 1958 brought to a close Batavier Line's 128-year-old Rotterdam–London passenger link. *Laurence Dunn*

coasting service. January 1946 Rotterdam–Harwich service. June 1947 Rotterdam–London, later fitted with new short mainmast. Joined by Zeeland's *Koningin Emma* summer 1948 and *Oranje Nassau* 1949–51 (thrice weekly). 1951–58 lone service (c50 first class passengers only). Boiler trouble led to withdrawal after final London departure 12 April 1958; laid up in Rotterdam. Autumn 1959 sold to Ver Utrechtse Ijzerhandel for scrap; demolition commenced January 1960.

Batavier III (1939)

Built: 1939 by Scheepswerf De Noord, Alblasserdam
Length: 283ft 6in oa/267ft 0in bp
Breadth: 43ft 8in
Depth/draught: 23ft 10in/16ft 3½in
Gross tonnage: 2,687
Machinery: 3-cylinder Werkspoor compound
Boilers: 2 se, 996lb/sq in
Power: 3,000ihp
Speed: 15kt
Hull: Flush deck
Passengers: 88 first, 71 second, 24 third
History: Launched 2 March 1939 after low water level caused postponement from 28 February; entered service 16 June. Laid-up in Rotterdam after start of World War 2. May 1940 seized by German forces and used as safety ship by German navy. 1 January 1941 troop transport to Norway under F. Laeisz management. 15 October 1942 mined and sunk c20 miles south of Aalborg, no survivors.

Holland Steamship Co

Amsterdam–London/Hull, etc
1885–1974   Hollandsche Stoomboot Maatschappij
Funnel colours: Yellow with black top

Hollandsche Stoomboot Maats (Holland Steamship Co or HSM for short) was formed in Amsterdam in 1885 to run a steamship service to London. Previous companies involved in this trade had been the Amsterdam Steamship Co of 1855 and the Screw Steamer Co which had first despatched its 70ft paddle steamer *De Beurs* to London as far back as 1827.

HSM commenced operating with the 1879 built 754-ton *Fijenoord*, bought from the Netherlands Steamship Co and renamed *Ijstroom*, thus starting the familiar *-stroom* (River) syle of nomenclature. A new ship – *Amstelstroom* – quickly joined the service which became twice weekly; the London berth being Brewer's Quay upstream from the Tower, though this was later changed to Hay's Wharf on the other side of the Pool next to London Bridge.

HSM also ran services to the Humber and the south and west coasts of the UK, the latter mainly

for cargo only. Passenger carriage became intermittent between the wars and ceased altogether after World War 2, though the Company's many cargo vessels continued to trade until 1974 when operations ceased.

Amstelstroom (1885)

Built: 1885 by Netherlands Steamship Co, Rotterdam
Length: 228ft 8in
Breadth: 28ft 5in
Depth: 14ft 8in
Gross tonnage: 787
Machinery: 2-cylinder compound
Power: 130nhp
Speed: 11kt
Hull: 2 decks, raised foc'sle and poop
Passengers: First and second class
History: Entry into service enabled twice-weekly service; scheduled North Sea canal entrance to Blackwall Point in 16 hours. 1905 reboilered and sold to D. Dimokas & Co Piraeus; renamed *Irini*. 1908 sold to D.G. Goudis, renamed *Spetsai*. 1909 renamed *Spezia;* 1913 renamed *Spetzai*. Later transferred to Hellenic Steam Nav Goudi (J. Leonidas, Manager); lost during war. Raised, renamed *Spetsai,* transferred to Hellenic Co of Maritime Enterprises (A. Palios, Manager). 1928 sold to A.K. Riggas; renamed *Volos*. 1930 absorbed by Hellenic Coast Lines. 7 December 1933 foundered near Cape Spartivento bound Piraeus–Savona.

Holland Steamship Co's British-built *Ijstroom* of 1898 had an unusual 'four-island' profile. Her Dutch-built counterpart *Maasstroom* was very similar but had a slightly thinner funnel with a deeper black top. Regulars on the Amsterdam–London service, they each mounted six deck cranes for speedy cargo handling.
World Ship Society

Ijstroom (1898), Maasstroom

Built: 1898/1900 by R. Thompson & Son, Sunderland/Rijkee & Co, Rotterdam
Length: 230ft 5in/228ft 5in
Breadth: 32ft 2in/33ft 10in
Depth/draught: 14ft 7in/15ft 3in
Gross tonnage: 960/1,034
Machinery: 3-cylinder triple expansion
Boilers: 2
Power: 181nhp/1,300ihp
Speed: 12kt
Hull: Steel, 2 decks, 4-island type
Passengers: First, second and steerage
History: Near sisters. Departures Wednesday and Saturday from Brewers Quay, Pool of London (8am) and Amsterdam (4pm). 1912 *Ijstroom* swept against London Bridge, losing mainmast and damaging funnel. Service continued during World War 1. 1922 *Ijstroom* sold to Cie de Nav France-Irlande, Brest; renamed *Banba*. 1 July 1923 wrecked off Newfoundland Coast bound Sydney NS-Granville. 23 January 1918, *Maasstroom* damaged by German air raid on London, one lost. Post World War 1, 12 passengers only. February 1935 sold to Van Heyghen Freres, Ghent for scrap.

Amstelstroom (1910)

Built: 1910 by Maats, Fijenoord, Rotterdam
Length: 271ft 8in
Breadth: 37ft 1in
Depth: 16ft 1in
Gross tonnage: 1,413
Machinery: 3-cylinder triple expansion
Boilers: 1
Power: 203nhp
Speed: 13kt
Hull: Three-island type, long bridge and poop.
History: Fitted with refrigeration machinery. Served Amsterdam–London/Hull. 23 March 1917 damaged by gunfire from German torpedo boats V44, G86 and G87 and abandoned c50 miles northwest of Ijmuiden. 27 March found drifting c20 miles east-southeast of N Hinder L/V by submarine UB10 and sunk by torpedo.

Zaanstroom, Lingestroom

Built: 1913/1917 by Rotterdam Drydock Co, Rotterdam
Length: 243ft 7in/242ft 4in
Breadth: 37ft 1in/37ft 2in
Depth/draught: 17ft 4in/16ft 7in
Gross tonnage: 1,657/1,480
Machinery: 3-cylinder triple expansion
Boilers: 1se
Power: 200nhp
Speed: 13kt
Hull: Combined foc'sle and bridge, poop.
Passengers: 12 first class, later increased to 25.
History: Near sisters. 18 March 1915 *Zaanstroom* captured in North Sea by submarine U28 and taken to Zeebrugge by prize crew. Used as distilling ship by German navy. 5 October 1918 scuttled. 1919 raised by Belgians and sold to Soc Navale Charbonniere; renamed *Westland*. 1922 sold to Scheepvaart en Steenkolen Maats, Holland. July 1925 sold to United Baltic Corporation; renamed *Baltannic*. UK–Baltic States service (12 passengers). World War 2 to New Zealand as refrigerated feeder ship. 1949 sold to ICI Ltd; storage hulk for explosives in Loch Torridon. 1958 sold to West of Scotland Shipbreaking Co Troon; arrived in tow 7 May. *Lingestroom* post World War 1 service Amsterdam–Pool of London (Enderby's Wharf). 1937 sold to Thesen's Steamships Co, Capetown; renamed *Griqua* 1938. Then largest and most powerful South African coaster, Capetown–Belgian Congo passenger cargo service 1948 sold to Colonial Steamships Co, Port Louis, Mauritius; renamed *Chamarel*. 2 September 1949 explosion and fire St Denis, Reunion, whilst unloading petrol; capsized and sank.

Lingestroom (1917), photographed passing Erith in the early 1930s. *Laurence Dunn collection*

Argo Line

Bremen/Hamburg–London/Hull/Leith
1857–1897	Norddeutscher Lloyd AG
1897–1922	Argo DS Gesellschaft (1896)
1923–1925	Roland Linie AG
1925–1933	Norddeutscher Lloyd AG
1933–1936	Argo Reederai AG
1936–1952	Argo Reederei, Richard Adler AG
1952–	Argo Reederei, Adler & Sohnen

Funnel colours: 1857 Buff (NDL)
    1897 Black
    1923 Buff with black top
    1925 Buff
    1933 Buff with yellow eight-pointed star on green band under black top

The well-known firm of Norddeutscher Lloyd was formed on 20 February 1857 as a result of a merger between three local Weser concerns and an insurance company. Six ships all with bird names were ordered from Palmer's, Newcastle for the UK trade, also two larger ships for a service to New York. On 28 October 1857 the three-masted steamer *Adler* became the first NDL ship in foreign trade when she left Nordenham for London. By the end of the following year she had been joined by *Mowe, Falke, Schwalbe, Condor* and *Schwan* and between them they had made 64 round voyages to London and 93 to Hull. Their success was such that they were soon lengthened.

Germany became a unified nation-state in 1871 and this led to an increase in trade with the result that by 1876 the annual number of round voyages to the UK had risen to a total of 236. In 1879 *Condor* was run down by a sailing ship whilst serving in the Company's Baltic service, and later sank; in 1881 the four oldest steamers plus the fairly new *Strauss* (1872) were sold to DFDS.

In 1885 NDL accepted a subsidy for its Far East service which had started in 1880 and this obliged it to build newer and faster ships. At the same time the Company was also building new express steamers for its New York service, and so in order to realise capital for these costly ventures the decision was taken to dispose of the UK trade. In 1897 after 40 successful years that part of the business was sold to the newly-formed Argo Steamship Co of Bremen (1896) along with the seven remaining 'birds'. These were:

Reiher
Built 1870 Earle's; 225ft × 28ft; 872gt

Mowe
Built 1882 J.C. Tecklenborg; 211ft × 32ft; 940gt

Condor/Schwan
Built 1884 J.C. Tecklenborg; 225ft × 30ft; 1,230gt

NDL's Stettin-built *Albatross* of 1893 had a more rakish appearance than subsequent ships built for Argo. Pictured in the Humber she could carry 20 first class and 35 second class passengers. *Author's collection*

Adler
Built 1884 Flensburg SB; 240ft × 31ft; 1,336gt

Albatross/Falke
Built 1893/94 Stettin SB; 213ft × 30ft; 1,083gt

They could carry about 25 first and 35 second class passengers and were all constructed of iron, except the last two which were of steel. These two also differed in being propelled by triple expansion instead of compound engines.

The most interesting of the seven was the *Adler* (Eagle) which had been launched from the Flensburg Shipbuilding Co's yard in February 1884, performing her trials in Flensburg Bay on 9 April. She was unusual in having two funnels which made her something of a novelty in the Bremen–UK trade; her flush-decked hull was built on the spar deck principle and incorporated a straight stem and counter stern.

Her first class accommodation was placed amidships with berths for 16 passengers in a saloon which was described as 'being decorated in polished oak and Hungarian ash with Brussels carpets on all floors'. Additional sleeping arrangements were provided for 30 second class passengers in the forward tween-deck.

Her cargo holds were well ventilated and were fitted up for the carriage of livestock, which had made up a good part of NDL's North Sea trade during the preceding years. Main propulsion was by means of a two-cylinder compound engine which produced 250nhp for a speed of about 12kt.

After only two years service under Argo colours she was sold to the Lombard Steamship Co London and placed under the management of J. White. Her engines were tripled in 1903 with a 225nhp unit from G. Clark & Co, South Shields and she was given new boilers at the same time. The following year she was resold to Cie Generale Transatlantique which renamed her *Ville De Nantes* and placed her in local service from St Nazaire. She remained thus for over 20 years and was finally sold for scrap in 1926 being broken up early the following year.

Schwalbe

Built: 1898 by Bremer Vulkan, Bremen
Length: 235ft 5in
Breadth: 31ft 0in
Depth: 17ft 6in
Gross tonnage: 1,178
Machinery: 3-cylinder triple expansion
Power: 135nhp
Hull: 1 deck with raised foc's'le and poop
Passengers: 140 in three classes
History: December 1916 lost after collision at Haugesund

Sperber

Built: 1899 by Bremer Vulkan, Bremen
Length: 234ft 8in
Breadth: 31ft 0in
Depth: 20ft 0in
Gross tonnage: 1,265
Machinery: 3-cylinder triple expansion
Power: 850ihp
Speed: 11kt
Hull: 1 deck and spar deck; three-island type
Passengers: 14 first, 24 second, 80 third
History: 21 March 1916 wrecked Havringe bound Bremen–Oxelosund

Strauss

Built: 1899 by Bremer Vulkan, Bremen
Length: 185ft 0in
Breadth: 29ft 5in
Depth: 17ft 8in
Gross tonnage: 903
Machinery: 3-cylinder triple expansion
Power: 650ihp
Speed: 10kt
Hull: 1 deck and spar deck
Passengers: 10 first, 24 second, 64 third
History: Launched July, trials 13 August. 1919 sold

Argo Line's *Strauss* (1899) hurries down the Thames en route from St Katherine's Dock to Bremen. Her Bremer Vulkan built contemporaries *Schwalbe* and *Sperber* differed in having a raised boat deck and several deck cranes. *Adler* of 1900, a single ship, differed in having a long bridge deck incorporating No 2 hold.
World Ship Society

Oldenburg–Portuguese Line; renamed *Oldenburg II* then *Hyamonte* in 1922. 1925 sold to Luke Thomas & Co, London. 1926 transferred to Cowasjee, Dinshaw & Bros, Aden. 4 October 1942 sunk in collision in Red Sea.

Adler (1900)

Built: 1900 by Bremer Vulkan, Bremen
Length: 235ft 6in
Breadth: 31ft 1in
Depth: 19ft 0in
Gross tonnage: 1,304
Machinery: 3-cylinder triple expansion
Power: 136nhp/850ihp
Speed: 11kt
Hull: 2 decks, three-island type
Passengers: 18 first, 24 second, 84 third
History: Launched 31 March and delivered in May. After World War 1 she was surrendered to Shipping Controller, London; repurchased 1921. 1938 renamed *Aar* to allow name to pass to new ship. Sold to F. Italo Croce, Genoa; renamed *Ezilda Croce*. May 1950 scrapped at Savona.

Bussard

Built: 1906 by Henry Koch, Lubeck
Length: 245ft 9in
Breadth: 36ft 2in
Depth: 19ft 4in
Gross tonnage: 1,494
Machinery: 3-cylinder triple expansion
Power: 152nhp (2 boilers)
Speed: 11kt
Hull: 1 deck and spar deck, three-island type
History: Launched 2 June, trials 11 July. 1917 sold to Leonhardt & Blumberg, Hamburg; renamed *Otto Leonhardt*. 1924 resold locally to K.W.E. Sturm; renamed *Brigitte Sturm*. 1928 sold to Heckmann & Sturm, Hamburg. 1929 sold to August Bolten, Hamburg. 1936 sold to Richard Borchardt; renamed *Richard Borchardt*. January 1938 missing when bound Nordenham–Pasajes.

Schwan (1907)

Built: 1907 by AG Neptun, Rostock
Length: 240ft 8in
Breadth: 33ft 9in
Depth: 11ft 8in
Gross tonnage: 1,212
Machinery: 3-cylinder triple expansion
Power: 161nhp/1,000ihp (2se boilers, 210lb/sq in)
Speed: 11kt
History: Launched 11 September, trials November. After World War 1 surrendered to Shipping Controller, London but returned 1921. 1938 renamed *Pinguin* to allow name to pass to new ship. April 1949 reinstated Bremen–Hull service. April 1954 broken up by W. Ritcher, Hamburg.

Reiher (1909)

Built: 1909 by Bremer Vulkan, Bremen
Length: 220ft 7in
Breadth: 32ft 5in
Depth: 13ft 7in
Gross tonnage: 1,045
Machinery: 3-cylinder triple expansion
Power: 179nhp
Speed: 11kt

The Seebeck-built *Mowe* of 1913 followed the *Schwalbe/Schwan* line of development and had accommodation for about 40 passengers. Like most Argo ships she was interchangeable between the UK and Baltic services and is shown here in Stettin in NDL colours sometime during the period 1925–33. Note her mix of derricks and four deck cranes.
Author's collection

Hull: 1 deck, short foc'sle and combined bridge/poop.
History: Launched 5 October, trials 4 November 1938. Renamed *Flamingo* to allow name to pass to new ship. 1939 requisitioned, becoming Scout V-109. December 1940 became *Sperrbrecher 39* (blockade runner), later No 139. 13 February 1945 mined west of Lindesnaes on northeast coast of Denmark.

Möwe

Built: 1913 by G. Seebeck AG, Geestemunde
Length: 241ft 5in
Breadth: 36ft 0in
Depth: 18ft 9in
Gross tonnage: 1,251
Machinery: 3-cylinder triple expansion
Power: 220nhp/1,350ihp (2 boilers)
Speed: 11kt
Hull: 2 decks, three-island type
Passengers: About 40
History: Launched December 1912, trials March 1913. On London run before World War 1, Baltic services afterwards. End 1926 sold to Cie des Messageries Maritimes; renamed *Marechal Gallieni*. Based at Diego Suarez for Madagascar coastal feeder service. 24 September 1942 seized by UK government; returned 1945. Traded Madagascar–East African ports before returning to former coastal service. September 1954 sold for scrapping at Bombay.

Greif, Phönix

Built: 1913 by Stettiner Oderwerke, Stettin
Length: 235ft 0in
Breadth: 32ft 0in
Depth: 13ft 0in
Gross tonnage: 1,165/1,116
Machinery: 3-cylinder triple expansion
Power: 205nhp/1,250ihp
Speed: 11½kt
Hull: 1 deck, raised foc'sle and combined bridge and poop
Passengers: About 44
History: Launched December 1912/28 January 1913; trials February/12 April. Bremen–Hull service before World War 1.

Greif seized 1914 by USSR at Reval; returned 1918. 1919 surrendered to Shipping Controller, London. 1920 sold to Tyne-Tees SS Co; renamed *Dunstanburgh* (12 passengers). Leith–Hamburg service. 1938 sold Stanhope SS Co (Manager J.A. Billmeir); renamed *Stanburgh*. 4 November explosion in petrol cargo, stranded off Sete bound Barcelona. Refloated and towed to Toulon for scrapping.

Phönix requisitioned 1914, becoming Scout V-106, later *Sperrbrecher 36* then *136*. November 1942 mined off St Nazaire; raised. 22 November 1944 stranded near Memel.

Habicht, Adler (1938)

Built: 1938 by Nordseewerke, Emden/Lubecker Maschinenbau, Lubeck
Length: 245ft 4in/249ft 2½in
Breadth: 39ft 6in
Depth: 12ft 5in
Gross tonnage: 1,377/1,494
Machinery: 2-cylinder compound with LP turbine by A.G. Weser
Boilers: Coal-fired
Power: c1,250ihp
Speed: 12kt
Hull: Short raised foc'sle and bridge deck
Passengers: c40
History: Launched 8 March/16 March 1938;

Above left:
The compact looking *Habicht* **and her three near sisters marked Argo Line's return to large-scale passenger carrying in 1938, accommodation being provided for about 40. An evolved** *Mowe* **with extra hatch between bridge deck and mainmast, she was twice bombed and sunk during World War 2.**
Laurence Dunn collection

Left:
Adler **lasted until 1984 as the Greek school ship** *Savilco,* **moored at Paleon Faliron near Piraeus. Comparison with the view of** *Habicht* **shows the extent of alterations made in 1953 during her conversion to a motor ship by Wm H. Muller.**
Author

delivered May. Bremen–Hull service (twice weekly). *Habicht* World War 2 blockade pilot *Kiel No 4*, later *H-409* then *DC-09*. December 1944 bombed and burnt out in Libau; raised and towed to Kiel. May 1945 sunk in air raid. 1946 raised; surrendered to Holland. 1947 acquired by N.V. Maats Zeevaart, Rotterdam. 1948 entered service as *Hagno* (manager Hudig & Veder). 1954 sold to Smith's Coasters Pty Ltd, Durban; renamed *Induna*. 1961 laid-up at Durban; scrapped December 1962. *Adler* World War 2; Seedienst Ostpreussen at first, then accommodation ship. August 1944 to May 1945 ambulance carrier in Baltic. Surrendered to UK; renamed *Empire Coningsby* (manager GSN Co) and taken to Hull. 1946 sold to Wm H. Muller & Co, Rotterdam; renamed *Margeca*. 1947 renamed *Wickenburgh*. 1953 rebuilt as motor ship; new funnel, white hull. 1963 sold Scandinavian–Baltic & Mediterranean Shipping Corp, Piraeus (manager: F. Georgopoulis & A. Athandssiades); renamed *Nissos Thassos*. 1970 renamed *Savilco*. 1979 sold Pythagora Cia Naviera SA; static school of navigation at Paleon Faliron. October 1984 reported sold to Greek shipbreakers at Eleusis.

Schwan (1938), *Reiher* (1938)

Built: 1938 by Howaldtswerke, Kiel
Length: 245ft 2in
Breadth: 38ft 6in
Depth: 12ft 5in
Gross tonnage: 1,311/1,304

Machinery: 2-cylinder compound with LP turbine by A.G. Weser
Boilers: Coal-fired.
Power: c1,250ihp
Speed: 12kt
Hull: Short raised foc'sle and bridge deck.
Passengers: c40
History: Launched June/July 1938; delivered July/September. Bremen–UK service. *Schwan* World War 2 Scout V-101. October 1940 became blockade runner *Sperrbrecher 31*. 1942 rebuilt Aarhus, later *Sperrbrecher 131*. September 1947 surrendered to UK and taken to Grimsby. 1948 sold to Atkinson & Pickett Ltd, Hull and towed to Grangemouth. 27 December badly damaged by fire during refit. September 1949 sold to Currie Line Ltd, Leith; renamed *Rhineland*. Re-entered service in September with mainmast at aft end of bridge deck and kingpost on poop. 1956 sold to D. Hendry & Son, Glasgow; renamed *Herriesbrook*. Sold to Smith's Coasters Pty Ltd, Durban; renamed *Inyoni* 1957. September 1961 broken up at Isipingo, Natal. *Reiher* 1939 acted as World War 1 auxiliary minelayer *Koningin Louise* in unfinished film (dummy second funnel and false superstructure). World War 2 pilot ship, later minesweeper depot ship. 27 December 1946 badly damaged by fire in Copenhagen. 1948 sold to Alpina Transports & Affretements SA. Antwerp; renamed *Alpina*. 1952 sold Cie Charles Le Borgne, Antwerp; renamed *Augustin le Borgne*. 22 August fire in cargo. 1956 sold Compania Nav Francisco N, Puerto Cortez; renamed *Francis N*. 1957 rebuilt as motor ship. 1958 sold to Hanimex, Hamburg (Manager H. Vogemann). October 1959 sold to Erich Drescher, Hamburg. November sold to Compania Nav Paolina SA, Beirut; renamed *Fulchera*. 1968 broken up in Italy.

Fasan started life as a 10-passenger cargo ship in 1936, becoming a World War 2 hospital ship until sunk during an air raid. A postwar rebuild incorporating a new bow section resulted in a changed appearance with new tapered funnel and accommodation for over 40 passengers.
Laurence Dunn collection

Fasan

Built: 1936 by Howaldtswerke AG, Kiel
Length: 243ft 8in
Breadth: 38ft 5in
Depth: 15ft 1in
Gross tonnage: 1,410
Machinery: 2-cylinder compound with LP turbine
Boilers: Coal-fired
Power: 1,100ihp
Speed: 12kt
Hull: Short raised foc'sle
Passengers: Over 40
History: Launched 17 April 1936; trials June. 1,275gt/10 passengers. World War 2 naval hospital ship. 27 July 1943 sunk during air raid at Hamburg. 1944 raised but again sunk during air raid on 21 November. 1946 raised minus forepart. December 1949 re-entered service after complete rebuild by A.G. Weser, Bremen (new forepart and increased passenger accommodation). Bremen–Hull, later Baltic trade. 1958 sold Hellenic Mediterranean Lines; renamed *Media*. Marseilles–Eastern Mediterranean ports (75 uniclass, 78 dormitory, 87 deck passengers). 1968 broken up in Italy.

Adler was one of West Germany's first postwar deliveries following the lifting of building restrictions in 1950. She and her two sisters had simple but homely accommodation for up to 60 passengers and differed from the prewar ships in their altered masting arrangement, lower bridge and streamlined funnel. Both *Adler* and *Falke's* powerful diesels were rumoured to have been originally intended for U-boats. *Mowe*, the last of the trio, was steam driven, with a correspondingly taller funnel.
Laurence Dunn

Adler, Falke, Möwe (1950)

Built: 1950 by A.G. Weser; Seebeck, Bremerhaven
Length: 248ft 7in
Breadth: 39ft 6in
Gross tonnage: 1,461 (Mowe 1,437)
Machinery: 2 x 6-cylinder MAN diesels (*Mowe* 4-cylinder compound with LP turbine by Ottensener Eisenwerk AG, Hamburg
Boilers: Oil-fired, 1,500lb/sq in (*Mowe* only)
Power: 3,000bhp (*Mowe* 1,250shp)
Speed: 14kt (*Mowe* 12½kt)
Hull: Short raised foc'sle and bridge deck
Passengers: 60 (*Mowe* 56)
History: Launched June/22 July/September; trials 17 August (max 17 kt)/30 September/25 November. Bremen, Hamburg–Hull, London (from July 1952) and Finland (July 1952 *Adler* carried 62-strong German Olympic equestrian team to Helsinki). 1954 *Adler* Bremen–Leith fortnightly. Later *Mowe* mainly in Baltic trade. *Adler* and *Falke* bi-weekly Bremen–Hamburg–Hull (September 1963 joined by 12 passenger *Whitby Abbey*). February 1966 *Mowe* sold to Eckhardt & Co, Hamburg for scrap. September 1966 *Adler* and *Falke* withdrawn and sold to Dacema Lines Inc, Cebu; renamed *Athena* and *Demeter* and left Rotterdam for Manila 29 November and 5 January 1967. 1973 *Demeter* sold to Aboitiz Shipping Corp, Cebu (manager Cebu-Ormoc Ferry Inc); renamed *Emilia*. 9 November 1974 caught fire off Mindoro bound Manila–Ormoc, passengers evacuated and fire extinguished 10 but later beached at Batangas and abandoned as CTL. 1975 *Athena* renamed *Maligaya*. 1978 sold to Solid Shipping Corp, Manila. Scrapped 1979.

DFDS

Copenhagen/Esbjerg–Newcastle/Hull/Grimsby/
London/Antwerp/Dunkirk
1866–   Det Forenede Dampskibs-Selskab A/S
Funnel colours: Black with broad red band
   1967–   blue circle with white maltese cross
   added to red band

The well known Danish shipping company Det
Forenede Dampskibsselskab (United Steamship
Co or DFDS for short) was formed in Copenhagen
towards the end of 1866 by the amalgamation of
several Danish shipping concerns. Over the
succeeding years the company prospered and by the
turn of the century controlled one of the largest
fleets in the world.

One of the earliest services linked the Danish
capital with London but after the new port of
Esbjerg was completed in 1873, DFDS – anxious to
take part in the cattle export trade via this shorter
route – ordered a new paddle steamer from Gourlay
Bros. The 627-ton *Riberhuus* entered service
between Esbjerg and Thames Haven upon
completion in 1875, but she carried only a handful
of passengers.

Unsatisfactory lairage facilities at Thames Haven
led DFDS to approach the Great Eastern Railway
for permission to call at Harwich instead;
agreement was reached and *Riberhuus* sailed for
the Essex port on 2 June 1880. Later that year the
new Parkeston Quay was completed and
thenceforward the Esbjerg service terminated
there.

In 1882 DFDS applied for a Gothenburg–
Harwich service but the proposal was rejected.
However, government backing in the shape of a
subsidy enabled the Esbjerg service to be increased
to three departures a week in 1889. Success was
such that in 1912 the subsidy was withdrawn.

DFDS made shipping history when the company
introduced *Parkeston,* the world's first short sea
passenger motor ship, to the Harwich run in 1925.
The sale of *Kronprinsesse Ingrid* in 1968 ended
DFDS' long and successful association with the
traditional North Sea passenger ship.

Koldinghuus . DFDS

Koldinghuus

Built: 1883 by Lobnitz & Co, Renfrew
Length: 276ft 2½in
Breadth: 30ft 1in
Depth: 14ft 0in
Gross tonnage: 1,069
Machinery: 4-cylinder compound oscillating
Power: 1,600ihp
Speed: 14kt
Hull: Iron
Passengers: c70 berths aft
History: Maiden voyage from Esbjerg 18 July,
1883. Reserve ship from 1901. Last (572nd)
crossing from Esbjerg 5 January 1903. Hulked
1904. Sold for scrap in Copenhagen August 1906.

N.J. Fjord, Ficaria, Primula

Built: 1896 by Lobnitz & Co, Renfrew
Length: 271ft 6in oa/260ft 4in bp
Breadth: 34ft 1in
Depth/draught: c15ft 0in/17ft 3in
Gross tonnage: 1,425/1,530/1,531
Machinery: 3-cylinder triple expansion
Boilers: 2
Power: 2,300ihp
Speed: 14kt
Hull: Steel, flush deck
Passengers: c70 first class, c300 emigrants
History: Launched 14 May/7 September/5
November 1896. Trial speed 15kt. *N.J. Fjord*
regular Esbjerg–Harwich service, sisters irregular –
Ficaria from 1903, *Primula* from 1907 after period

on Copenhagen–Newcastle service. World War 1 laid up, later tramping Denmark–UK. 1916 *N.J. Fjord* passed between UK and German fleets before Battle of Jutland. May 1917 *N.J. Fjord* torpedoed by U-boat in North Sea bound Blyth–Odense (with coal). 1922 *Primula* refitted (74 first, 26 second class passengers) for new weekly Esbjerg–Antwerp/Dunkirk service. *Ficaria* trading mainly in Baltic; 12 July 1932 laid up Esbjerg; November 1934 sold to Hughes Bolckow for scrapping at Blyth. February 1938 *Primula* sold to Clayton & Davie Ltd for scrapping at Dunston-on-Tyne.

J.C. La Cour

Built: 1901 by Elsinore Shipbuilding Co, Elsinore
Length: 270ft 7in
Breadth: 36ft 7in
Depth: 15ft 0in
Gross tonnage: 1,635
Machinery: 3-cylinder triple expansion
Power: 3,600ihp
Speed: 15kt
Hull: Steel, 1 deck and awning, short raised foc'sle
Passengers: 112 berths (76 first class)
History: Esbjerg–Harwich service. Laid-up Denmark during World War 1, afterwards mainly relief ship but occasionally on Copenhagen–Oslo service. Final call Harwich 1931. Laid up Esbjerg. 1933 sold to Blyth Shipbreakers for scrap.

A.P. Bernstorff

Built: 1913 by Elsinore Shipbuilding & Engineering Co, Elsinore
Length: 291ft 9in
Breadth: 41ft 8in
Depth/draught: 25ft 8in/17ft 3in
Gross tonnage: 2,316
Machinery: 4-cylinder triple expansion
Boilers: 4
Power: 3,300ihp
Speed: 15½kt
Hull: 2 decks, raised foc'sle
History: 12 August 1914 service suspended because of World War 1. Traded to Manchester and UK west coast ports; laid up; Denmark–Norway service. Postwar charter to UK government (six weeks) for repatriation of PoWs. First commercial voyages Copenhagen–Hull, then twice weekly Esbjerg–Grimsby. 1919 resumed Harwich run. 1920 Government charter to carry guests to Abenra Fjord to accompany King Christian X and Queen

Completed at Elsinore in 1913, the 2,316-ton *A.P. Bernstorff* reflected advances made in shipbuilding since the delivery of *J.C. La Cour* 12 years previously. Early success was cut short by World War 1, which also killed plans for a sister. She went on to survive both wars, including a period as a German ambulance carrier in World War 2, and was eventually scrapped in 1957, after a successful career of 40 years during which she served on several North Sea routes.
Laurence Dunn collection

Alexandrine for return of South Jutland celebrations. End 1922 assisted rudderless Norwegian steamer *Modig* in North Sea. 1925 major overhaul by Frederikshavn Vaerft & Flydedok; new Howden forced draught boilers (15% coal saving). Later transferred to weekly Esbjerg–Antwerp/Dunkirk service (84 first, 60 second class passengers). Laid up in Esbjerg World War 2. Early 1943 seized by German forces; 20 December 1944–May 1945 served as ambulance carrier *Renate*. 1946 postwar refit then relief sailings Harwich service. 2 February 1947 rescued 19 survivors from Danish steamer *J.C. Jacobsen* in North Sea. 1949 replaced by *Kronprinsesse Ingrid;* transferred to new weekly Copenhagen–Newcastle service. September 1950 used as floating hotel off Leith by Copenhagen Municipal Orchestra for Edinburgh Festival. 1952 Esbjerg–Newcastle. 1957 withdrawn and sold to Eisen und Metal KG for demolition in Hamburg (commenced June).

Power: 2,600ihp
Speed: 14kt
Hull: Steel deck, short raised foc'sle
Passengers: 112 first, 78 second
History: Built with sister *Kong Haakon* for new service Stettin–Copenhagen–Oslo. Early 1920 transferred to Esbjerg–Harwich service (134 first, 68 second, 220 third class passengers). Replaced by *Parkeston* and resumed original service. Laid up World War 2, 1942 German troop transport. Summer 1945 chartered by UK Government for trooping and repatriation duties: Tilbury–Ostend/ Hook of Holland. 1947 sold to Bore Line, Abo/ Turku; renamed *Bore II.* Refitted with two small funnels, yellow hull; Finland–Aland–Sweden service. 1965 sold to Finland Steamship Co; renamed *Silja II.* Summer 1966 Helsinki–Travemunde service (62 first class, 138 tourist, 30 deck passengers). Laid up and sold June 1967 to Helsingin Romuliike for scrap.

Dronning Maud

Built: 1906 by Burmeister & Wain, Copenhagen
Length: 273ft 0in
Breadth: 38ft 2½in
Depth/draught: 22ft 9in/16ft 9in
Gross tonnage: 1,779
Machinery: 4-cylinder triple expansion
Boilers: 4

Although built for DFDS' new Stettin–Copenhagen–Oslo service in 1906 *Dronning Maud* (originally with flush deck) spent several years on the Harwich run in the 1920s, thereby justifying her inclusion in this book. A neat little ship, she served for a while as a German troop transport in World War 2 before returning to the North Sea to fulfil a postwar charter by the British Government for repatriation duties. Sold to Finland in 1947 she sailed the waters of the Baltic until broken up in 1967 at the ripe old age of 61. *Author's collection*

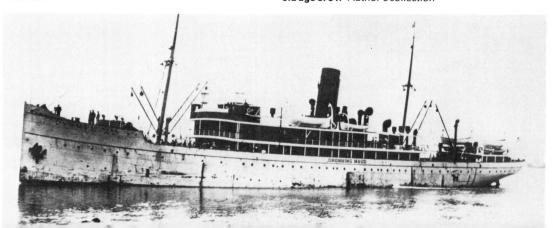

Parkeston, Jylland, Esbjerg, England

Built: 1925/1926/1929/1932 by Elsinore
Shipbuilding & Engineering Co
Length: 321ft 0in oa/306ft 4in bp
Breadth: 44ft 2½in
Depth/draught: 28ft 6in/17ft 4in
Gross tonnage: 2,762 (*England* 2,750hp)
Machinery: 2 x 6-cylinder B&W diesels
Power: 3,800bhp
Speed: 16kt
Hull: Short raised foc'sle
Passengers: 124 first, 60 third (plus 20 cars)
History: *Parkeston* maiden voyage Esbjerg–
Harwich 8 October 1925 (16½kt average)
inaugurated daily service. *Jylland* m/v 26 June 1926.
Esbjerg m/v 25 April 1929. *Esbjerg* in collision with
Dutch *Prinses Juliana* off Harwich 29 June 1935.
Jylland in collision with THV *Patricia* at Harwich 15
February 1936. Proposed Copenhagen–Leith–
Iceland service by *Parkeston* cancelled because of
World War 2. All laid up Esbjerg; *Esbjerg* and
Parkeston later moved to Frederikshavn then all to
Copenhagen (south Harbour). Seized by German
navy 1 January 1944, renamed and taken Germany
for trooping/target ship duties. *England* as
Grenadier bombed and sunk at Kiel 27 August
1944; raised after war, towed Flensburg for engine
removal, then Odense for scrapping. *Jylland* as
Musketier sunk by dive-bombers off Travemünde
10 May 1945 (c800 refugees lost). *Parkeston* as
Pionier and *Esbjerg* as *Kurassier* Allied prizes at
Lubeck 1945; returned Denmark but *Esbjerg* mined
25 July 1945 about seven miles from Stevns Light en
route Copenhagen. Raised 1946 and sold 1947 to
Cia Trasmediterranea, Spain. Rebuilt as *Ciudad de
Ibiza* (3,059gt, 405 passengers) for Barcelona–Ibiza
service. Later Barcelona–Menorca. 1978 sold Cia
D.Ricardo Villanova, Valencia for scrap. *Parkeston*
reopened Esbjerg–Harwich service (weekly at first)
4 December 1945. May 1947 stern damaged by mine
en route for dry-docking at Elsinore. 1952

Externally, the 2,762-ton *Parkeston* was an obvious
development of *A.P. Bernstorff* but her completion at
Elsinore in 1925 created a sensation for she was the
world's first short-sea passenger ship to be motor
driven. Her two B&W diesels brought considerable fuel
savings – 18 tons of oil per day compared with *A.P.
Bernstorff's* 55 tons of coal – and engine room staff were
reduced by 10. Her unique place in the annals of shipping
history was further enhanced by a 50-year career and she
is pictured here in her postwar state with extra
accommodation aft. Note also the extension to her
original short funnel. *Laurence Dunn collection*

transferred Esbjerg–Newcastle service (274
passengers). April 1953 returned Harwich service
for about a year in place of fire damaged *Kronprins
Frederik* (sailings reduced to five per week).
September 1964 sold Akers MV, Oslo; worker
accommodation ship *Aker II*. 1975 sold Paul
Bergsoe for scrap (commenced Masnedo 15
September).

Kronprins Frederik, Kronprinsesse Ingrid

Built: 1940–46/1949 by Elsinore Shipbuilding Co,
Elsinore
Length: 375ft 0in oa/353ft 9in bp
Breadth: 49ft 9in
Depth/draught: 25ft 10in/18ft 6in
Gross tonnage: 3,985/3,968
Machinery: 2 x 10-cylinder B&W diesels
Power: 8,400bhp
Speed: 20½kt/21kt
Hull: Long raised foc'sle merged into
superstructure; 2 decks
Passengers: 138 first, 146 second (plus 33 cars)
History: *Kronprins Frederik* launched by namesake
20 June 1940 (originally two sisters proposed).
Moved Sydhamn, Copenhagen and stripped of
valuable fittings for safekeeping during World War
2. May 1945 towed to Elsinore for completion. May

Although launched in June 1940, six years passed before the sleek-lined *Kronprins Frederik* made her debut. A development of *Kronprins Olav* built for the Oslo service in 1937, she introduced new standards of comfort and elegance to the England route. Note how the foc'sle has been extended to merge into the streamlined superstructure, also the extensive use of glazed screening between heavy upright stanchions. A speed of over 20kt was provided by twin B&W diesels, reducing the passage time to 18–19 hours.
Author's collection

1946 trials; m/v June with sponsor aboard. *Kronprinsesse Ingrid* launched 17 January 1948 by Princess Margrethe. All-welded hull. M/v 13 June 1949. Cost at £600,000 approximately double *Kronprins Frederick's*. 1951 *Kronprinsesse Ingrid* landed Danish Royal Family at Dover for wedding of Prince Philip/Princess Elizabeth. *Kronprins Frederick* 19 April 1953 electrical fire at Harwich, capsized outwards from quay, approximately one-third of accommodation gutted. Raised 26 August and towed to Elsinore 11 September. Repairs took approximately eight months. *Kronprinsesse Ingrid* 20 April 1954 fire when 18miles north of Smith's Knoll, extinguished. April 1964 *Kronprins Frederick* replaced by new car ferry *England* after 1,430 crossings; transferred Esbjerg–Newcastle service and first arrival Tyne 27 June inaugurated new passenger terminal at Newcastle Quay. *Kronprins Frederick* 1966 major refit, fitted with bow thruster and passive stabilising tanks; spring 1966 replaced *Kong Olav* on Copenhagen–Faroes/Iceland service. December 1966 *Kronprinsesse Ingrid* withdrawn pending arrival car ferry *Winston Churchill;* transferred to Newcastle service summer 1967/68. 1969 sold to Costas Spyrou Latsis, Piraeus;

renamed *Mimika L.* Piraeus–Rhodes service (22 hours) via Mykonos, Patmos, Leros, Kalymnos, Kos. 1976 *Kronprins Frederick* sold Arab Navigators Co, Egypt; renamed *Patra*. Red Sea pilgrim trade. Lost by fire 24 December 1976 c50 miles north of Jeddah, bound Suez (102 lives lost). 1977 Costas Latsis failed, *Mimika L.* laid up. Sold to Dodekanissos Shipping Enterprises SA then Astir Shipping Enterprises; 1978 renamed *Alkyon* (Seagull). Piraeus–Rhodes service. Late 1980 sold to Dimitrios Ventouris SA, Piraeus. October 1983 laid up in Piraeus. 23 April 1984 sailed for Karachi; arrived 9 June for scrapping.

Kronprinsesse Ingrid followed her sister from Elsinore in 1949 though her cost at around £600,000 was almost double. Her slightly lower tonnage and marginal speed advantage were attributed to an all-welded hull, while external differences included longer bulwarks forward and modernised cranes aft. Following a spell on the Newcastle service she was sold to Greece in 1969, becoming the orange-funnelled *Mimika L* pictured here off Vouliagmeni on a return sailing from Rhodes to Piraeus. After giving over 35 years' service she ended her days at Gadani Beach in the summer of 1985.
Author

In addition to its main passenger services to Harwich and later Newcastle, DFDS also ran a number of other North Sea services on which passengers were carried. These emanated from Copenhagen or Esbjerg and up to the time of World War 1 were generally served by a variety of elderly cargo steamers with limited passenger accommodation. In 1921 new services were started between Esbjerg and London (Hay's Wharf) and Leith. At the same time sailings on the established Esbjerg–Humber route were increased to two per week and the original Copenhagen–London service was speeded up to a direct two-day passage via the Kiel canal. All these routes were operated by a number of cargo/passenger ships, the more important of which are detailed below.

Dagmar

Built: 1903 by R. Stephenson & Co Ltd, Newcastle
Length: 290ft 6in
Breadth: 40ft 0in
Depth/draught: 25ft 7in/19ft 5in
Gross tonnage: 2,387
Machinery: 3-cylinder triple expansion by Wallsend Slipway
Boilers: 2
Power: 1,900ihp
Speed: 12kt
Hull: 1 deck and awning deck, raised foc'sle and bridge deck
Passengers: 27 first, 20 second (as built 36/18/200)
History: Originally built as *Irkutsk*, and with two Caledon built sisters *Kurgan* and *Wologda* ran in the DFDS-controlled Lassman Bros service between St Petersburg and London. In 1910 passed to the management of Helmsing and Grimm, Riga

The passenger/cargo steamer *Dagmar* was formerly *Irkutsk*, one of three Russian registered sisters built for the Leningrad–London butter trade in 1903.
Laurence Dunn collection

and renamed *Imperator Nicolai II*. Taken over by DFDS in 1920 and renamed *Dagmar*. Served mainly on the Copenhagen–London run and became a war loss in 1941.

Flora

Built: 1909 by Burmeister & Wain, Copenhagen
Length: 253ft 6in
Breadth: 34ft 7in
Depth/draught: 16ft 9in/16ft 1in
Gross tonnage: 1,218
Machinery: 3-cylinder triple expansion
Boilers: 2
Power: 1,400ihp
Speed: 12kt
Hull: 2 decks, three-island type
Passengers: 26 first, 4 third
History: After World War 1 ran from Esbjerg to Grimsby and later London. On Copenhagen–Newcastle route in early 1930s. Taken over by UK Ministry of Shipping in 1940 and renamed *Flora II* under Ellerman's Wilson management. 2 August 1942 torpedoed by U.254 south of Iceland while on a voyage from Reykjavik to Hull.

Margrethe

Margrethe, broadly similar in design to *Dagmar,* started life as the DFDS emigrant steamer *Moskov.* Renamed in 1925, she became a familiar site in UK east coast ports over the next 30 years. *Laurence Dunn collection*

Built: 1914 by Elsinore Shipbuiding & Engineering Co Ltd
Length: 380ft 8in
Breadth: 40ft 6in
Depth/draught: 25ft 5in/20ft 3in
Gross tonnage: 2,441
Machinery: 3-cylinder triple expansion
Boilers: 3
Power: 1,500ihp
Speed: 12kt
Hull: 3 decks, raised foc'sle
Passengers: 10 first, 66 second (as built 10/78/628)
History: Originally built as *Moskov* for emigrant trade. After World War 1 ran from Danzig to

Vidar, a World War 1 completion, served the Polish emigrant trade after the Armistice but later became a regular North Sea trader. Note the difference in design from *Margrethe*. *Laurence Dunn collection*

Copenhagen or Southampton with *Vidar*. Renamed *Margrethe* in 1925 and put on Esbjerg–Grimsby service. From 1927 to start of World War 2 on Copenhagen–London service. After war on London, Antwerp services. Sold to Eisen und Metall KG Lehr & Co for breaking at Bremerhaven in April 1959.

Vidar

Built: 1915 by Burmeister & Wain, Copenhagen
Length: 252ft 8in
Breadth: 37ft 0in
Depth/draught: 16ft 10in/17ft 3in
Gross tonnage: 1,353
Machinery: 3-cylinder triple expansion
Boilers: 2
Power: 1,600ihp
Speed: 13½kt
Hull: 2 decks, well-deck type
Passengers: 31 first, 4 third
History: After World War 1 used as an emigrant carrier between Danzig and either Copenhagen or Southampton. Later ran from Esbjerg to Grimsby but in 1930s was mainly on Esbjerg–London

service. Bombed on 30 January 1940 with the loss of 15 lives on a voyage from Newcastle to Esbjerg. Torpedoed and sunk 31 January 1940 by U.21, c37 miles east of Duncansby Head bound Newcastle-Esbjerg, 15 lost.

Hroar

Built: 1923 by Fredrikhavns Vaerft & Flydedok A/S
Length: 253ft 8in
Breadth: 37ft 2½in
Depth: 16ft 9in
Gross tonnage: 1,401
Machinery: 3-cylinder triple expansion
Boilers: 2
Power: 196nhp
Speed: 13½kt
Hull: 2 decks, well-deck type
Passengers: 27 first, 12 second
History: The only ship of this type built for DFDS between the wars, and was the opposite number of Ellerman Wilson's *Spero* with which she generally alternated on the Copenhagen–Hull service. Occasionally on other routes such as Copenhagen–Le Havre in 1927 and Esbjerg–Grimsby in 1930. Survived air attack on 1 February 1940; later laid up in Copenhagen. After war again on Hull service with occasional visits to London interspersed with periods in Baltic trade. Laid up in Copenhagen 6 February 1960 and broken up by Bruges Shipbreaking Co in May.

Hroar, with accommodation for about 40 passengers, was the only ship of her type built for DFDS between the wars. She started life on the Copenhagen–Hull run and is seen here on one of her infrequent visits to London after World War 2. Designwise she was a development of *Vidar*. *Laurence Dunn collection*

Thule Line/Swedish Lloyd

Gothenburg–Granton/London/Harwich
1870–1916   Angfartygs Aktiebolaget Thule
1869–1978   Fornyade Angfartygs Aktiebolaget
   Svenska Lloyd
Funnel colours: White with black top and gold 5
   pointed star on blue disc

Angfartygs Aktiebolaget Thule (Thule Steamship Co) was formed in Gothenburg on 23 March 1870 by a group of local businessmen headed by August Leffler. The new company's first ships were the wooden, Swedish-built *Ingeborg* and the iron steamer *Frithjof*, built at Newcastle. A further steamer, *Kung Ring,* was the first to adopt the later familiar white funnel with its distinctive gold star set on a blue circle.

The Thule Line ships traded between Gothenburg and the Scottish port of Granton near Leith. The choice of the latter was forced upon them as Thos Wilson & Son was too strong to allow competition into Hull, and London was already served by J.W. Wilson, an Englishman resident in Gothenburg, who had started a live cattle export business in the mid-1860s.

In 1879 Thule took delivery of its first passenger steamer named *Bele,* and after the Company's acquisition of Wilson's 'London Line' and its ships in 1882 several newer and larger ships were added to this run. 1910 saw the inauguration of a summer call for passengers at Harwich, but six years later during World War 1 Thule Line was absorbed by

Fornyade Angfartygsakt Svenska Lloyd (Swedish Lloyd) which was anxious to obtain a stake in the North Sea passenger business.

The Company's turbine sisters *Britannia* and *Suecia* of 1929 set new standards and these were followed by two larger post-World War 2 passenger ships, the diesel *Saga* and turbine *Patricia.* However, increasing air traffic led to the latters' disposal in the mid-1950s leaving the older pair to continue until the arrival of new car ferries in 1966.

Bele

Built: 1879 by Motala Co, Gothenburg
Length: 231ft 10in
Breadth: 30ft 7in
Depth: 16ft 2in
Gross tonnage: 1,342
Machinery: 2-cylinder compound
Boilers: 2se, 70lb/sq in
Power: 900ihp
Speed: 12kt
Hull: Steel, flush deck, 1 deck and spar deck
Passengers: 30 first amidships, 12 second aft
History: Launched October 1879. M/v Gothenburg–Granton. 1882 transferred to London (Millwall Dock) service. 1892 replaced by *Thule* and returned to Granton service. 1916 to Swedish Lloyd. July 1921 lost off west coast of Greenland.

Thule Line's first passenger steamer *Bele* was at the time of her construction in 1879 one of the first ships to come from a Swedish shipyard. Her initial service was between Gothenburg and Granton (Edinburgh) – Wilson Line competition being too strong to allow the use of Hull, whilst London was already served by the ships of Gothenburg-based J.H. Wilson. The latter's 'London Line' ships were acquired by Thule in 1882 and *Bele* was moved south. *Author's collection*

Thorsten – a steel version of *Bele* with raised foc'sle and bridge deck – joined the newly-acquired London service in 1882. She could carry over 50 passengers, mainly in first class, and alternated on weekly sailings with the earlier ship, calling at Tilbury during the summer months with cargo being handled at the traditional Blackwall berth. During World War 1 she was captured by another former North Sea passenger ship, *Vienna*, then operating as the German navy raider *Meteor*, but was later released on account of her neutrality.
World Ship Society

Thorsten

Built: 1882 by Motala Co, Gothenburg
Length: 262ft 2½in oa/248 ft 7in bp
Breadth: 32ft 4½in
Depth: 16ft 4in
Gross tonnage: 1,666
Machinery: 2-cylinder compound
Boilers: 2se, 70lb/sq in
Power: 1,600ihp
Speed: 12kt
Hull: Steel, part iron beams, raised foc'sle and bridge deck
Passengers: 40 first amidships, 15 second aft
History: Gothenburg–London service. 1909 replaced by *Saga* and transferred to Granton service. 1916 to Swedish Lloyd; 16 June captured by German auxiliary cruiser *Meteor* (ex-*Vienna*), later released. 1921 sold to Hans Diedrich Schmidt (manager A. Schmidt), Pernau. 1925 scrapped.

Thule

Built: 1892 by Messrs Wigham Richardson, Low Walker, Tyneside
Length: 282ft 5in
Breadth: 37ft 8in
Depth: 15ft 9in
Gross tonnage: 1,969
Machinery: 3-cylinder triple expansion
Boilers: 2se, 160lb/sq in
Power: 2,760ihp
Speed: 14kt
Hull: Steel, spar deck, raised foc'sle and bridge deck
Passengers: 50 first, 25 second
History: Launched 29 February 1892; trials 26 May. Gothenburg–London service. May 1910 Harwich (Parkeston Quay) call (summer only) inaugurated. 1916 to Swedish Lloyd. 1920 extensive refit –

The British-built *Thule* of 1892 replaced *Bele* on the London run. A development of *Thorsten* she was appreciably larger and was propelled by triple expansion instead of compound engines. In 1910 she and *Balder* inaugurated a summer call for passengers at Parkeston Quay, thus shortening the journey to Gothenburg, although DFDS had failed to get permission to run on this route as far back as 1882. Rebuilt in 1920 with new bridge and enlarged boat deck, she later ran to the Tyne before donning Italian colours in 1925, and was finally lost in her 50th year during World War 2.
World Ship Society

Right:
Glasgow-built for Thule's Granton service in 1898, the stiff-looking *Balder* could be described as a modernised *Bele*. Main structural differences were a short well-deck forward hidden by high bulwarks, a repositioned foremast, and two pairs of deck cranes.
Author's collection

Below right:
Following an extensive rebuild in 1930 *Balder* became the almost new-looking *Northumbria* and traded regularly to Newcastle's Swedish Wharf until seized by the Germans in Norway in 1940. Postwar passenger sailings to the Tyne were resumed in the summers of 1949 and 1950 by the chartered Svea steamer *Ragne* (1919). *Laurence Dunn collection*

superstructure enlarged and modernised. August re-instated Harwich call with *Balder*. c1921 transferred to Newcastle service (inaugurated 1920). 1925 sold to Ernesto Fassio & C. Villain; renamed *Franca Fassio*. Weekly Genoa–Barcelona service. July 1929 owners re-registered as Villain & Fassio. 1935/36 chartered to Tirrenia Co to replace tonnage requisitioned for Abyssinian War. 4 October 1940 torpedoed by RN submarine off Capo Noli.

Balder/Northumbria

Built: 1898 by Messrs Blackwood & Gordon, Port Glasgow
Length: 246ft 2in
Breadth: 34ft 1in
Depth: 14ft 0in
Gross tonnage: 1,378
Machinery: 3-cylinder triple expansion
Boilers: 2se, 170 lb/sq in
Power: 920ihp
Speed: 12kt

Hull: Steel, 1 deck, raised foc'sle and long bridge/poop
Passengers: 58 first amidships, 39 second aft, 12 third foc'sle
History: Launched 23 June 1898; trials 15 September (12½kt). Gothenburg–Granton service. 7 May 1910 transferred to Harwich/London service. 1 April 1911 collided with and sank *Malaga* (1,614gt) in fog off Gravesend. 1916 to Swedish Lloyd. August 1920 re-instated Gothenburg-Harwich service. 1923 transferred to Newcastle service (25 first, 28 second, 64 third class passengers). 1930 major refit: renamed *Northumbria*. Laid up during Depression. Summer 1938 re-instated Harwich calls. April 1940 seized by German forces in Norway. October 1943 bombed and sunk during Allied air raid on Gdynia.

Saga (1909)

Built: 1909 by Swan Hunter & Wigham Richardson, Tyneside
Length: 322ft 5in

121

The elegant Swan Hunter-built *Saga* was the last and largest passenger steamer built for Thule Line before the Swedish Lloyd take-over in 1916. A logical development of *Thule,* though about 1,000 tons larger and with a short hidden well-deck forward, she replaced *Thorsten* on the London run in 1909. Her original funnel was later heightened, and during the latter half of World War 1 she was chartered by Moore McCormack to inaugurate a New York–Rio passenger service. After a brief spell on the Newcastle run she resumed her London sailings and was sold to CGT in 1929. *World Ship Society*

Breadth: 46ft 2in
Depth/draught: 19ft 6in/20ft 1in
Gross tonnage: 2,809
Machinery: 3-cylinder triple expansion by Neptune Works
Boilers: 2se, 170 lb/sq in
Power: 4,000ihp
Speed: 15kt
Hull: 2 decks, raised foc'sle and long bridge/poop
Passengers: 85 first amidships, 55 second aft, 30 steerage
History: Launched 21 April 1909; trials June. Gothenburg–London service. 1916 to Swedish Lloyd; several voyages to east coast USA for grain. End 1916 chartered by Moore McCormack Line for new New York–Rio de Janeiro passenger service. 1919 returned Sweden and opened Gothenburg–Newcastle service before reverting London service. 1929 sold Compagnie Generale Transatlantique; renamed *Mayenne*. Mediterranean cargo service. 1943 war loss.

Patricia (acquired 1919)

Built: 1901 by Stabilimento Technico, Trieste
Length: 344ft 0in
Breadth: 43ft 0in
Depth/draught: 24ft 4in/20ft 6in

Gross tonnage: 2,981
Machinery: 3-cylinder triple expansion
Boilers: 5se, 180 lb/sq in
Power: 5,000ihp
Speed: 16½kt
Hull: Steel, 2 decks and awning deck, raised foc'sle and poop
Passengers: 76 first, 226 third
History: Built as *Mongolia* for Chinese Eastern Railway Co, Russia (sister *Manchuria*). Vladivostok/Port Arthur–Shanghai express service (120 passengers). Evaded Japanese navy February 1904 and reached Port Arthur. Hospital ship during siege. Surrendered Japan; renamed *Kanto Maru* (auxiliary). Later returned to Russia. 1910 transferred to Russian East Asiatic Co. May 1910 sold to Government of Western Australia for £40,000; refitted at Liverpool and renamed *Western Australia*. Fremantle–Wyndham service. 1915 ambulance carrier UK–France under Royal Mail

After adventurous service in Far Eastern and Australian waters the 3,000-ton *Patricia* was purchased by Swedish Lloyd in 1919 to augment the Company's newly-acquired passenger fleet. A major internal refit altered her little externally save for losing her original turtle-back foc'sle and receiving new boats in gravity davits. Initially on the Newcastle emigrant run, she was soon altered again for the London service on which she sailed for nine years before being sold to United Baltic Corporation and renamed *Baltavia*. *Author's collection*

then Union Castle management. 1917 exchanged PoWs between Leith and Copenhagen. Became troopship. 1919 sold to Swedish Lloyd for £90,000; renamed *Patricia*. Major refit – turtle-back foc'sle removed and boats raised. Inaugurated new Gothenburg–Newcastle emigrant service with *Saga*. Late 1920 transferred to London service (116 first, 434 second, 22 third class passengers). 1929 sold to United Baltic Corporation; renamed *Baltavia*. Pool of London–Baltic ports service (18 first, 60 second, 372 third class passengers). 1935 sold for scrap.

Suecia, Britannia

Built: 1929 by Swan Hunter & Wigham Richardson, Tyneside
Length: 376ft 4in oa/360ft 0in bp
Breadth: 50ft 1in
Depth/draught: 28ft 6in/20ft 4in
Gross tonnage: 4,216
Machinery: 3 Parsons SR geared turbines driving single shaft
Boilers: 4se, 220lb/sq in
Power: 5,700shp
Speed: 17½kt (19kt max)
Hull: 2 decks, raised foc'sle, ice strengthened
Passengers: 220 first class amidships, 45 second class aft

History: Launched Wallsend 24 January/Walker 27 February 1929. M/v Gothenburg–London 15 June/22 June. Thrice-weekly service summer, weekly winter. Passengers landed at Tilbury Stage, cargo at Millwall Dock. Later fitted with bilge keels to reduce rolling. 1937 converted to oil-firing by Eriksbergs. March 1937 *Suecia* sunk by newly launched tanker *Kollbjorg* while shifting berth in Eriksbergs yard, raised and re-entered service June. 29 December 1938 *Britannia* grounded in fog 1½ miles from Southend Pier. Both laid up World War 2 apart from one safe conduct voyage each. March 1945 requisitioned by UK Government for troop/refugee service London–Antwerp and Hull–Cuxhaven; released February 1946 and re-entered London service after short refit. Hulls painted white spring–autumn 1947. c1950 foc'sle extended to bridge. 1953 fitted with new third class smokeroom aft. 1954 major engine overhaul. 1956 passenger accommodation altered (127 first, 124 tourist, plus 92 summer dormitory). October 1966 sold to Hellenic Mediterranean Lines, Piraeus; renamed *Isthmia/Cynthia*. Service Marseilles – Genoa – Piraeus – Alexandria – Port Said – Beirut. 1970 *Isthmia* laid up Kynosura. 1972 sold to Turkish shipbreakers; delivered to Istanbul 2 November, demolition commenced at Kartal October 1973. 1973 *Cynthia* sold to Italian shipbreakers; arrived Savona 22 October, demolition commenced at Vado Ligure yard in November.

Left:
Suecia, first of two splendid Tyne-built turbine steamers to appear in 1929. Outwardly almost identical (her sister *Britannia* had a small curved plate where her bridge deck dropped to promenade deck level), the two ships' internal decor reflected the styling of the countries after which they were named. Originally heavy rollers until fitted with larger bilge keels, they soon established a popular following on their thrice-weekly summer and weekly winter sailings. *Author's collection*

Left:
A 1958 view of *Britannia* showing the extent of successive postwar alterations: extended foc'sle, removal of kingposts midships and aft, new boats abreast mainmast, and the addition of a third class smokeroom on the poop. Outstaying their younger and larger partners, the two sisters continued on the London run until 1966 when they were replaced by car ferries and sold to Greece. *John G. Callis*

Acquired from Greece in 1935 as *Patris II,* the second *Patricia* became a frequent visitor to the Thames during the summer months leading up to World War 2. Following a charter voyage to Italy for the Swedish navy in 1940 she was purchased by the latter and converted into a submarine depot ship at considerable cost. *Laurence Dunn*

Patricia (acquired 1935)

Built: 1926 by Swan Hunter & Wigham Richardson Ltd, Tyneside
Length: 345ft 0in
Breadth: 47ft 6in
Depth/draught: 26ft 3in/20ft 0in
Gross tonnage: 3,902
Machinery: 2 sets, 3-cylinder triple expansion
Boilers: 2se, 210lb/sq in
Power: 2,900ihp
Speed: 14kt
Hull: 2 decks and teak weatherdeck, raised foc'sle and long bridge/poop
Passengers: 112 first, 80 second, 52 third class
History: Launched 19 October 1925; trials 19 January 1926. Built as *Patris II* for Byron Steamship Co, London (Embiricos). Service Marseilles–Genoa–Piraeus–Alexandria–Cyprus–Beirut (100 first, 150 second class, plus deck passengers). 1935 sold to Swedish Lloyd; renamed *Patricia*. Refitted by Eriksbergs for Gothenburg–London summer service. 1940 chartered by Swedish Government to escort home four destroyers purchased from Italian navy. Stopped by RN and escorted into Kirkwall; released and returned to Sweden. Sold to Swedish navy for £117,500. May–September 1941 converted to submarine depot ship for up to nine submarines (500 berths) – cost of £387,500 caused storm of protest. Berthed Stockholm in summer, Karlskrona in winter. Often acted as target ship for destroyers, submarines and FPBs. Mid-1971 replaced by purpose-built *Alvsborg* and scrapped.

Saga (1946)

Built: 1940–46 by Gotaverken A/B (Hull by Lindholmen A/B), Gothenburg
Length: 420ft 10in oa/390ft 0in bp
Breadth: 55ft 4in
Depth/draught: 32ft 11in mld/18ft 11in
Gross tonnage: 6,458
Machinery: 4 x 8-cylinder Gotaverken diesels geared to one shaft
Power: 6,700bhp
Speed: 18½kt
Passengers: 160 first, 80 second, 100 third, plus 60 portable summer berths
History: Hull launched at Lindholmen yard under subcontract 10 October 1940. Completed Gotaverken May 1946. M/v Gothenburg–London 20 May. Largest ship to berth in Upper Pool (New Fresh Wharf). Accommodation partly air-conditioned. Designed with cruising in mind – first cruise to Bergen and Hardangerfjord Whitsun 1946. October 1946 left Gothenburg/London for

Although advance publicity pictures showed her with a black hull, the elegant 6,500-ton *Saga* had an all-white livery when finally delivered by Gotaverken in 1946, her construction having been delayed by the war. A motor ship, her general arrangement nevertheless owed a lot to the successful 1929-built sisters. Designed also with cruising in mind she had a comfortable 18kt service speed for a 35-hour North Sea passage, investigations having shown that any further increase in speed, if awkward arrival times were to be avoided, would require at least 24kt. After disposal she served CGT and later Bulgaria with little external change, save for a new promenade deck aft. *Laurence Dunn*

one-month cruise to Canaries, Casablanca, Southern Spain and Lisbon setting pattern for future winters. 1949 accommodation on shelter deck altered to single cabins with private facilities. December 1956 sold to Compagnie Generale Transatlantique because of air competition and increased running costs; renamed *Ville de Bordeaux*. Bordeaux–Casablanca service. 1960 transferred to Marseilles/Nice–Corsica service (181 first, 144 tourist, 66 fourth class passengers). 1964 sold to Navigation Maritime Bulgare, Varna; renamed *Nessebar*. Varna–Marseilles service, later Varna–Istanbul–Port Said. 1970s ownership changed to Balkanship State Passenger Lines (Balkanturist management). 1975 sold to Brodospas for scrap; arrived at Split 25 December.

Patricia (1951)

Built: 1951 by Swan Hunter & Wigham Richardson, Tyneside
Length: 454ft 2in oa
Breadth: 58ft 0in
Depth/draught: 31ft 9in mld/19ft 0in
Gross tonnage: 7,775
Machinery: 3 sets Parsons SR geared turbines geared to one shaft
Boilers: 2 Babcock & Wilcox watertube, 450lb/sq in
Power: 8,650shp
Speed: 19kt
Hull: Short raised foc'sle, 3 decks and promenade deck
Passengers: 166 first, 78 second, 100 third aft, plus 64 dormitory
History: Launched end 1950; completed 4 May 1951. Inaugurated new London Pier at Gothenburg on arrival. Short Whitsun cruise to Stockholm, inspected by King Gustav. Joined other three ships in Gothenburg–London service. Designed for cruising in winter – first cruise ex-Gothenburg 13 September 1951 for Tilbury and Mediterranean ports. Second cruise ex-Tilbury 8 October for Mediterranean including Istanbul (26 days, 7,750

Patricia, Swedish Lloyd's third Tyne-built passenger ship (coincidentally the third to hold the name *Patricia*), was at 7,775 tons the largest North Sea passenger steamer ever built when delivered by Swan Hunter in 1951. A development of *Saga* with raised foc'sle, she was arguably the better looking, her appearance being helped by the raising of her boats in gravity davits.
Skyfotos

miles). Winter 1952 experimental cruise to Bermuda. Winters 1953/54 and 1954/55 chartered to US for New York–West Indies cruising. Summer 1955 chartered to Hapag Lloyd Travel for two Mediterranean cruises because of decline in North Sea passenger traffic, but forced to return to Gothenburg to lay up because of Suez Crisis. 1957 sold to Hamburg Amerika Line; renamed *Ariadne*. Converted to full-time cruise ship (249 passengers) – foc'sle extended to bridge, fitted swimming pool and partial air-conditioning. First cruise 1958. December 1960 sold to McCormick Shipping Corp, Panama (manager, Atlantic Cruise Lines Inc) for 14-day Caribbean cruises. May 1961 sold to Ariadne Shipping Co Ltd, Monrovia (manager, Eastern Steamship Corp, Miami). 1963 major refit; fitted with full air-conditioning (239 passengers). Seven-day cruises Miami–Nassau/Jamaica, Miami–Puerto Rico/Virgin Is alternate weeks. 1969 sold to Ares Shipping Corporation. 1971 based at Port Everglades. Winter 1972/73 laid up; owners Minos Navigation Ltd. Summer 1973 sold to Bon Vivant Cruises SA (Chandris); renamed *Freeport II*. December 1973 to Piraeus for refit; renamed *Bon Vivant*. New mast and funnel, superstructure extended, interior altered for 380 passengers, gross tonnage 6,725. Chartered to Flagship Cruises for Caribbean cruising 1974/75. Spring 1976 began 14-day cruises from Venice–Greek Islands, Istanbul, Alexandria, Dubrovnik. 8 January 1977 arrived at Dubai as hotel ship for Dubai Maritime Corporation, Panama (Chandris). Laid up at Piraeus early 1978. Spring 1979 transferred to Gilda Maritime Corporation, Monrovia; renamed *Ariane*. Seasonal cruises from Piraeus. Laid up Piraeus 15 October 1979–spring 1982. Proposed series of seven-day cruises from Genoa cancelled; returned to lay up on 7 June.

Gotha Line

Gothenburg–Antwerp
1869–1971 Fornyede Angfartygs Aktiebolaget
    Gotha (F. Sternhagen)

Fornyede Angfartygs Aktiebolaget Gotha (Gotha Line) was established in Gothenburg in 1869 by F. Sternhagen. Services were introduced to Holland and Belgium but heavy ship losses forced the Company into liquidation. It was reconstituted in 1872 and the Rotterdam and Antwerp routes reinstated on a weekly basis.

In 1927 the cargo ship *Burgundia* was refitted to carry about 30 persons and 1930 saw the introduction of the purpose-built *Belgia*. Between them the two ships maintained a weekly summer service to Antwerp until 1939 when World War 2 brought it to a close.

Burgundia

Built: 1920 by Kockums M/V, Malmo
Length: 256ft 0in
Breadth: 38ft 4in
Depth/draught:: 16ft 5in/16ft 7in
Gross tonnage: 1,668
Machinery: 3-cylinder triple expansion
Boilers: 2se, 185lb/sq in
Power: 750ihp
Speed: 10kt

Belgia*. Col R.C. Gabriel collection*

Hull: 1 deck, three-island type
Passengers: c30
History: Originally cargo ship (sister *Ardennia* 1921). Converted 1927 to carry passengers. Gothenburg–Antwerp service (summer only). 28 March 1938 minor collision at Ymuiden. Last visit to Antwerp March 1940. 10 May 1942 bombed off Emden; repaired at Oskarshamn. 11 August 1944 damaged by mine in Weser. After World War 2 passenger accommodation removed; traded under G.A. Bratt management. 1961 sold to Jacobson Ltd, Malta; renamed *Jan Pawl*. 1964 sold to Malta Maritime Services Ltd; renamed *Robertina*. 1967 sold to Norsk Skipsopphugnings for scrap; demolition commenced Grimstad in October.

Belgia

Built: 1930 by Nya Varvs Oresund, Landskrona
Length: 286ft 7in
Breadth: 40ft 2½in
Depth: 16ft 8in
Gross tonnage: 2,023
Machinery: 4-cylinder compound by Akt
            Lindholmen-Motala
Boilers: 2
Power: 124nhp
Speed: 12kt
Hull: 2 decks, raised foc'sle
Passengers: c60
History: Delivered April 1930. M/v 16 May Gothenburg–Antwerp. Alternated with *Burgundia* on weekly schedule in summer. 11 December 1934 grounded in Scheldt; refloated. Laid up Gothenburg end October 1939; passenger service withdrawn. Later traded as cargo ship, last visit to Antwerp March 1940. Convoy service Clyde–Gibraltar then UK coasting. 26 January 1941 bombed and set on fire near Sunk L/V bound Thames–Sunderland, six crew lost. Burnt out and drifted ashore but later refloated and towed to Harwich. Patched up and towed to Tyne for repairs. August 1941 acquired by MoWT; renamed *Empire Bell* (1,741gt). 25 September 1942 torpedoed and sunk by U442 c90 miles southeast of Cape Kötlutangi, Iceland.

Fred Olsen Line

Oslo/Arendal–Grangemouth
1886–1901   Steamship Co Faerder Ltd
1901–   Fred Olsen & Co
Funnel colours: Black with red band and blue and
white houseflag

In 1886 the Oslo-based Steamship Company Faerder Ltd inaugurated a passenger/cargo service to Grangemouth with the 1875 Doxford built steamer *Faerder*. The venture was initially successful and two more steamers followed in quick succession from the Grangemouth Dockyard. In building these however the inexperienced company appears to have over-reached itself and help was sought from the young Fred Olsen who had already earned a reputation in shipping circles. He accepted and took over the running of Faerder Line's ships in 1903, thus beginning a long association with the North Sea passenger business.

Olsen built three more steamers for the Grangemouth service but finally abandoned it (after World War 1 losses) in favour of the more profitable Newcastle service (qv).

Scotland (1889), *Norway* (1891)

Built: 1889/1891 by Grangemouth Dockyard Co, Grangemouth
Length: 197ft 6in/202ft 8in
Breadth: 29ft 1in/30ft 1in
Depth: 14ft 6in to main deck
Gross tonnage: 889/919
Machinery: 3-cylinder triple expansion by Hawthorn & Co, Leith/Dunsmuir & Jackson, Govan
Boilers: 2 steel, 160lb/sq in
Power: 700/1,000ihp
Speed: 11½kt (contract)
Hull: Steel, 1 deck and awning deck
Passengers: c65 first, 25 second, a few third class and emigrants
History: Launched 14 June 1889/13 February 1891; trials 15 October 1889/12 May 1891. Accommodation amidships, electric light. Oslo–Grangemouth service. 1903 sold to Fred Olsen because of financial problems. 15 February 1904

The elegant *Norway* built at Grangemouth in 1891 was the second of two similar passenger ships for Faerder Line's Oslo–Grangemouth service. Flush-hulled with a pleasing sheer, she could accommodate about 100 passengers amidships and was electrically lit. Running costs proved too much for the two ships' owner and led to their disposal to the young and successful Fred Olsen, thereby starting his long association with the North Sea passenger business.
Col R.C. Gabriel collection

Olsen preferred continuity with ship names, so a new passenger steamer, the first built to his order, took on that of *Scotland* from the 1889-built ship when launched at Grangemouth in 1904. A larger development of *Norway,* her career came to a premature end when she was wrecked near Arendal in 1911. *Fred Olsen*

Scotland wrecked near Thorshavn bound Leith-Faroes. 1909 *Norway* sold to W. Eadie, Glasgow. Later sold to Luke Thomas & Co, Aden; renamed *Cetriana.* Later sold to Cowasjee Dinshaw Bros Ltd, Aden; East African service. July 1923 struck rock south of Kismayu when bound Kilindini–Kismayu and foundered. Passengers and crew saved and landed at Kilindini.

Scotland (1904)

Built: 1904 by Grangemouth Dockyard Co, Grangemouth
Length: 215ft 5in
Breadth: 32ft 1in
Depth: 20ft 10in
Gross tonnage: 1,104
Machinery: 3-cylinder triple expansion
Boilers: 2 steel
Power: 933ihp
Speed: 11kt
Hull: Steel, 1 deck and spar deck
History: Launched 17 May 1904. First passenger steamer built for Fred Olsen. Oslo–Grangemouth service. 22 April 1911 wrecked Langesund near Arendal in fog, bound Grangemouth. Passengers

and crew saved but ship and cargo, which included Norwegian exhibits for Glasgow Historical Exhibition, abandoned as total loss.

Norway (1910), *Scotland* (1912)

Built: 1910/1912 by Nylands Mek Verksted, Oslo
Length: 231ft 10in
Breadth: 35ft 8in
Depth: 22ft 10in
Gross tonnage: 1,447/1,490
Machinery: 3-cylinder triple expansion
Boilers: 2
Power: 1,500ihp
Speed: 13kt
Hull: 2 decks
History: *Norway* ordered 1909 to replace 1891-built namesake. *Scotland* ordered 1911 after loss of 1904-built namesake. Oslo–Grangemouth service. 19 March 1916 *Scotland* wrecked off May Island. 26 May 1917 *Norway* torpedoed and sunk 11 miles west of Holmengraa bound Leith-Holmengraa. Service terminated.

Olsen's third *Scotland,* completed by Nylands M/V in 1912 to replace her wrecked namesake, was a sister of the second *Norway,* delivered by the same yard two years previously. While retaining a flush hull, they were much more robust looking ships with greater freeboard, solid bulwarks forward, and an enlarged house aft. Both had short lives and the Grangemouth service was not resumed after World War 1, Olsen thence forward concentrating his UK service on Newcastle with its better connections to both north and south.
Author's collection

Oslo/Kristiansand–Newcastle
1867–1906   Ostlandske Lloyd
1906–   Fred Olsen & Co (A/S Ganger Rolf)

Det Ostlandske Lloyd (East Norway Lloyd) was founded by Rolf Andvord of Oslo in 1867 to operate a coastal shipping service. Later, new services to Antwerp and Newcastle were started leading to the purchase of several second-hand steamers, some of which were altered to carry passengers.

In 1890 the Company's first purpose-built passenger/cargo ship *Sterling* joined the Newcastle service, which was further supplemented two years later by the purchase of the Liverpool–London steamer *Graceful*. Difficulties arose however and in 1906 the Lloyd agreed to sell both its Newcastle and Antwerp services, along with the ships that maintained them, to Fred Olsen, thereby making him one of the leading North Sea passenger ship operators.

Under Olsen guidance the Oslo–Newcastle service flourished and the motor-driven sisters *Black Prince* and *Black Watch* of 1938 were widely acknowledged as outstanding examples of short sea passenger ships. Sadly they failed to survive World War 2 but two fine replacements, *Blenheim* and *Braemar*, joined the route in 1951/52, the latter destined to become the last conventional North Sea passenger ship in service until replaced by a car ferry in 1975.

Sterling

Built: 1890 by S. & H. Morton & Co, Leith
Length: 210ft 0in
Breadth: 30ft 1in
Depth: 21ft 3in to awning deck
Gross tonnage: 1,047
Machinery: 3-cylinder triple expansion
Power: 130nhp

Speed: 12kt
Hull: Steel, 1 deck and awning deck
History: Launched 16 September 1890. Oslo–Newcastle service. 1906 sold to Fred Olsen. 1906 sold to Damps Thore, Copenhagen (manager Thor E. Tulinius). 1915 sold to Rederi Aktiebolaget Artemis, Stockholm (manager Otto Hellsten); renamed *Themis*. About 1917 sold to Icelandic government (manager H/f Eimskipafilag Islands); renamed *Sterling*. 1 May 1922 wrecked in Seydisfjord.

Sovereign

Built: 1886 by Sir Raylton Dixon, Middlesbrough
Length: 244ft 2in
Breadth: 33ft 4in
Depth: 16ft 4in
Gross tonnage: 1,047
Machinery: 3-cylinder triple expansion by
                 T. Richardson & Sons, Hartlepool
Boilers: 2se, 150lb/sq in
Power: 1,000ihp
Speed: 12kt
Hull: 1 deck and awning deck, 1 short raised foc'sle
Passengers: 112 as built
History: Built as *African* for Union Line's South African coastal service. 1893 sold to F.H. Powell & Co; renamed *Graceful*. Liverpool–London service. 1902 sold to Ostlandske Lloyd; renamed *Sovereign* and fitted with taller funnel. Oslo–Newcastle

Delivered by Fredriksstad M/V in 1907, *Sterling* was Olsen's first passenger new-building to be designed specifically for the Newcastle service. Departures on the 'Royal Mail Route' were scheduled from the Tyne via Arendal every Friday evening and the single fare was three guineas. Note *Sterling's* exceptionally tall funnel. *Fred Olsen*

Built by Nylands M/V in 1912 as a replacement for the old *Sovereign, Bessheim* was an enlarged *Sterling* with a raised foc'sle, shorter funnel and repositioned mainmast. Pictured here at Fred Olsen's berth in the Tyne, she was the crack steamer on the Olso run until joined by her more modern sister *Blenheim* in 1923, the latter being identifiable by a different window arrangmenet and solid bulwarks amidships. Note the very tall masts for carrying the W/T aerial.
Author's collection

service (weekly each way with *Sterling*). 1906 sold to Fred Olsen. 1912 sold to Bergen Line; renamed *Zeta*. Bergen–Continent service. 1914 voyage to Newcastle with stranded tourists. Post-World War 1 opened new Bergen–Antwerp service (extension of Rotterdam service) in place of prewar German service by Neptun Line. 1931 sold for scrap.

Sterling (1907)

Built: 1907 by Fredriksstad Mek Verksted, Fredriksstad
Length: 231ft 1in
Breadth: 34ft 1in
Depth: 22ft 2in
Gross tonnage: 1,323
Machinery: 3-cylinder triple expansion
Boilers: 2
Power: 1,350ihp
Speed: 13kt
Hull: Steel, 1 deck and spar deck
History: First Olsen passenger ship built in Norway. Oslo–Newcastle service (via Arendal). 25 March 1922 wrecked near Tvedestrand when bound Newcastle.

Bessheim, Blenheim (1923)

Built: 1912/1923 by Nylands Mek Verksted, Oslo
Length: 256ft 0in
Breadth: 36ft 2in
Depth/draught: 22ft 9in/19ft 0in
Gross tonnage: 1,781/1,807
Machinery: 3-cylinder triple expansion
Boilers: 2
Power: 1,750ihp
Speed: 14kt
Hull: 2 decks, short raised foc'sle
Passengers: c80 first, a few second

History: *Bessheim* replaced *Sovereign* in Oslo–Newcastle service. *Blenheim* virtual repeat to replace lost *Sterling*. Weekly sailings each way on Saturdays, later twice weekly Tuesday/Saturday from June to September (sea passage Tyne Dock–Arendal 32hr + 10hr passage up Oslofjord). 1938 replaced by *Black Prince/Black Watch*. 22 April 1941 *Blenheim* destroyed by fire in Porsanger Fjord during German invasion. 21 November 1941 *Bessheim* torpedoed and sunk off Hammerfest. Early 1948 wreck of *Blenheim* raised and towed to Bodo. Sold to local company which, unable to obtain foreign currency for repairs abroad, sold wreck to Bruges shipbreakers in August 1949.

Black Prince, Black Watch

Built: 1938 by Akers Mek. Verksted, Oslo
Length: 365ft 5in
Breadth: 53ft 4in
Depth: 26ft 6in
Gross tonnage: 5,035
Machinery: 2 x 9-cylinder B & W diesels
Power: 7,000bhp
Speed: 18kt
Hull: 1 deck and shelter deck, long raised foc'sle, cruiser stern
Passengers: 185 first, 65 second
History: *Black Prince* launched December 1937 by Crown Princess Martha; trials May, delivered June. *Black Watch* delivered December. Largest ships built in Norway. Interiors considered most ingenious of any North Sea passenger ship. Galley placed beneath main dining saloon with interconnecting lift. Portable bulkheads used to adapt dining area to suit number of passengers. Extensive deck space. 1 July 1938 *Black Prince* inaugurated new improved service Oslo–Newcastle via Kristiansand. Open sea passage 23hr. 1939 laid-up in Oslo because of World War 2. 1941 seized by German navy and used as accommodation ships. 21 December 1942 *Black Prince* (renamed *Lofjord*)

bombed and badly damaged by fire during allied air raid on Danzig. 4 May 1945 *Black Watch* sunk off Harstad by aircraft from HMS *Trumpeter* whilst acting as submarine depot ship. After World War 2 wreck of *Black Prince* minus engines salved by Svitzers and towed to Frederisktad, Denmark. Deemed unworthy of restoration to passenger ship status by owners and towed to Antwerp in May 1947. Plans for conversion to fruit ship for Sigurd Herlofson abandoned. End 1951 wreck sold to Messrs Dohmen & Abetz for demolition at Burcht.

Blenheim (1951), *Braemar*

Built: 1951/1953 by John I Thornycroft & Co Ltd, Southampton (hulls) and completed by Akers Mek Verksted, Oslo
Length: 374ft 0in oa/335ft 0in bp
Breadth: 53ft 2in
Depth/draught: 29ft 0in/17ft 8in
Gross tonnage: 4,766/4,776
Machinery: 8-cylinder B & W diesel
Power: 4,600bhp
Speed: 16½kt
Hull: 2 decks, long raised foc'sle
Passengers: c100 first, 106/150 second, 36 group (+ c40 cars in hold)

History: Launched Woolston 16 August 1950/end November 1952; entered service February 1951/May 1952. Replaced *Bali/Bretagne*. Air-conditioned, fitted sauna. Oslo–Newcastle via Kristiansand twice weekly each way, increased to thrice weekly June–September. 21 May 1968 *Blenheim* caught fire c220 miles east of Dundee, passengers evacuated and later transferred to *Braemar* and *Spero* (Ellerman's Wilson). Superstructure gutted, towed Kristiansand and laid-up. 1969 sold A/S Uglands Rederi; renamed *Cilaos* and converted to car-carrier at Grimstad (2,404gt). Le Havre–Reunion service. 1974 transferred to Ocean Car Carriers Pte Ltd, Singapore. Mainly employed Mediterranean–South America occasionally returning North European waters for shuttle services out of Rouen. 1981 sold Demolition Tonnage Ltd, London; resold Pakistan breakers, Gadani Beach and arrived Karachi 8 September. 1974/75 *Braemar* last traditional North Sea passenger ship in service. September 1975 replaced by car ferry *Borgen* and sold to Dashwood Finance Co Ltd, Manila acting for Peninsular Tourist Shipping Corp; renamed *The Philippine Tourist* and converted 1976 by Bataan Shipyard & Eng. Co for use as floating casino in Manila Bay (manager: Manila Bay Enterprises). 1978 replaced by *Philippine Tourist* (Ex *Fairsky*); renamed *The Philippine Tourist 1* and towed to Cebu City. Winter 1979/80 returned to Manila after *Philippine Tourist* gutted by fire and laid up.

Fred Olsen acquired Ostlandske Lloyd's Antwerp service in 1906, along with the old steamers *Anvers*, *Frigga* and *Memento*. These were soon replaced by new ships but it was not until 1926 that the route was transformed by the introduction of the funnel-less *Brabant*, Norway's first North Sea passenger ship to be motor driven. *Bretagne* of 1937 brought new standards of luxury but she was destined to be the last passenger ship built for the Antwerp service which became cargo only following her sale to Greece in 1958.

Brüssel, Brabant (1907)

Built: 1907 by Fredriksstad Mek Verksted, Fredriksstad
Length: 241ft 7in
Breadth: 35ft 1in
Depth/draught: 20ft 6in/17ft 6in
Gross tonnage: 1,489/1,492
Machinery: 3-cylinder triple expansion
Boilers: 2
Power: 1,200ihp
Speed: 12kt
Hull: Steel, spar deck type with short raised foc'sle
Passengers: 37 first amidships, 15 second aft, 24 third tween-decks
History: First Olsen ships built for Oslo–Antwerp service. 15 January 1917 *Brabant* mined and sunk c2 miles southeast Flamborough Head bound Oslo-London. *Brussel* ran Antwerp service alone 1919–1922. Replaced by new MS *Brabant* 1926. 1927 sold Finland Line, Helsinki; renamed *Norma*. 1964 sold Helsingin Romuliika, Helsinki for scrap; demolition commenced September.

Paris (1910)

Built: 1910 by Akers Mek Verksted, Oslo
Length: 241ft 6in
Breadth: 37ft 2½in
Depth: 20ft 6in
Gross tonnage: 1,634
Machinery: 3-cylinder triple expansion
Boilers: 2
Power: 1,000ihp
Speed: 12kt
Hull: 2 decks, three-island type (long bridge deck)
History: Oslo–Antwerp service. 15 April 1917 torpedoed and sunk c100 miles west of Greitingen. Norway bound Bergen-Garston.

Paris (1922), *Biarritz*

Built: 1922 by Akers Mek Verksted, Oslo
Length: 255ft 8in
Breadth: 39ft 8in
Depth: 16ft 10in
Gross tonnage: 1,752
Machinery: 3-cylinder triple expansion
Boilers: 2
Power: 169nhp
Speed: 13kt
Hull: 1 deck, three island type (long bridge deck)
History: Weekly Oslo–Antwerp service. 1937 *Biarritz* replaced by new *Bretagne;* transferred to

On acquiring the Antwerp passenger service of Ostlandske Lloyd in 1906 along with its three old steamers *Anvers, Frigga* and *Memento,* Fred Olsen immediately ordered two new steamers from Fedriksstad M/V. The aptly named *Brussel* (seen here) and her sister *Brabant* entered service in 1907. Despite their cargo ship looks they could carry about 75 passengers in three classes. After her sale to Finland in 1927 *Brussel* lasted with little alteration until 1964.
Fred Olsen

Constructed in Olso by Olsen's own shipyard, Akers M/V, the *Paris* of 1910 was a beamier version of the Fredriksstad sisters but her design incorporated three masts and a raised poop. Her career was cut short by World War 1, her loss in April 1917 occurring exactly three months after that of *Brabant*. *Fred Olsen*

Oslo–Rotterdam service (with *Bali*). 25 January 1940 *Biarritz* torpedoed and sunk by U.14 c18 miles northwest of Ijmuiden. *Paris* seized by German forces; converted to minesweeper depot ship MRS.4. 12 March 1945 torpedoed and sunk off Haugesund by MTB 5.

Having gone from two masts to three it was even more unusual that the next ships built by Akers for Olsen's Antwerp service should be four-masters. A little larger than her earlier namesake, the second *Paris*, seen here in the Scheldt, had higher well-deck bulwarks and one pair of boats repositioned above the poop. Her sister *Biarritz* joined *Bali* on the Rotterdam run in 1937 but both sisters became war losses. *Laurence Dunn*

Brabant (1926)

Built: 1926 by Akers Mek Verksted, Oslo
Length: 282ft 0in oa/270ft 6in bp
Breadth: 41ft 2½in
Depth: 22ft 6in
Gross tonnage: 2,335
Machinery: 2 x 6-cylinder Akers/B & W diesels
Power: 2,300bhp
Speed: 13kt
Hull: Three island type, cruiser stern
Passengers: 70 first amidships, 30 third aft
History: Delivered March 1926. First Norwegian North Sea passenger motor ship (after trials with two small diesel cargo ships on Rotterdam service). Oslo–Antwerp service (passage time approximately two days). Later fitted with small funnel and mainmast removed. 1940 seized by

German forces; used as accommodation ship at Horten. Later trials ship then armed transport. October 1944 survived mining in Skagerrak. Resumed Antwerp service after World War 2. 1951 passenger figures shown as 80 in three classes; joined by *Bali*. December 1954 sold Sudan Navigation Co; renamed *Suakin*. Port Sudan–Jeddah–Suez trade with pilgrims and cargo. 1971 sold Hussein Mohammed Fayez; renamed *Radwa*. 1972 sold Pakistani breakers; demolition commenced Gadani Beach in December.

Bali (acquired 1935)

Bergen–Rotterdam service: for details and history see *Alnwick* p 78.

The handsome flush-decked *Bretagne* of 1937 was destined to be the last Olsen passenger ship built for the Antwerp service but at 3,785 tons she was also the largest. A single screw motor ship, she could be described as a mini prototype for the larger Newcastle run sisters *Black Prince* and *Black Watch* which she helped to replace after World War 2, not returning to her designed service until 1953. After becoming the Greek *Massalia* in 1958 she ran between Marseille and Eastern Mediterranean ports until withdrawn in 1967, the only outward change being extra boats abreast the mainmast and on the poop, plus a black painted hull.
Laurence Dunn

Bretagne

Built: 1937 by Akers Mek Verksted, Oslo
Length: 314ft 1½in oa/299ft 10in bp
Breadth: 45ft 10in
Depth/draught: 29ft 4in to upper deck/18ft 1in
Gross tonnage: 3,285
Machinery: 9-cylinder B & W diesel
Power: 3,500bhp
Speed: 16kt
Hull: 1 deck and flush shelter deck, cruiser stern
Passengers: 88 first amidships, 26 second aft, 34 third tween-decks summer/10 winter
History: Entered service April 1937. Partnered *Brabant* on Oslo–Antwerp service (weekly each way on Saturdays). After World War 2 transferred to direct Oslo–Newcastle service to replace war losses (150 passengers). 1951 joined by new *Blenheim*. 1953 replaced by *Braemar;* returned to Oslo–Antwerp service. 1958 sold Hellenic Mediterranean Lines, Piraeus; renamed *Massalia*. Marseilles – Genoa – Piraeus – Limassol – Beirut – Port Said – Alexandria – Piraeus – Genoa – Marseilles service (82 first, 90 tourist, 84 dormitory, 90 deck passengers). Later called at Haifa instead of Beirut and first two classes merged into 'uniclass'. April 1967 withdrawn and laid up Piraeus area. Spring 1974 scrapped at Eleusis by P. Skounis & I. Efthimiou.

P.G. Halvorsen

Bergen/Stavanger–Newcastle
1871–1890   Kulkompagnet af 1871
1890–1892   P. G. Halvorsen Ltd
Funnel colours: Buff (*Britannia*)

P.G. Halvorsen was originally employed by Bergen Line but later became the driving force behind the expansion of the Company's associated ship repair business into the fully fledged shipbuilding concern Bergens Mek Verksted. In 1871 he set up a Bergen partnership entitled Kulkompagnet af 1871 (Coal Co of 1871) in order to import coal from the UK. The following year he was forced to resign from BMV by Bergen Line which resented his interference in technical matters for which he lacked any training.

Halvorsen decided to concentrate on his shipowning activities and in 1879 set up a regular weekly service to the Tyne, building two new ships: the 709-ton *Johan Sverdrup* in 1880 and the larger *Norge* two years later. Passengers began to be carried in increasing numbers and in 1887 Halvorsen applied for a Government grant for a mail service linking Bergen, Stavanger and Newcastle. The Storthing refused and stood by their decision when he tried again the following year.

Counter proposals were put forward and eventually after much discussion the Government agreed to pay Halvorsen for two trips a week in a joint service to Newcastle with Bergen Line and Nordenfjeldske. He immediately put in hand a fast new passenger ship *Britannia*, built to his own design, which failed to live up to expectations and her unpopularity, coupled with the loss of *Norge*, forced the company into liquidation in 1892.

Norge

Built: 1882 by Rostocker AG, Rostock
Length: 200ft 0in
Breadth: 28ft 0in
Depth: 14ft 8in
Gross tonnage: 893

Machinery: 2-cylinder compound by Borsig & Co, Berlin
Power: 130nhp
Speed: 11kt
Hull: Iron, awning deck type
Passengers: 15–20 later increased to 80–100
History: Bergen–Newcastle weekly service. 1 June 1890 made first Halvorsen sailing from Bergen in new joint mail service with Bergen Line and Det Nordenfjeldske. 26 December 1891 wrecked Tynanger bound Newcastle-Stavanger.

Britannia

Built: 1890 by Laxevaags Engineering & Shipbuilding Co, Bergen
Length: 275ft 0in oa/254ft 1in bp
Breadth: 34ft 1in
Depth: 14ft 9in
Gross tonnage: 1,555
Machinery: 3-cylinder triple expansion by B.W. Maclachlan, Glasgow
Boilers: 4
Power: 2,800ihp
Speed: 15kt
Hull: Steel, flush deck, clipper bow
Passengers: 180 first
History: Launched 23 January 1890; trials 17kt at 3,600ihp. M/v Bergen–Newcastle 2 June. Unsatisfactory in service because of excessive vibration and poor sea-keeping. 1892 sold to US owner via brokers C.H. Pile & Co, London; renamed *America*. 1893 sold to Brazilian navy; renamed *Andrada*. Converted to armed merchant cruiser – 2 × 4.7in, 6 × 6pdr, 6 × 1pdr, 4 torpedo tubes, Sims Edison dirigible torpedo. After 1900 downgraded to transport. 1916 sold to E.G. Fontes & Co, Rio de Janeiro; renamed *America;* Brazilian coastal trade. Broken up about 1930.

Britannia as *Andrada*. *Author's collection*

Bergen Line

Bergen/Haugesund/Stavanger–Newcastle
1851– Det Bergenske Dampskibsselskab
Funnel colours: Black with three white rings

Det Bergenske Dampskibsselskab (The Bergen Steamship Co) was formed in Bergen on 12 December 1851, due mainly to the efforts of local businessman, Consul Michael Krohn.

The new Company's first steamship was the paddle-driven *Bergen* which made its maiden sailing to Hamburg on 13 February 1853 with 150 passengers. In October 1854 she was joined by the larger paddler *Norge* (575 tons) but disaster struck in 1855 when the new ship was run down by *Bergen* off Kristiansand with the loss of 40 lives.

The Company survived this tragedy and soon afterwards took delivery of its first screw-steamer, *Nordstjernen* (North Star), which began the traditional 'heavenly body' style of nomenclature. Designed for a new Bergen–Trondheim service, she began her career on the Hamburg run in place of *Norge*.

In the late 1880s Krohn tried to form an amalgamation with two other shipping companies – Trondheim's Det Nordenfjeldske and Oslo-based Det Sondenfjeldske, which operated from East Norway to Hamburg and Hull. His efforts were unsuccessful but the former agreed to co-operate in 1857 and a year later joined Bergen Line's Hamburg service. Det Sondenfjeldske went its own way but in 1866 was forced to withdraw from the Hull route after a rate war with the more powerful Wilson Line. No other Norwegian foray into the England trade was made until 1879 when Halvorsen established a weekly service between Bergen and Newcastle. A later stab at a summer passenger/cargo service to Leith by Det Stavangerske's *Kong Olaf* in 1887 was short-lived.

Following unsuccessful attempts by Halvorsen to obtain a government subsidy in 1887 and 1888, Bergen Line with a promise of Nordenfjeldske's co-operation proposed a weekly service from Trondheim and Bergen to the UK for an annual payment of Kr150,000. After further discussion

parliamentary agreement was finally reached on 14 June 1888 with Bergen Line's proposal being accepted for a service to Newcastle, but Halvorsen would also be paid for two trips a week from Bergen and Stavanger.

Bergen Line ordered a new ship from Germany but opened the new joint service on 31 May 1890 with the purchased *Mercur*. Two years later the luckless Halvorsen's sailings were absorbed and the Newcastle route went from strength to strength with several new ships being added.

After World War 1 agreement was reached with Ellerman's Wilson Line outlining the Company's sphere of influence in the North Sea and further notable events included the opening of the new Tyne Commission Quay terminal in 1928 and the delivery of the large motor ship *Venus* in 1930. A summer car ferry service was introduced in 1966 but *Leda* (1953), Bergen Line's only postwar conventional passenger steamer, continued until withdrawn in 1974.

Mercur

Built: 1883 by Motala Co, Gothenburg
Length: 207ft 0in
Breadth: 29ft 8in
Depth: 21ft 5in
Gross tonnage: 972
Machinery: 2-cylinder compound
Boilers: 2
Power: 155nhp
Speed: 12kt
Hull: Iron and steel, 1 deck
History: Built for Det Sondenfjeldske's Christiania–Hamburg service. 1889 sold to Bergen Line. 31 May 1890 opened new mail service Bergen–Newcastle. 1895 replaced by *Vega*, thereafter employed on North Cape cruises. 1902 new boilers. Later became cargo steamer. 1948 sold Kupath Hacoperativim, Tel-Aviv. 28 March 1950 foundered in heavy weather 3 miles off Capo Suvero bound Messina–Genoa.

The part iron, part steel *Neptun* (1890) originally had a fully rigged foremast but is shown after the removal of her yards. Like most Bergenske ships she was built with cruising in mind and spent the majority of her 38-year life as a white-hulled summer 'tourist' steamer, interspersed with winter cargo sailings. *Author's collection*

Neptun

Built: 1890 by J.C. Tecklenborg, Geestemunde
Length: 218ft 9in
Breadth: 30ft 0in
Depth/draught: 22ft 8in/14ft 10in
Gross tonnage: 959
Machinery: 3-cylinder triple expansion by H. Paukseh AG, Landsberg
Boilers: 2se
Power: 220nhp
Speed: 13kt
Hull: Steel, 1 deck and awning deck
History: Ordered after acquisition of mail contract. Entered service June 1890. Summer cruising. c1899 replaced by *Hera*, thereafter cruising Bergen–North Cape in summer, cargo ship in winter. September 1914 single voyage Bergen–Newcastle with stranded tourists. 1928 sold to Stavanger Shipbreaking Co for demolition.

Mira

Built: 1891 by A. & J. Inglis, Glasgow
Length: 202ft 2½in
Breadth: 30ft 2½in
Depth: 15ft 1in
Gross tonnage: 966
Machinery: 3-cylinder triple expansion
Boilers: 2se
Power: 188nhp

Speed: 13kt
Hull: Steel, 2 decks and awning deck
History: Completed June 1891. Trondheim–Bergen–Newcastle service. 1903 transferred to Hamburg service, replaced by *Irma* 1905. July 1906 carried King Haakon and Queen Maud from Trondheim to Christiania after their Coronation. Summer cruising, winter cargo ship on Newcastle/Hamburg routes. 1927 entered coastal express service after major refit. 1937 replaced by *Nordstjernen* and placed in reserve. Late 1939 survived bombing attack in North Sea. 9 April 1940 seized by German forces in Bergen; became accommodation ship. February 1941 returned to coastal service. 4 March shelled and sunk by HMS *Bedouin* near Narvik during Lofoten Raid.

Venus (1893)

Built: 1893 by C.S. Swan & Hunter, Wallsend
Length: 230ft 8in
Breadth: 31ft 2½in
Depth: 11ft 9in
Gross tonnage: 1,067
Machinery: 3-cylinder triple expansion by Wallsend Slipway Co
Boilers: 1de 160lb/sq in
Power: 246nhp
Speed: 13½kt
Hull: Steel, flush deck
History: Trondheim–Bergen–Newcastle service. 1903 reboiled (195nhp). 1917 laid up because of

Venus (1893) shown with heightened funnel, was specifically designed for the Newcastle run, her timely arrival enabling her owners to absorb the bankrupt Halvorsen's share of the joint service. *Vega* was similar but lacked bulwarks aft. *Author's collection*

unrestricted German blockade of UK waters. March 1918 experimental round voyage to Newcastle, evaded blockade but laid up for remainder of hostilities. 1919 returned to Newcastle service. 1930 renamed *Sylvia*. 1931 replaced by new *Venus* and put into reserve. 1933 broken up in Norway.

Vega (1895)

Built: 1895 by J. L. Thompson & Sons, Sunderland
Length: 233ft 2½in
Breadth: 32ft 1in
Depth: 12ft 0in
Gross tonnage: 1,164
Machinery: 3-cylinder triple expansion by J. Dickinson & Sons, Sunderland
Boilers: 1de, 175lb/sq in
Power: 222nhp
Speed: 13kt
Hull: Steel, 1 deck and spar deck
History: Launched 9 March 1895; trials 28 May (14 kt average). Hull fitted with bilge keels to reduce rolling. Passenger accommodation lit by electricity and fitted baths and shower baths. Trondheim–Bergen–Newcastle service extended in high summer to North Cape on 'yachting cruises'. 1909 reboilered; 16 November 1916 stopped by German submarine near Stavanger; machinery in cargo deemed contraband and sunk by gunfire. Passengers and crew later picked up by Danish ship.

Irma

Built: 1905 by Sir Raylton Dixon & Co, Middlesbrough
Length: 244ft 0in
Breadth: 32ft 9in
Depth: 13ft 3in
Gross tonnage: 1,322
Machinery: 3-cylinder triple expansion by J. Dickinson & Sons, Sunderland

Boilers: 1de
Power: 245nhp
Speed: 13kt
Hull: 1 deck and spar deck
Passengers: 230 max including 120 first
History: Launched 5 January 1905; trials 8 April. Originally intended for Bergen–Hamburg service but primarily on Newcastle service (B&N Royal Mail Route: three sailings weekly). 4 October 1911 fire in forward hold about 100 miles from Tyne bound Bergen; extinguished but forced to return Newcastle. In summer often extended voyage to Trondheim with a west coast fjords cruise. February 1917 laid up. 26 November 1918 reopened Newcastle service. 1921 withdrawn and transferred to full-time cruising with purpose-built *Meteor* and later *Stella Polaris*. Refitted late 1920s. 1931 transferred to coastal express service as replacement for *Hera*. 13 February 1944 torpedoed and sunk off Hestkjaer by Norwegian MTB, 25 passengers and 36 crew lost.

Jupiter, Leda (1920)

Built: 1915/1920 by Lindholmens Varv A/B, Gothenburg, and Sir W.G. Armstrong, Whitworth Co, Walker-on-Tyne
Length: 305ft 1in
Breadth: 41ft 8in
Depth/draught: 18ft 9in/17ft 0in
Gross tonnage: 2,625/2,519
Machinery: 3-cylinder triple expansion/1 HP and 1 LP double-reduction geared turbines
Boilers: ?/3se 220lb/sq in
Power: 309nhp/2,800shp (3,500shp max)
Speed: 15/15½kt
Hull: Long raised foc'sle and combined bridge/poop, 1 deck
Passengers: 225/94 first, 47 third
History: *Jupiter* ordered summer 1914, completed end 1915. Entered service January 1916 Bergen–Newcastle service (26hr, sailing Thursday and returning Saturday). 1917 laid up in Bergen.

The handsome *Irma* (1905) was an improved and enlarged *Vega*, marking the final evolution of Bergenske's early North Sea passenger ship design phase. At that time the 'B&N Line Royal Mail Route' provided three sailings a week to Albert Edward Dock Newcastle, with single fares from Stavanger and Bergen at £4 and from Trondheim at £6.10s. After cruising in the 1920s and subsequent coastal service, *Irma's* loss by torpedo from a Norwegian MTB in 1944 was a wartime tragedy. *Author's collection*

November 1917 chartered by UK government for Aberdeen–Bergen service; armed and dazzle-painted. Returned early 1919 and resumed Newcastle service 18 January. *Leda* ordered 10 May 1919; launched by Lady Mayoress of Newcastle 4 May 1920; trials autumn (17kt). First North Sea passenger steamer with geared turbines. Entered service Newcastle run December 1920. 1 October 1923 *Leda* grounded in Vatlestrom near Bergen, flooded forepeak and extensive keel damage. Late 1920s both refitted and interiors modernised. May 1931 *Leda* replaced by new *Venus* and transferred to Bergen–Hamburg service. November 1933 *Leda* transferred to Bergen–Rotterdam service. Summer 1938 *Jupiter* replaced by new *Vega* and transferred to Bergen–Rotterdam service allowing *Leda* to return to Hamburg service. January 1937 *Jupiter* rescued crew of *Veni* (Haugesund) assisted by *Venus* and *Leda* rescued crew of *Karmt* (Haugesund) in severe North Sea gales. 31 July 1940 *Leda* seized by German navy; 17 September transferred to F Laeisz management; May 1944–January 1945 naval service; returned Laeisz for repatriation of refugees from East Prussia. 25 March 1945 *Leda* sunk by Russian artillery off Stettin; wreck raised and towed Lubeck. January 1949 sold to Eisen und Stahl AG and left for Bremerhaven in tow 16 December. *Jupiter* lying in

The 16kt Lindholmen-built *Jupiter* marked a great advance in Bergen Line's North Sea service but lacked the grace of her predecessors. Ordered before World War 1 her construction was delayed and she was not delivered until the end of 1915. Sold to Greece in 1955, she became George Potamianos' successful cruise ship *Hermes,* with larger funnel and extra superstructure in place of her well-deck. *Author's collection*

Copenhagen at end World War 2. Refitted and returned to Newcastle run 9 March 1946 replacing former Iceland steamer *Lyra.* Summer 1948 transferred to seasonal Bergen–Antwerp service, Newcastle service in winter. 1953 replaced by new *Leda* and transferred to Norwegian coastal cruise service connecting with Newcastle sailings. 1955 sold to Epirotiki Steamship Navigation Co 'George Potamianos' SA: renamed *Hermes.* Converted to cruise ship – new funnel, superstructure extended over well-deck (2,557gt: 265 passengers). Chartered to French Co for Marseilles–Odessa service. Laid up winter 1956. 1957 hotel ship at Ydra for filming of 'Boy on a Dolphin'. Summer 1958 seven-day 'culture' cruises to Black Sea. 4 March 1960 caught fire during refit at Piraeus, towed out and beached Sileniai Bay, Salamis. 9 March refloated and later sold to Brodospas for breaking up at Split.

Leda **was a turbine driven sister of** *Jupiter* **with more extensive passenger accommodation, high bulwarks round her forward well-deck and raked masts and funnel. After the arrival of** *Venus* **in 1931 she ran to Hamburg or Rotterdam, finally becoming a war loss off Stettin whilst in German hands in the final months of World War 2.** *Author's collection*

Venus (1931)

Built: 1931 by Elsinore Shipbuilding & Engineering Co, Elsinore
Length: 412ft 0in oa/398ft 6in bp; later 420ft 6in oa
Breadth: 54ft 2in
Depth/draught: 26ft 6in/20ft 0in
Gross tonnage: 5,406; later 6,269
Machinery: 2 x 10-cylinder B&W diesels
Power: 10,250bhp
Speed: 19kt
Hull: 1 deck and flush shelter deck
Passengers: 201 first amidships, 76 second
History: Trials Hveen measured mile, Oslofjord (20.64kt at 11,000bhp). Fastest motor ship in world. Entered service May 1931 Bergen–Newcastle (twice weekly each way). January 1937 rescued crew of *Trym* (Trondheim) in North Sea gale and on return voyage assisted *Jupiter* in rescue of crew of *Veni* (Haugesund). Laid up September 1939 because of excessive War Risks premium demand. 1940 requisitioned by German forces for one month after invasion. March 1941 requisitioned for conversion to submarine depot/target ship; Baltic service. 15 April 1945 sunk at Hamburg during Allied air-raid (direct hit on forehatch, holed by near miss). September 1945 salvage operations started, raised and towed to Elsinore. Major rebuild; new bow section (one deck higher, raked stem) fitted in ex-German drydock at Aarhus, new funnels, new accommodation (135 first, 278 tourist), garage for 30 cars. May 1948 re-entered service. December 1948 inaugurated first of regular winter cruises Plymouth–Madeira–Teneriffe (260 one class passengers). November 1950 two private charter 14-day cruises to Mediterranean from Liverpool and Dublin. 1953 fitted with stabilisers. 23 March 1955 blown ashore in Plymouth during gale; refloated 26th. UK cruising terminal changed to Southampton. Spring 1965 repainted white with yellow funnels, twice weekly summer service Stavanger–Newcastle with hydrofoil connection to Bergen. Summer 1966 replaced by new car ferry *Jupiter* and transferred to weekly Bergen–Rotterdam service. Winter week-end sailings to Newcastle. Autumn 1968 withdrawn after final cruise from Southampton. Sold to Shipbreaking Industries Ltd; arrived Faslane 19 October for demolition.

Vega (1938)

Built: 1938 by Cantieri Riuniti dell'Adriatico, Trieste
Length: 424ft 7in
Breadth: 58ft 4in
Depth/draught: 28ft 5in/20ft 0in
Gross tonnage: 7,287
Machinery: 2 x 10-cylinder CRDA-Sulzer diesels
Power: 12,400bhp
Speed: 20kt
Hull: 2 decks and shelter deck, long raised foc'sle
Passengers: 217 first amidships, 248 second aft
History: Launched ; trials 28–30 April 1938 (21.75kt max); delivered May. Inaugural cruise to Oslo via Palermo and Algiers. Carried King of Norway and members of Storthing on coastal trip to Bergen. 2 June m/v Bergen–Newcastle (four sailings a week each way with *Venus*). September 1940 laid up because of excessive War Risks premium demand (Kr76million per annum with *Venus*). 11 September 1940 seized by German forces; returned 16 October. 18 March 1941 seized by German navy and taken to Baltic as submarine depot ship. 4 May 1945 bombed and sunk by Allied aircraft in Eckernfjord during evacuation of refugees from East Prussia.

Astrea

Built: 1941 by A/B Crichton-Vulkan, Turku
Length: 313ft 2in
Breadth: 44ft 1in
Draught: 19ft 4in
Gross tonnage: 3,190
Machinery: 7-cylinder Krupp diesel
Power: 3,250bhp
Hull: Long raised foc'sle

Passengers: 70 first, 70 second

History: Ordered by Finland Line for Turku–Hull service (34 first, 16 third class passengers). Launched 16 September 1939; delivery delayed by World War 2. 1940 damaged by air raid. Completed 16 May 1941 and laid up. 17 February 1944 sold to Stockholms Rederi Svea which agreed to resell to Bergen Line after World War 2. Rebuilt by Finnboda Varv, Stockholm. 17 September 1945 completed and sold to Bergen Line. October maiden voyage Bergen–Newcastle; repatriating Norwegian civilians with *Lyra*. January 1946 normal weekly service Bergen–Newcastle via Haugesund and Stavanger. April 1953 replaced by *Leda;* transferred to Bergen – Haugesund – Stavanger – Rotterdam service (second class passengers only). 1966 replaced by *Venus.* 1967 sold to P/f Skipafelagid Foroyar, Thorshavn; renamed *Tjaldur* (Panamanian flag) for Copenhagen–Faroes service. 18 July 1969 major engine breakdown en route Thorshavn; towed Aalborg. Sold to H.P. Heuvelman for scrap and arrived Krimpen, New Waterway in tow 6 September; demolition commenced 22nd.

Leda (1953)

Built: 1953 by Swan Hunter & Wigham Richardson Ltd, Wallsend
Length: 436ft 8in oa/420ft 7in bp
Breadth: 57ft 2½in
Depth/draught: 26ft 2in/20ft 0in
Gross tonnage: 6,670

Machinery: 2 sets DR Parsons steam turbines by Wallsend Slipway & Engineering Co.
Boilers: 2 oil-fired Babcock & Wilcox, 450lb/sq in
Power: 13,000shp
Speed: 22kt
Hull: 2 decks, long raised foc'sle, aluminium superstructure
Passengers: 19 first, 384 tourist (+ 65 cars max)

History: Launched 3 September 1952 by Princess Astrid; trials 23 March 1953. Fitted with stabilisers. Pre-service visits to Oslo, London, Leith. April 1953 replaced *Astrea* and *Jupiter* in Bergen–Stavanger–Newcastle service (twice weekly all year round). Early 1954 record passage Newcastle–Stavanger 16hr 27min quay to quay. 10 May–13 June 1963 out of commission for repairs to turbine blades; replaced by chartered aircraft. Mid-1960s thrice weekly summer service. Early 1970s winter service reduced to weekly (September–May). Autumn 1974 withdrawn; laid up in Bergen (replaced by chartered DFDS *England*). 1977 sold to Stord Vaerft A/S; shipyard worker accommodation ship. 1979 sold to Kuwait Livestock Trading & Transport Co; renamed *Najla*. Proposed conversion to livestock carrier shelved. May 1979–September 1980 accommodation ship at Stornoway; laid up in Norway. 1981 sold to Dolphin (Hellas) Shipping SA, Piraeus; 13 April left Kristiansand for Chalkis in tow of tug *Hansa*. (Ge). Laid up. Summer 1982 towed to Piraeus area; renamed *Albatross*. 1983/84 converted to cruise ship: gross tonnage 6471/484 passengers. Renamed *Allegro* for winter cruise programme from South America, which failed. Returned to Piraeus and renamed *Albatross* 1985. Summer 1985 cruising in North European waters. Still in service.

The impressive *Leda,* turbine-driven like her earlier namesake, was built by Swan Hunter in 1953 to replace the ageing *Jupiter*. She was the first North Sea passenger ship to incorporate stabilisers, and although her large funnel and tripod masts lent an air of modernity, her design was an obvious development of the prewar *Vega*.

Iris, formerly *Ingerid,* newest and largest of Burger & Zoon's three Holland–Norway passenger ships acquired by Bergen Line in 1907, continued in the Rotterdam trade until World War 2. Her previous running mate *Flora* (ex-*Olaf Kyrre*) was soon transferred to the Iceland run and became a war loss in 1917 whilst *Ceres* (ex-*Lerfos*) lasted until scrapped in 1935. *Iris* herself was lost in **1944.** *Author's collection*

Bergen/Haugesund/Stavanger–Rotterdam

In 1907 Bergen Line took over Burger & Zoon's Stoomvaart Maats Noorwegen which operated a passenger/cargo sercice between Rotterdam and Bergen. The deal included three ships, namely *Ingerid, Flora* and *Ceres* but the latter two were lost in World War 1. *Ingerid,* renamed *Iris* was joined by the purpose-built *Ariadne* in 1930 but both were lost during World War 2. Postwar service was maintained by *Astrea* and finally by *Venus* from 1966 until 1968 when the latter was withdrawn and broken up.

Iris

Built: 1901 by Gourlay Bros, Dundee
Length: 236ft 0in
Breadth: 32ft 1in
Depth: 15ft 6in
Gross tonnage: 1,213
Machinery: 3-cylinder triple expansion
Boilers: 2
Power: 900ihp
Speed: 13kt
Hull: 2 decks, short raised foc'sle and combined bridge-poop
Passengers: 50 first, 30 second (aft)

History: Built as *Ingerid* for D. Burger & Zoon's Rotterdam–Norway service; original gross tonnage 1,095. 1907 sold to Bergen Line; renamed *Iris.* Bergen–Haugesund–Stavanger–Rotterdam service. September 1914 Bergen–Newcastle voyage with stranded tourists. February 1917 laid up. 1918 returned to Rotterdam service (sailing Bergen pm Saturday/Rotterdam noon Wednesday). Late 1920s major refit. 4 October 1944 struck submerged rock near Newfoundland when bound Hebron–Cape Harrison, Labrador. Total loss.

Ariadne

Built: 1930 by Nylands Verksted, Oslo
Length: 271ft 3in
Breadth: 38ft 2in
Depth: 19ft 4in
Gross tonnage: 2,029
Machinery: 3-cylinder triple expansion
Boilers: 2
Power: 234ihp
Speed: 14kt
Hull: 2 decks, three-island type, cruiser stern
History: Bergen–Stavanger–Rotterdam service, occasionally extended in summer to Aalesund and Trondheim. 15 April 1940 requisitioned by military and sailed to Tromso for orders. 13 June 1940 bombed and sunk by six German aircraft en route to join Lerwick-bound convoy: one crew and one passenger lost.

The *Ariadne* was built specifically for Bergen Line's Rotterdam service in 1930. Her outward appearance was rather stiff when compared with the elegance of her older consort *Iris* but her cruiser stern was an innovation shared with the contemporary *Venus.* *Bergen Line*

Nordenfjeldske

Trondheim/Bergen-Newcastle
1890–   Det Nordenfjeldske
    Dampskibsselskab
Funnel colours: Black with broad red band
    bordered by two narrow white bands

Det Nordenfjeldske Dampskibsselskab (Northern Steamship Co) was founded on 28 January 1857 by two leading Trondheim businessmen, Hans Jensen and Jelmer Lundgreen, who had been impressed by the apparent profitability of a shipping venture following the extension of Bergenske's Hamburg service to their native town. Their first steamer was the second-hand *Nidelveen* which was soon joined by the Dumbarton-built *Haakon Jarl*.

After a year's trading the new Company's shareholders rejected a merger bid proposed by Bergenske but co-operation remained close and at the end of 1858 Nordenfjeldske joined the latter's Hamburg service. Further co-operation involved the taking over of the Government run coastal service northwards from Trondheim and by 1870 this had been extended to Vadso, giving a continuous 1,725-mile service from Hamburg.

In May 1888 Nordenfjeldske agreed to join Bergenske in a projected mail service to the UK, this being a counter proposal to one put forward by P.G. Halvorsen, a Bergen shipowner engaged in the Newcastle coal trade. After much parliamentary argument the three parties agreed on a joint service to Newcastle, for which Nordenfjeldske ordered a new steamer, *Ragnvald Jarl*, from Wigham, Richardson. In October 1921 the Company ceased North Sea passenger operations to concentrate on cargo services and the Coastal Express service.

Ragnvald Jarl

Built: 1890 by Messrs Wigham Richardson Ltd,
    Low Walker
Length: 233ft 0in oa/225ft 0in bp
Breadth: 30ft 2½in
Depth: 16ft 7½in
Gross tonnage: 1,084
Machinery: 3-cylinder triple expansion

Boilers: 150lb/sq in
Power: 160nhp
Speed: 12kt
Hull: Steel, 1 deck and awning deck
History: Launched at Neptune Yard 22 March 1890; trials 22 May (13kt on Whitley mile). M/v first week of June, Trondheim–Bergen–Newcastle service (one round voyage every two weeks). 1902 reboilered. 1907 replaced by *Haakon VII* and transferred to Hamburg service (extended to include Norwegian fjord cruises in summer). During World War 1 returned to Newcastle service until laid-up early 1917. 1920 sold to Hijos de Jose Taya, Barcelona; renamed *Capitan Revuelta*. Mediterranean service. 1922–24 ownership transferred to Jacinto and Umberto Mitats. Reverted to Jose Taya until broken up in 1930.

Haakon VII

Built: 1907 by Trondheims Mek Verksted,
    Trondheim
Length: 250ft 4in
Breadth: 33ft 2in
Depth: 21ft 7in md
Gross tonnage: 1,347
Machinery: 3-cylinder triple expansion
Boilers: 2
Power: 293nhp
Speed: 13kt
Hull: 1 deck and spar deck
Passengers: 144 in two classes
History: Delivered May 1907. Trondheim–Bergen–Stavanger–Newcastle service. 1910 fitted with W/t. In summer Trondheim–Bergen section included a cruise via Hardanger, Sogn and Geiranger fjords. End July 1914 Bergen–Newcastle sailing cancelled by owners fearing naval action in North Sea. Service resumed after Government guaranteed all mail ships against War Risks following outbreak of World War 1. Laid up early 1917. Resumed normal service after World War 1. October 1921 withdrawn and transferred to coastal express service. Late pm 6 October 1929 wrecked between Melsholmen and Stavenes in storm; 17 lost. Wreck salvaged April 1930, condemned and towed to Stavanger for demolition late summer.

Index